live
second

365 Ways to Make Jesus First

An I Am Second Daily Reader

Doug Bender

THOMAS NELSON
Since 1798

NASHVILLE   DALLAS   MEXICO CITY   RIO DE JANEIRO

© 2012 by e3 Partners Ministry

Published in Nashville, Tennessee, by Thomas Nelson. Thomas Nelson is a registered trademark of Thomas Nelson, Inc.

Thomas Nelson, Inc., titles may be purchased in bulk for educational, business, fund-raising, or sales promotional use. For information, please e-mail SpecialMarkets@ ThomasNelson.com.

Scripture quotations are taken from the Holy Bible, New International Version®, NIV®. Copyright © 1973, 1978, 1984, 2011 by Biblica, Inc.™ Used by permission of Zondervan. All rights reserved worldwide. www.zondervan.com.

Library of Congress Control Number: 2012950518

ISBN: 978-1-4002-0480-9

Printed in the United States of America

12 13 14 15 16 QG 6 5 4 3 2 1

To Norm Miller and Gary Hall

In appreciation to Norm Miller whose generosity and vision inspired the I am Second movement and to Gary Hall who first told my father, Gary Bender, the great message of our God, enabling me to share that message with you.

Also a giant thanks goes to everyone involved in making this book possible: Bryan Norman and his team at Thomas Nelson, Mike Jorgensen, John Humphrey, and the whole I Am Second staff, Nancy Nelson with her careful eye to detail, Curtis Sergeant whose wisdom and teaching is reflected in this book, Tom and Kitti Rau for all the coffee, to our many supporters, and the ever creative launch team who helped get the word out. I could not be more honored to have such a great team around me.

Contents

How This Book Works

This book contains 365 daily readings that challenge you to consider what life would look like if Jesus were first. This book is for anyone looking to discover meaning in life, your mission on this planet, or the cure to life's difficulties. You do not need to believe in Jesus to start this journey, but I think you will be challenged by his message before you trek too far. I believe the power of his love, the vastness of his forgiveness, and the strength of his presence will inspire you to rethink your relationship with God.

Wherever you are, let this book take you one step further in your journey with God. I believe and hope this book will be much more than a daily reading, that it will be a guidebook for travelers, a handbook for seekers, and a motivational manual for the uninspired. This book may not always soothe your soul, but I think it will always inspire your reflection and challenge your daily routine.

Everyday Read

If you have never used a book of this type, it is important to know that it is meant to be read a little each day and not in large chunks. Each day spend only a few minutes reading one day's entry and spend the rest of your time reflecting on its application. Each entry is meant to serve as a nugget of contemplation for your daily growth, not your evening speed read. And remember, while it is meant to be read every day, life gets the best of all of us. If you fall behind or miss a day, just pick back up where you left off and continue the journey wherever you stopped.

Group or Individual

Life is a team sport, not an individual event. I encourage you to spend at least one day a week pointedly discussing the themes and lessons of this book with a few friends. To assist in these conversations, the first entry of every week is designed to work as a group discussion guide. While it works perfectly well as an individual study, like life, you will get the most out of it when you enjoy it with others. Going through this book with a group will dramatically increase the effect it will have on your life. For more information on how a discussion group like this might function or how you can start one with your friends, check out our free resources at www.iamsecond.com/groups.

The Bible

Each entry is created to help you discover the meaning and application of a passage from the Bible. A key verse from that passage will be provided in the entry and a reference for the complete passage provided below. I encourage you to read the whole passage before reading the entry each day. For those of you unfamiliar with looking up Bible passages, there are plenty of great smart phone apps (YouVersion®) and websites (www.biblegateway.com) that provide free electronic Bibles and Bible resources.

Talk with God

Many entries have a suggested prayer. Take these words as a guide for your conversation with God. If the words of the written prayer do not reflect your heart, then do not pray them. Take them as a suggestion only. Find the words that best express your heart. Use what is written only as a starting place.

In addition to these prayers, the last entry of every week is a copy of one of the Bible's prayers. They are prayers from Jesus, from his disciples, from the prophets, the poets, and the songwriters of God's book. I believe the breadth of their honesty and depth of their meaning will enrich your conversations with God.

Live and Tell

As I have said already, this book is meant to be a guide for your reflection and a source of inspiration for your daily spiritual growth. To help you in that endeavor, each entry concludes with "Live It" and "Tell It" questions. Give these questions the time they deserve. Think about how what you are learning could impact your life and how you could pass on what you discover. You will find this book full of action points. Use your discernment to know how much you can do and what you choose to do. While it is important to apply what you are learning, do not overwhelm yourself with too many applications or goals that are too large. Pace yourself.

Practice It

At the end of Day 1 each week, you will be encouraged to *Practice It*. This is an opportunity for you to get a bit interactive. Find a partner. If you have a small group you are meeting with, then ask someone from your group, or if not then ask a friend or spouse. Ask that person to help you practice any of the more challenging commitments you make. If there is a difficult conversation you need to have, then ask that friend to let you practice having that conversation with them so you can build confidence for the real-life encounter. If you have a habit or behavior you need to change, ask this friend to help walk you through an action plan for the coming weeks.

Social Media

For those of you familiar with the online social network Twitter, "hashtags" are the string of letters at the end of many tweets that help organize the Twitter world. Whenever you use a hashtag, you and everyone else on Twitter can search for the tweets of others who are discussing the same topic under that hashtag. If you want to share your thoughts or prayers after any given reading, simply compose a tweet and include with it #IAS + the entry title, and others will be able to search for and read your insights. For example, the third entry is titled "image." If you would like to share a thought about that entry, you can tweet that thought along with the hashtag #IASimage and others will be able to search for your thoughts.

Bonus Content

For training tools, free downloads, group discussion guides, and other bonus content register at iamsecond.com/livesecondbonus.

Introduction

No Other

I am the Lord,
*   and there is no other. . . .*
I, the Lord, speak the truth;
*   I declare what is right. . . .*
Ignorant are those who carry about idols of wood,
*   who pray to gods that cannot save. . . .*
Turn to me and be saved,
*   all you ends of the earth;*
*   for I am God, and there is no other. . . .*
Before me every knee will bow;
*   by me every tongue will swear.*
They will say of me, "In the Lord alone
*   are deliverance and strength."*
All who have raged against him
*   will come to him and be put to shame.*

—Isaiah 45:18b, 19b, 20b, 22, 23b–24

Maybe you believe in God. Maybe you believe in the idea of God. Maybe you don't know what you believe. Wherever you stand, know that the God of the Bible, the God who sent his Son, Jesus, to die so that whoever believes in him may live, that this God demands nothing less than everything from you. He allows no other god— not money, not success, not comfort or pleasure, not any other god by any other name. He offers deliverance and strength, unconditional and unimaginable love, a deep and personal relationship, a path through this life and into the next. But in return he asks for everything. He must be your top priority, your chief concern, and your only God. He must be First.

Tweet using #IASnoother to share your thoughts.

Discover God

Weeks 1–5

Week 1: Perfect Ruin
Week 2: Abraham
Week 3: Coming Hero
Week 4: Firstborn
Week 5: Death and Life

God created everything. The stars, the planets, the earth, and every-thing in it. Then he made a special creation, people. He dressed this creation in his own image and granted them the title of sons and daughters. He had one rule: don't eat from a certain tree. Simple. Clear. But that first man and that first woman thought themselves above his rule and chose their own way, created their own rules, and became their own rulers. They exchanged goodness and eternity for evil, pain, and eventually death. Through their choice, creation fell to perfect ruin. And with every evil thought, with every selfish motive, with every prideful choice, and with every violent act, we too have eaten their fruit and separated ourselves from the one true God. But God never forgot his special creation and has worked a plan to bring us back. He spoke to Abraham, David, Isaiah, and others, telling them the path of forgiveness, of life and restoration. And he promised a Savior, a Hero who would come and show us that path. He promised his very own Son. This is the story of our God and the rescue of his people . . .

Day 1: Creation

Watch the Tony Evans Film

iamsecond.com/tonyevans

What did you like about, identify with, or learn from Tony's story?

In the beginning, God created the heavens and the earth. . . . And he made mankind in his own image.

—Genesis 1:1, 27

Read the whole passage in Genesis 1:1–28.

What It Says
1. What did you like about this passage?
2. What did you not like or find confusing about this passage?

What It Means
3. What does this passage teach about people?
4. What does this passage teach about God?

Live It. How will you live more Second today?
Tell It. How will you share what you have learned?

Practice It. Get with a friend or someone in your group. Practice or role-play your "Live and Tell" commitments.

Day 2: Image

God created mankind in his own image,
in the image of God he created them;
male and female he created them.

—Genesis 1:27

Read the whole passage in Genesis 1:24–31.

We look like God. We resemble the Creator of the universe. When we ignore the hurting, oppose the neglected, and forget the unwanted, we are not just sinning against some vague moral code; we insult God's masterpiece—the one thing on this planet, and perhaps the universe, made to look like him. Violence, prejudice, selfishness, hateful language, they stain the canvasses painted to reflect God. We honor a few, our favorites. We erect museums for Picasso and Raphael, Halls of Fame for our athlete superstars. But what have we done for everyone else? What have we done for the artwork living next door or sitting in the adjacent cubicle? Have we looked the beggar on the street corner in his eyes and treated him with the respect he deserves? Do we see the thousands of people around us each day and stand in awe at God's creation?

Talk with God

God, so often I forget the love and passion you poured into making my neighbors and coworkers, my friends and even my enemies. Help me see them and love them the same way you do.

Live It. How will you live more Second today?
Tell It. How will you share what you have learned?

🐦 Tweet using #IASimage to share your thoughts.

Day 3: Ruin

For dust you are,
and to dust you will return.

—Genesis 3:19

Read the whole passage in Genesis 3:1–24.

Our years unlimited, our stretch through time free and unend-ing—this was our destiny. Death and sickness were never meant to mar this world. But all was ruined when the father of humanity chose a different path. It wasn't enough for Adam to be like God, to be created in his image. He wanted right and wrong to be his choice. His desire came at a terrible yet promised price: death. Maybe not immediate, but sure nonetheless. Sickness, famine, war, somehow death would come to him and all his descendants. We may blame Adam for sending us down an unretreatable path, but we continue his journey with every prideful thought, with every hateful action, and with every drop of greed. We too are Adam. We too earn our rightful place in death and make clear our need for grace.

Talk with God

God, forgive me for my pride and my failures.

Live It. How will you live more Second today?
Tell It. How will you share what you have learned?

🐦 Tweet using #IASruin to share your thoughts.

Day 4: **Hate**

*The L*ORD *said, "What have you done? Listen! Your brother's blood cries out to me from the ground."*

—**Genesis 4:10**

Read the whole passage in Genesis 4:1–16.

Hatred has many faces. It wears anger and intolerance, pride and impatience, insults and gossiping. The same seed that blossoms into murder begins with small bits of jealousy, rudeness, and neglect. The same root that makes us argue with our neighbors is what matures into war and genocide. The same lack of love that causes abuse and slavery comes from those simple, quiet, but hateful thoughts in our heads. While few of us will ever commit murder, all of us carry the seed from which it springs. Peace will only rule our lives when the love of God finds a place in our hearts, our homes, and our relationships. So let us begin the process of changing hate to love. We can start with a kind word or an honest apology. We can start with humbleness or respect. But wherever we start, love is the medicine for our lives and the prescription for our predicaments.

Talk with God

Forgive my lack of love, God. Help me to love others as you have loved me.

Live It. How will you live more Second today?
Tell It. How will you share what you have learned?

🐦 Tweet using #IAShate to share your thoughts.

Day 5: **Divine Despair**

The LORD saw how great the wickedness of the human race had become on the earth, and that every inclination of the thoughts of the human heart was only evil all the time. The LORD regretted that he had made human beings on the earth, and his heart was deeply troubled.

—Genesis 6:5–6

Read the whole passage in Genesis 6:5–22.

We may convince ourselves that our wrongs, our failures, or our sins affect only us, that they don't hurt anyone else. But they offend God. The Creator, the infinite and eternal being, feels misery at our wickedness. God created humanity to be kind, wise, and good rulers of the earth, to love our neighbors and our God. But too often we hurt rather than heal. We create disunity and strife rather than love and goodness. We use our mouths to gossip rather than defend or encourage. We spend our thoughts on vengeance and greed instead of forgiveness and contentment. But how would our lives and even our world change if God were First, if we thought of his love before we swung our fists, waged our wars, or sought our glory, wealth, and comfort? How would our lives change if the concerns of others and the will of God came before our own?

Talk with God

God, teach me to make you my first thought and your love my chief concern.

Live It. How will you live more Second today?
Tell It. How will you share what you have learned?

🐦 Tweet using #IASdivinedespair to share your thoughts.

Day 6: Reset

Then Noah built an altar to the LORD and, taking some of all the clean animals and clean birds, he sacrificed burnt offerings on it.

—Genesis 8:20

Read the whole passage in Genesis 7–8.

God flooded the whole earth, filled it with carnage and destruction. God's wrath nearly destroyed all life. But as his anger waned and the seas receded, Noah stepped out and committed to a different future, a different path for humanity. The first family began with a forbidden fruit, but Noah's family would start with a sacrifice, a promise to obey, a commitment that God would be their God. What direction have we chosen for our family? Along what path are we leading our children or our siblings? Does our temper get the best of us? Does impatience rather than kindness color our relationships? Does laziness or ingratitude stress and corrode our bond? What road are we traveling with our family, the one that leads to obedience and love or the one that ends in a flood?

Talk with God

God, help me influence my family to follow, obey, and love you.

Live It. How will you live more Second today?
Tell It. How will you share what you have learned?

🐦 Tweet using #IASreset to share your thoughts.

Day 7: Cosmos

When I consider your heavens,
*   the work of your fingers,*
the moon and the stars,
*   which you have set in place,*
what is mankind that you are mindful of them,
*   human beings that you care for them?*
You have made them a little lower than the angels
*   and crowned them with glory and honor.*
You made them rulers over the works of your hands;
*   you put everything under their feet:*
all flocks and herds,
*   and the animals of the wild,*
the birds in the sky,
*   and the fish in the sea,*
*   all that swim the paths of the seas.*
Lord, our Lord,
*   how majestic is your name in all the earth!*

—Psalm 8:3–9

God was not born from our imagination, but we through his. He is Creator, Master, and King. Though he grants us the right to rule over his creation and the freedom to manage his domain, we remain under his reign. We breathe with his consent, walk by his allowance, and rule through his grace.

Talk with God

Worship.

"Lord, how majestic is your name . . ."
God, I worship you because . . .

Tweet using #IAScosmos to share your prayers.

Day 1: The Promise

Watch the Whispering Danny Film

iamsecond.com/whisperingdanny

What did you like about, identify with, or learn from Danny's story?

> *I will make you into a great nation,*
>   *and I will bless you;*
> *I will make your name great,*
>   *and you will be a blessing.*
>
> **—Genesis 12:2**

Read the whole passage in Genesis 12:1–9, 15:1–21.

What It Says
1. What did you like about this passage?
2. What did you not like or find confusing about this passage?

What It Means
3. What does this passage teach about people?
4. What does this passage teach about God?

Live It. How will you live more Second today?
Tell It. How will you share what you have learned?

Practice It. Get with a friend or someone in your group. Practice or role-play your "Live and Tell" commitments.

Day 2: Childless

But Abram said, "Sovereign Lord, what can you give me since I remain childless and the one who will inherit my estate is Eliezer of Damascus? You have given me no children; so a servant in my household will be my heir."

—Genesis 15:2–3

Read the whole passage in Genesis 15:1–3.

Faced with old age and an old promise, Abram was still without children. God had promised to make Abram's descendants great. But still the childless Abram waited. Frustrated and impatient, he confronted God, reminding him of his promise. Too often we hide our needs or emotions from God. Angry about losing a job, frustrated with a family member, hurt by a friend, worried about money, we come to God with if-it's-your-wills and if-you-pleases. Nothing is hidden from God. He knows our pain, our anger, and our frustrations. But he wants us to plainly and honestly talk with him about our needs and our troubles without hidden meanings or veiled intent.

Talk with God

God, this is what is going on in my life and this is what I need . . .

Live It. How will you live more Second today?
Tell It. How will you share what you have learned?

🐦 Tweet using #IASchildless to share your prayers.

Day 3: Goodness

*He took him outside and said, "Look up at the sky and count the stars—if indeed you can count them." Then he said to him, "So shall your offspring be." Abram believed the L*ORD*, and he credited it to him as righteousness.*

—Genesis 15:5–6

Read the whole passage in Genesis 15:4–21.

God made Adam a promise: obey and you will live, but eat the fruit and death will come. Adam chose the latter. And with every selfish action and every hurtful thought, we choose the same. Death reminds us of our choice and of our inability to remedy our broken souls. Our attempts at goodness are never good enough, never perfect or blameless enough to erase the debt we owe. God requires absolute and complete goodness. The kind of goodness or "righteousness" that only God possesses and only he can grant. Abram shows us that it is through faith, through trusting God, that goodness is granted. It is not what we do but whom we trust that makes all the difference. Trusting ourselves or our own goodness will never suffice. Admitting our weakness and trusting God to forgive and grant his goodness is our only hope.

Talk with God

Forgive my feeble attempts at goodness. Teach me to trust you more, to have faith in you and not in my own good deeds.

Live It. How will you live more Second today?
Tell It. How will you share what you have learned?

Tweet using #IASgoodness to share your thoughts.

Day 4: **Child**

Sarah became pregnant and bore a son to Abraham in his old age, at the very time God had promised him. . . . Abraham was a hundred years old when his son Isaac was born to him.

—Genesis 21:2, 5

Read the whole passage in Genesis 21:1–7.

Finally the long-awaited promise came true. A child was born to an aged, desert-wandering couple who could only hope and trust in God's impossible promise. Sometimes we forget that the same God who created the universe, the same God who wrote the laws of physics and who sent his Son to die on a cross, is the same God who still works and moves in this world. The same God chronicled in the Bible still offers strength and rewards, relationship and forgiveness. The God who planned the rise and fall of empires has a plan for you and me. How might our lives be different if we lived with this at the front of our minds? How might the way we treat our families, do our jobs, or interact with others change if we believed that the God who loved Abraham loves us as well?

Talk with God

Thank you for loving me, for knowing me, for caring for me, and for having a plan for my life.

Live It. How will you live more Second today?
Tell It. How will you share what you have learned?

🐦 Tweet using #IASchild to share your thoughts.

Day 5: **The Test**

Take your son, your only son, whom you love—Isaac—and go to the region of Moriah. Sacrifice him there as a burnt offering on a mountain I will show you.

—Genesis 22:2

Read the whole passage in Genesis 22:1–8.

Abraham prayed for a child until he was one hundred years old. God gave him Isaac. But even Abraham's only son could not come before God. God will not share his glory or his position. Sunday church is not enough. Evening prayers or the occasional holiday won't suffice. God is not a fan club to be joined, an idea to be "liked," or a hobby to be toyed with. He is either First in our lives, or we are strangers and enemies. He is a jealous God and does not share top honors with anyone. He demands nothing less than absolute priority. Either we and everything we hold dear take second place to him, or we stop pretending that he is our God.

Talk with God

God, you are First. My family, my career, my possessions, my friends, everything and everyone in my life are second place to you.

Live It. How will you live more Second today?
Tell It. How will you share what you have learned?

Tweet using #IASthetest to share your thoughts.

Day 6: Is He First?

Now I know that you fear God, because you have not
withheld from me your son, your only son.

—Genesis 22:12

Read the whole passage in Genesis 22:1–19.

What takes priority in your life? What makes you hesitate when
God says, "Give it up." Perhaps it's an old wound or a long-held
grudge. Maybe it's pride. Maybe it's your comfort, career, or possessions. Everyone has tests. Everyone has those moments when
God asks, "Am I still First?" What will you say when that moment
comes? Would you pass the test? If God asked, would you sell your
house or quit your job? Would you risk financial stability, relational
connections, or career opportunities if God asked you to prove that
he was still First in your life?

Talk with God

God, I want to make you First in my life. I struggle and I stumble
and I need your help, but I want to be Second.

Live It. How will you live more Second today?
Tell It. How will you share what you have learned?

Tweet using #IASishefirst to share your thoughts.

Day 7: Will You Really?

Then Abraham approached God and said: "Will you sweep away the righteous with the wicked? What if there are fifty righteous people in the city? Will you really sweep it away and not spare the place for the sake of the fifty righteous people in it? Far be it from you to do such a thing—to kill the righteous with the wicked, treating the righteous and the wicked alike. Far be it from you! Will not the Judge of all the earth do right?"

—Genesis 18:23–25

God is not shocked by our grievances or deaf to our concerns. Abraham challenged God's actions and questioned his plans. He insisted God maintain his justice and preserve his people. He demanded that God act like God. The ancient saints approached God with reverence, but also with boldness and honesty. Can we say the same about our own interactions with God?

Talk with God
Ask.

"Will you really . . . ?"
God, because I know this about you, I ask that you . . .

🐦 Tweet using #IASwillyoureally to share your prayers.

Day 1: Failure

Watch the Christian Hosoi Film

iamsecond.com/christianhosoi

What did you like about, identify with, or learn from Christian's story?

> *One evening David got up from his bed and walked around on the roof of the palace. From the roof he saw a woman bathing. The woman was very beautiful . . .*
>
> **—2 Samuel 11:2**

Read the whole passage in 2 Samuel 11:1–27.

What It Says
1. What did you like about this passage?
2. What did you not like or find confusing about this passage?

What It Means
3. What does this passage teach about people?
4. What does this passage teach about God?

Live It. How will you live more Second today?

Tell It. How will you share what you have learned?

Practice It. Get with a friend or someone in your group. Practice or role-play your "Live and Tell" commitments.

Day 2: **King**

"There is still the youngest," Jesse answered. "He is tending the sheep."

—1 Samuel 16:11

Read the whole passage in 1 Samuel 16:1–13.

God choose David to be king of his people. He was a simple, small boy who herded sheep. He smelled of green pastures and open fields. He fought lions and fended off thieves. He did not possess a kingly stature, experience in battle, or knowledge of palace politics. He was just a boy, the youngest of eight sons, but he loved his God—and it was that love and that childlike trust that made him special. God does not use our measurements. He does not value beauty above humility. He does not measure wit and charisma above faith and integrity. God sees the core of our hearts and measures the substance of our being and the truth of our character.

Talk with God

Father, teach me to rely on your strength, your guidance, not my own. Make me the leader you desire by making me the follower you demand.

Live It. How can you live more Second today?
Tell It. How will you share what you have learned?

Tweet using #IASking to share your thoughts.

Day 3: Forever

Your house and your kingdom will endure forever before me;
your throne will be established forever.

—2 Samuel 7:16

Read the whole passage in 2 Samuel 7:1–29.

From shepherd boy to mighty king, from lowly child to hero of his nation, God made the name David synonymous with fame and greatness. Despite all his failures, God made David a promise that he and his descendants would be established forever. Though history journeyed on, his kingdom fell, and his throne all but ceased to exist, God's promise would stand. One day a man would come, a Savior and Prophet, a Hero and King. A morning would dawn when David's line would once again sit on the throne and that throne, would forever endure. They would call that man the Christ or Messiah; we might have called him Hero. God never forgets his people and never fails in his promises. He will follow through on what he commits. No matter how tough life gets or how dreary the day becomes, we can find courage in the fact that God will come through in the end.

Talk with God

You never forget. You never abandon. Despite our failures and through all our mistakes, you still remember your special creation. And for that I praise and thank you.

Live It. How will you live more Second today?
Tell It. How will you share what you have learned?

🐦 Tweet using #IASforever to share your thoughts.

Day 4: Caught

You are the man!
   —2 Samuel 12:7

Read the whole passage in 2 Samuel 11:1–12:14.

It started with a glance, a stray eye, a chance look. The spark grew and the flame fanned. David, known as the man after God's heart, took what was not his and destroyed what could not be fixed. If there was a person who understood God's heart, who knew God's will, who believed in God's law, it was David. But no amount of understanding or faith, no amount of courage or strength, will, or discipline, could root out the blackness that hid in his human heart. Even the best of humanity lay dark and broken at the core. A remnant of goodness, a glimpse of godlike beauty remains, but it is tainted and dirtied by sin. Such stains can only dissolve with God-sized solutions and God-designed remedies. We can only hope for God's grace and beg for his mercy. We cannot erase our wrongs or wipe out their effects on others. We must simply trust and hope in God for forgiveness.

Talk with God

I too have failed. Failed to keep your laws, failed to love my neighbor, to keep pure my mind, to give you my strength. Forgive my failure.

Live It. How will you live more Second today?
Tell It. How will you share what you have learned?

🐦 Tweet using #IAScaught to share your thoughts.

Day 5: Prince of Peace

And he will be called
Wonderful Counselor, Mighty God,
Everlasting Father, Prince of Peace.
He will reign on David's throne
and over his kingdom,
establishing and upholding it
with justice and righteousness
from that time on and forever.

—Isaiah 9:6–7

Read the whole passage in Isaiah 9:1–7.

The forbidden fruit eaten, the world flooded and restarted, the children of Abraham straying, and the kings of Israel failing—in short, humanity had failed. God saw the hopelessness of the human race, the debt of its sin and the surety of its punishment. So God made a promise, the promise of a Savior. This Savior would be called Counselor, God, Father, and Prince. He would come and be the Hero who rescues his people and the Savior who wins the battle. When we are disappointed by friends, hurt by our family, angered at our own failures, we can be encouraged that our Hero will neither fail nor disappoint. Jesus succeeds where we all fail. He holds true when others falter. He is the solid rock on which our life can find security.

Talk with God

You knew our sin, you saw our plight, and you sent your Son to rescue us. For that I can only praise you.

Live It. How will you live more Second today?
Tell It. How will you share what you have learned?

🐦 Tweet using #IASprinceofpeace to share your thoughts.

Day 6: In Our Place

But he was pierced for our transgressions,
he was crushed for our iniquities;
the punishment that brought us peace was on him,
and by his wounds we are healed.
We all, like sheep, have gone astray,
each of us has turned to our own way;
and the LORD has laid on him
the iniquity of us all.

—Isaiah 53:5–6

Read the whole passage in Isaiah 53:1–12.

Despite his offer of forgiveness, his message would not be heard. This promised Hero would be betrayed, beaten, and murdered. He would be pierced for our failures, crushed for our mistakes, and punished for our sin. But through his death would come life. We owe an infinite debt to God, a payment for our evil, restitution for the chaos we plunged this world into. This Hero would be the answer to that debt and the hope of this world. Through this Hero God promised forgiveness no matter how messy our lives or how big our sins. He offered it freely. We can wallow in our guilt, run from our past, or hide from our faults; but God offers to wash it all away, if we let him.

Talk with God

Thank you for providing a way for my sins to be forgiven.

Live It. How will you live more Second today?
Tell It. How will you share what you have learned?

🐦 Tweet using #IASinourplace to share your thoughts.

Day 7: Savior

My soul glorifies the Lord
*   and my spirit rejoices in God my Savior,*
for he has been mindful
*   of the humble state of his servant.*
From now on all generations will call me blessed,
*   for the Mighty One has done great things for me—*
*   holy is his name.*
His mercy extends to those who fear him,
*   from generation to generation.*
He has performed mighty deeds with his arm;
*   he has scattered those who are proud in their inmost thoughts.*
He has brought down rulers from their thrones
*   but has lifted up the humble.*
He has filled the hungry with good things
*   but has sent the rich away empty.*
He has helped his servant Israel,
*   remembering to be merciful*
to Abraham and his descendants forever,
*   just as he promised our ancestors.*

—Luke 1:46–55

No king can stand before his might. No mortal can wink at his strength. Nothing and no one can stand in his way. But despite his enormity, love is his name, kindness is his reputation. He could snuff out all life with a word and destroy all matter with a thought, but instead he loves. He remembers his people and extends mercy to the faithful.

Talk with God

Worship.

"My soul glorifies the Lord . . ."
God, I worship you because . . .

🐦 Tweet using #IASsavior to share your prayers.

Day 1: Birth

Watch the Jim Monroe Film

iamsecond.com/jimmonroe

What did you like about, identify with, or learn from Jim's story?

> *Today in the town of David a Savior has been born to you; he is the Messiah, the Lord.*
>
> **—Luke 2:11**

Read the whole passage in Luke 2:1–21.

What It Says
1. What did you like about this passage?
2. What did you not like or find confusing about this passage?

What It Means
3. What does this passage teach about people?
4. What does this passage teach about God?

Live It. How will you live more Second today?
Tell It. How will you share what you have learned?

Practice It. Get with a friend or someone in your group. Practice or role-play your "Live and Tell" commitments.

Day 2: My Son

This is my Son, whom I love; with him I am well pleased.

—Matthew 3:17

Read the whole passage in Matthew 3:1–17.

The Son of God became flesh and blood. He walked with angels. The universe bent to his will and shook at his voice. But he set it all aside and became a child. A feeding trough held him through his first night on earth. His hospital reeked of animal dung and donkeys. This wasn't the welcome of a hero, a king. This was the life of an impoverished child, a child born to a fleeing family in a conquered nation. He didn't bring an entourage. He didn't dress in glowing robes or a halo. Instead, he lived the simple life of a carpenter, and when the time was right, he stepped into the Jordan River and inaugurated his ministry. This heart of humbleness, submission, and sacrifice brought praise from his Father. How different our inner voices must be from his. How much time do we waste dreaming of our own grandeur or importance, our comfort or our popularity, when all the while the Father is most impressed with his Son, who gave up everything to die a carpenter?

Talk with God

Teach me to live a humble life, to attempt to bring greatness to your name, and to dream of growing your kingdom.

Live It. How will you live more Second today?
Tell It. How will you share what you have learned?

Tweet using #IASmyson to share your thoughts.

Day 3: Walker

Then he said to the paralyzed man, "Get up, take your mat and go home." And the man got up and went home.

—Matthew 9:6–7

Read the whole passage in Matthew 9:1–8.

Jesus made the blind see, the dead rise, and the lame walk. But he went further than that; he also forgave sins. While we may be able to forgive each other for certain offenses, only God can forgive in any absolute sense. We can forgive wrongs committed against each other by refusing to hold a grudge or press charges or require repayment. But we are never the only ones wronged. When we lie, cheat, steal, or mistreat someone, we not only hurt that person but also the one who created that person. We offend and sin against God. And no human can forgive sin against God. That is the right of God alone and one he freely exercises for all who ask him for forgiveness.

Talk with God

Thank you for offering your forgiveness. I confess my need for it.

Live It. How will you live more Second today?
Tell It. How will you share what you have learned?

Tweet using #IASwalker to share your thoughts.

Day 4: Sheep Keeper

I give them eternal life, and they shall never perish; no one will snatch them out of my hand. My Father, who has given them to me, is greater than all; no one can snatch them out of my Father's hand. I and the Father are one.

—John 10:28–30

Read the whole passage in John 10:1–30.

Every shepherd has two dangers. The danger of wandering sheep that drift from the fold and step into hazard's way and the danger of thieves who care nothing for the sheep, only for their bellies and their wallets. A good shepherd guards against both. Once placed in God's fold, a believer need never worry about falling or being snatched away. No amount of ignorance, stupidity, or temptation can drag us off. For though we, like sheep, all wander, we will never outpace our Shepherd. Jesus keeps us safe and holds us near. So when nagging doubts crop up about whether God still loves us, about whether Jesus really saved us, we can be assured and let our minds rest in this truth: the Shepherd still stands guard.

Talk with God

Continue to watch over me as my Good Shepherd. Keep me from dangers. Keep me from my own missteps. Keep me from wandering.

Live It. How will you live more Second today?
Tell It. How will you share what you have learned?

Tweet using #IASsheepkeeper to share your thoughts.

Day 5: Eyes Open

"Lord, I want to see," he replied.
   Jesus said to him, "Receive your sight; your faith has healed you."

—**Luke 18:41–42**

Read the whole passage in Luke 18:31–43.

He came to heal the sick, to restore the injured, and to give sight to the blind. But a good doctor does more than heal the symptoms; he addresses the cause of those symptoms. Blind eyes signal a broken world. Lame feet tell of an imperfect universe, one that allows pain and injury, injustice and suffering, an existence ruled by chaos and chance rather than order and benevolence. The Creator of the universe became part of that universe, a man who walked among his creatures. He did it all so that those who believe in him, those with faith in his strength could be healed of the disease of sin. We all have our symptoms. Physical or emotional, financial or relational, our jobs or our marriage, problems at school or at home. But while self-help books and celebrity doctors may offer treatments to soothe some of the pain, only Jesus can erase the disease itself.

Talk with God

Fix my broken world, Father. Provide for my needs. Heal my strained relationships and physical ailments, but most of all heal my soul stained with sin.

Live It. How will you live more Second today?
Tell It. How will you share what you have learned?

Tweet using #IASeyesopen to share your thoughts.

Day 6: **Looking**

The Son of Man came to seek and to save the lost.

—Luke 19:10

Read the whole passage in Luke 19:1–10.

Jesus came for those who know their lostness and who recognize their sickness. Healthy people do not go to the hospital. Those who do not know they are lost don't slow down to ask for directions. But if we admit our sickness and come clean about our lostness, Jesus offers eternal life in heaven. It is a gift that is neither earned by good deeds nor granted to those with good intentions. Heaven is not won when the good outweighs the bad nor given if we are not as bad as the next guy. We can put away all our dreams of impressing God and accept that we are already loved. We do not need to dress up to make him smile or clean up before he accepts us home.

Talk with God

I know my best deeds on my best days can never earn your favor. Forgive me of my failures and give me the strength to accept your grace.

Live It. How will you live more Second today?
Tell It. How will you share what you have learned?

🐦 Tweet using #IASlooking to share your thoughts.

Day 7: **Warned**

"You are my son;
today I have become your father.
Ask me,
and I will make the nations your inheritance,
the ends of the earth your possession.
You will break them with a rod of iron;
you will dash them to pieces like pottery."
Therefore, you kings, be wise;
be warned, you rulers of the earth.
Serve the LORD with fear
and celebrate his rule with trembling.
Kiss his son, or he will be angry
and your way will lead to your destruction,
for his wrath can flare up in a moment.
Blessed are all who take refuge in him.

—Psalm 2:7–12

God is full of kindness and grace, love and mercy. But his patience will not last forever. Judgment will come. We will be called to give an account of our lives. Whether or not we accept his existence or protest his deity, we will face his throne. Surrender is our only real option. Mercy is our only real hope. We have been warned.

Talk with God

Surrender.

"Be warned . . ."
God, I surrender my life and these plans . . .

🐦 Tweet using #IASwarned to share your prayers.

Day 1: One Way

Watch the Lecrae Film

iamsecond.com/lecrae

What did you like about, identify with, or learn from Lecrae's story?

> *I am the way and the truth and the life. No one comes to the Father except through me.*
>
> **—John 14:6**

Read the whole passage in John 14:1–14.

What It Says
    1. What did you like about this passage?
    2. What did you not like or find confusing about this passage?

What It Means
    3. What does this passage teach about people?
    4. What does this passage teach about God?

Live It. How will you live more Second today?
Tell It. How will you share what you have learned?

Practice It. Get with a friend or someone in your group. Practice or role-play your "Live and Tell" commitments.

Day 2: Coming Spirit

*Unless I go away, the Advocate will not come to you; but if
I go, I will send him to you. When he comes, he will prove
the world to be in the wrong about sin and righteousness
and judgment: about sin, because people do not believe in
me; about righteousness, because I am going to the Father,
where you can see me no longer; and about judgment,
because the prince of this world now stands condemned.*

—John 16:7–11

Read the whole passage in John 16:1–15.

Everyone has a certain moral compass, an internal guide im-
parted at birth and honed with time and culture. But this compass
warps with the onset of sin. Something about this broken world, our
imperfect upbringings, bad habits, and violated consciences turn
this moral guide into a guess-o-meter. It always points somewhere,
but north never stays true. That small voice in the back of our heads,
that gnawing guilt deep in our bellies, that pricking conscience hidden in our soul—we attempt to quiet these with societal excuses and
mental gymnastics. But the Advocate, the Spirit, cannot be silenced
or twisted. He brings sure conviction and correction. He provides
the resounding voice of God's law. He brings erring souls to Jesus
and straying children back to the Father. We must only listen for his
guidance and ready our ears for his wisdom.

Talk with God

Teach me the voice of your Spirit and the sound of your conviction.

Live It. How will you live more Second today?
Tell It. How will you share what you have learned?

🐦 Tweet using #IAScomingspirit to share your thoughts.

Day 3: **Last Dinner**

And he took bread, gave thanks and broke it, and gave it to them, saying, "This is my body given for you; do this in remembrance of me." In the same way, after the supper he took the cup, saying, "This cup is the new covenant in my blood, which is poured out for you."

—Luke 22:19–20

Read the whole passage in Luke 22:14–20.

The tearing of bread to remind us of his broken body and beaten corpse. The warmth and redness of wine to recall the blood he spilled to secure our salvation. Simple graphic reminders of a sacrifice that painted the world red and offered a path to God. For two thousand years, believers have eaten bread and drunk wine in remembrance of a slain Hero, the Savior sacrificed, the Son of God's death on a cross to bring forgiveness and life to all who believe. It reminds us to live a life worthy of his sacrifice. Inspires us to think of him whenever we eat, whenever we drink, whenever we do the everyday mundane tasks of our life. And it reminds us to shape our life around that memory.

Talk with God

God, I praise you for sending your Son, whose body was broken and blood was spilled to grant me new life.

Live It. How will you live more Second today?
Tell It. How will you share what you have learned?

🐦 Tweet using #IASlastdinner to share your thoughts.

Day 4: **Arrest and Trial**

"What crime has this man committed? I have found in him no grounds for the death penalty. Therefore I will have him punished and then release him." But with loud shouts they insistently demanded that he be crucified, and their shouts prevailed.

—Luke 23:22–23

Read the whole passage in Luke 22:47–71, 23:1–25.

"Not I," we all cry over the shouts of the mob. Surely we would never join such injustice, never allow such evil. We picture ourselves as one of the disciples, one of the good guys. But never Judas, never the mob, never Peter who abandoned his lord in his time of need. But no one in that crowd woke up that morning saying, "Today, I am going to lynch the Son of God." But lynch they did. Just days before, the crowded streets of Jerusalem roared with joyous raucous at the entrance of their Messiah, but now they shouted for his execution. Even unbelieving Pilate saw the injustice, though he refused to intervene. "You hypocrite," Jesus once said. "First take the plank out of your own eye, and then you will see clearly to remove the speck from your brother's eye." Perhaps our mental pictures should place our faces amidst the mob, with the unmoving Pilate, or with the scared Peter. Perhaps we think too highly of ourselves that we would not be swayed by a mob or moved by erring leaders.

Talk with God

God, give me the humbleness to see my failures, my weaknesses, and my mistakes with honest eyes.

Live It. How will you live more Second today?
Tell It. How will you share what you have learned?

🐦 Tweet using #IASarrestandtrial to share your thoughts.

Day 5: Execution

Father, into your hands I commit my spirit.

—Luke 23:46

Read the whole passage in Luke 23:26–56.

Jesus came because there was a price to a pay and a promise to fulfill. It was a promise that one day the world would end its wars and find peace from evil. It was a promise that rang true at Jesus' death and came to fruition at his resurrection. Through his death sin is forgiven, the chains of evil broken, and the debt of humanity erased. While this world persists, its evils will still prevail. But Jesus promises a new and unending life, a new world after this one, one without sickness or pain or trouble. He promises, for those who follow him, a new heaven and a new earth will be our future. We are offered it free and clear if only we accept it.

Talk with God

Teach me to spend my life never forgetting the sacrifice your Son offered.

Live It. How will you live more Second today?

Tell It. How will you share what you have learned?

🐦 Tweet using #IASexecution to share your thoughts.

Day 6: Risen

Why do you look for the living among the dead? He is not here; he has risen!

—Luke 24:5–6

Read the whole passage in Luke 24:1–8.

The grave could not hold him. Death could not defeat him. Hell could not prevail against him. Dead and buried for three days, Jesus, the coming Hero, the promised Messiah, the Son of God, sprang from his tomb alive and well. The debt of humanity's erring ways paid in full for all those who accept and believe. Jesus conquered death that we too may find victory over its hold. He offers hope when all else fails. He offers a future when all else ends. He offers what no one else can: eternal life. He offers it because he and he alone won over death. The question is, will we accept this offer? It is both free and exorbitant. Free in that he asks only for faith, for us to throw ourselves on his mercy and admit our inadequacy. Exorbitant because it cost the life and death of the Son of God, a price we did not pay but that was paid on our account.

Talk with God

Forgive me for my sins. Save me from my errors. I believe in the sacrifice of your Son. I commit to live the rest of my life never forgetting the price of my freedom.

Live It. How will you live more Second today?
Tell It. How will you share what you have learned?

🐦 Tweet using #IASrisen to share your thoughts.

Day 7: Every Knee

Who, being in very nature God,
did not consider equality with God something to be used
to his own advantage;
rather, he made himself nothing
by taking the very nature of a servant,
being made in human likeness.
And being found in appearance as a man,
he humbled himself
by becoming obedient to death—even death on a cross!
Therefore God exalted him to the highest place
and gave him the name that is above every name,
that at the name of Jesus every knee should bow,
in heaven and on earth and under the earth,
and every tongue acknowledge that Jesus Christ is Lord,
to the glory of God the Father.

—Philippians 2:6–11

He had everything to boast about. Every reason to come with pomp and power. He was the Son of God, the ruler of all existence. But he came to earth as a humble servant. No bright lights or big parades, just a small baby boy born in a barnyard stable. If Jesus did not boast, what right have we to?

Talk with God

Surrender.

"**. . . he** made himself nothing . . ."
God, I surrender my life and my plans . . .

Tweet using #IASeveryknee to share your prayers.

Session Two

Issues

Weeks 6–9
Week 6: Struggles
Week 7: Relationships
Week 8: Success
Week 9: Identity

Love. Success. Happiness. Everyone is looking for something. We search for it in pleasure, money, or relationships. We scour the earth for that thing that can fill our souls, bring meaning to our lives, and give us rest from life's troubles, but nothing works. Nothing can fill the vacuum in our chests. Relationships may soothe for a time, money may give pleasure for a while, but struggles, failure, and death overtake us all in the end. Nothing in this life can truly satisfy, truly last, or bring wholeness. But while this life will always be plagued with struggles, with broken relationships, and with a world of empty money, pleasure, and success, there is hope. A hope called Jesus. A Jesus who forgives our struggles, heals our relationships, and brings value to our work and meaning to our life.

Day 1: Clean

Watch the Brian "Head" Welch Film

iamsecond.com/brianwelch

What did you like about, identify with, or learn from Brian's story?

They saw the man who had been possessed by the legion of demons, sitting there, dressed and in his right mind.

—Mark 5:15

Read the whole passage in Mark 5:1–20.

What It Says
1. What did you like about this passage?
2. What did you not like or find confusing about this passage?

What It Means
3. What does this passage teach about people?
4. What does this passage teach about God?

Live It. How will you live more Second today?

Tell It. How will you share what you have learned?

Practice It. Get with a friend or someone in your group. Practice or role-play your "Live and Tell" commitments.

Day 2: Forgiven

Your sins are forgiven. . . . Your faith has saved you; go in peace.

—Luke 7:48, 50

Read the whole passage in Luke 7:36–50.

A woman walks in and pours a year's wages worth of perfume on Jesus' feet. A woman known in her community not for her generosity or goodness but for being a "sinner"—the kind of woman found on late-night street corners. Her scented offering became the expression of her faith, of her desire and gratitude for the forgiveness that Jesus brought. While the religious leaders of the day offered only condemnation, Jesus offered forgiveness and a path back to God. Jesus knew the greater the sinner, the greater the appreciation for the beauty of forgiveness. No matter our sin, no matter our history, our mistakes or our struggles, Jesus offers forgiveness. No life is too tattered, no soul too battered, no heart is too dirtied to be saved by the forgiveness of Jesus.

Talk with God

Forgive me for my failures and weaknesses and teach me to live a life of grateful response.

Live It. How will you live more Second today?
Tell It. How will you share what you have learned?

Tweet using #IASforgiven to share your thoughts.

Day 3: Confession

Therefore confess your sins to each other and pray for each other so that you may be healed.

—James 5:16

Read the whole passage in James 5:13–16.

The problem must first be recognized. We must admit that something is wrong. Without this confession, nothing more can happen. No one with a broken leg asks for running shoes. No one with an empty tank asks for new tires. They first confess the reason for their immobility and then proceed to address that reason. The cause of divorce, crime, violence, and poverty has but one root. The connection between sin and brokenness may not always be immediate or obvious; one bad thought does not always equal a stubbed toe or a jammed finger. But the root of the world's broken system is sin. And it is this confession that allows healing to commence both in our lives and in the lives of those around us.

Talk with God

Father, I confess to you my failures and promise to confess the same to those I have wronged.

Live It. How will you live more Second today?
Tell It. How will you share what you have learned?

Tweet using #IASconfession to share your thoughts.

Day 4: **Death to Sin**

Therefore do not let sin reign in your mortal body so that you obey its evil desires.

—Romans 6:12

Read the whole passage in Romans 6:1–14.

Jesus changes everything. With him, no longer can pride be our haven, nor selfishness our habit. Pleasure must cease its reign, and materialism must relinquish its hold on our hearts. Self must be made Second. He must be named First. Jesus is not a club one joins or a band one follows. He is not a sport one plays or a company one works at. He is King. He is Master. It is "Yes, sir." Not "I'll think about it." It is, "You lead. I'll follow. You speak. I jump." It is not Jesus and whatever. It is Jesus and obedience. It is death to sin and down with the tyranny of evil in our lives. Facing our struggles starts with naming our king. Will it be this world, this age, our habit of error and pattern of selfishness, or will it be God? We can serve but one.

Talk with God

God, I choose you as king. I choose you as the ruler of my life. It is you I wish to follow and you I wish to obey. Give me your patience, your strength, and your protection as I commit to you.

Live It. How will you live more Second today?
Tell It. How will you share what you have learned?

Tweet using #IASdeathtosin to share your thoughts.

Day 5: **Enslaved**

*Just as you used to offer yourselves as slaves to impurity
and to ever-increasing wickedness, so now offer yourselves
as slaves to righteousness leading to holiness.*

—Romans 6:19

Read the whole passage in Romans 6:15–23.

For some it is alcohol or drugs. For many, gossip, lust, or pride.
For others maybe shopping, television, or Twinkies. Everyone has a
deadly habit, a pattern of life and thought that enslaves us to sin and
evil. It captures our attention and makes us dependent on something other than God. That something cares not if we live, cares not
if we suffer or if we poison our future. It is without a heart, without
a care, without a desire that we succeed or live full lives. For it is
Jesus, and him alone, who came to bring us life to the fullest. He
is a demanding king and an exacting master, but one with our best
interest at heart. While few will see their struggle or their addiction
melt away at the moment of faith, all can be sure that trusting Jesus
means that sin no longer reigns supreme, that Jesus will one day
make us perfect.

Talk with God

God, start that process in me. You know my struggles, and you
know my addictions. Give me the freedom from those habits I so
desperately need.

Live It. How will you live more Second today?
Tell It. How will you share what you have learned?

🐦 Tweet using #IASenslaved to share your thoughts.

Day 6: **Addict**

I do not understand what I do. For what I want to do I do not do, but what I hate I do.

—Romans 7:15

Read the whole passage in Romans 7:14–25.

The apostle Paul, the theologian of the early church, the author of thirteen biblical books, a hero of the early faith, and a man who still struggled, still wavered, still found himself addicted to that which he hated. Often, we look at those who lead, especially leaders of churches and ministries, as superhuman. We imagine such leaders as without fault or at least serious fault, as beyond deep and disturbing problems. But there is something damaged and twisted in the heart of all of us, something that still rebels against God and his ways. That brokenness or twisted drive is sin, a force that pushes all of us toward destructive habits and compels all of us to do that which we hate. The mark of a follower of Jesus, of one who lives Second, is not perfection (though that will come in the end); it is the fight, the struggle to turn the tides of our desires toward the Maker of our souls.

Talk with God

God, give me the strength to fight the good fight, to run the good race, and to reach for the prize.

Live It. How will you live more Second today?
Tell It. How will you share what you have learned?

🐦 Tweet using #IASaddict to share your thoughts.

Day 7: Undeserved

*Praise the L*ORD*, my soul;*
    all my inmost being, praise his holy name.
*Praise the L*ORD*, my soul,*
    and forget not all his benefits—
who forgives all your sins
    and heals all your diseases,
who redeems your life from the pit
    and crowns you with love and compassion,
who satisfies your desires with good things
    so that your youth is renewed like the eagle's.
*The L*ORD *works righteousness*
    and justice for all the oppressed.

—Psalm 103:1–6

Confession is the act of acknowledging God's right to judge but trusting in his habit to forgive. Nothing we do or say can obligate God to forgive. We cannot be good enough to earn forgiveness or perfect enough to not need it. But if we humbly ask for it, he gives it every time.

Talk with God

Forgive.

". . . forgives all your sins . . ."
God, forgive me for . . .

🐦 Tweet using #IASundeserved to share your prayers.

Day 1: Forgive

Watch the Jeff and Cheryl Scruggs Film

iamsecond.com/
jeffandcherylscruggs

What did you like about, identify with, or learn from the Scruggses' story?

> *But we had to celebrate and be glad, because this brother of yours was dead and is alive again; he was lost and is found.*
> **—Luke 15:32**

Read the whole passage in Luke 15:11–32.

What It Says
1. What did you like about this passage?
2. What did you not like or find confusing about this passage?

What It Means
3. What docs this passage teach about people?
4. What does this passage teach about God?

Live It. How will you live more Second today?
Tell It. How will you share what you have learned?

Practice It. Get with a friend or someone in your group. Practice or role-play your "Live and Tell" commitments.

Day 2: Release

Then the master called the servant in. "You wicked servant,"
he said, "I canceled all that debt of yours because you
begged me to. Shouldn't you have had mercy on your fellow
servant just as I had on you?"

—Matthew 18:32–33

Read the whole passage in Matthew 18:21–35.

With deep wounds or unintentional annoyance, with old hurts or fresh cuts, with long struggles or slips of the tongue, whatever the case, whatever the relationship, however terrible the wrong, forgiveness is the answer. It may not be accepted. It may not change the other's behavior. It may not immediately restore the relationship. But forgiveness is what lets hurts heal, relationships begin recovery, and life to move on. Without it, loneliness will be our deepest friend, bitterness our home, and hurt our constant companion. God forgave all of our wrongs, all our sin, all our hurtful and painful offenses, all the darkness and violence, all the cruelty and neglect. He forgave it all. Surely, if God forgave every ounce of our own wrong, both secret and known, then we can forgive the comparably few wrongs that others have done to us.

Talk with God

Teach me to forgive as you have forgiven me.

Live It. How will you live more Second today?
Tell It. How will you share what you have learned?

🐦 Tweet using #IASrelease to share your thoughts.

Day 3: Love

"The most important commandment," answered Jesus, "is this: 'Hear, O Israel: The Lord our God, the Lord is one. Love the Lord your God with all your heart and with all your soul and with all your mind and with all your strength.' The second is this: 'Love your neighbor as yourself.' There is no commandment greater than these."

—Mark 12:29–31

Read the whole passage in Mark 12:28–34.

Love is not a feeling. It's not a romantic word. It's not a flippant or casual word. But a God-sized word. A word that captures all that Jesus said. All that he taught. All that he hoped to convey in this world. It is the anthem of God. The command above all other commands. The reason for our creation and the foundation of all relationships. The mark of our faith and the goal of our life. It is that thing for which we strive, that height we seek to climb, and that purpose for which we move and breathe and live.

Talk with God

I love you. Help me love more. Mark my life with love. Fill my breath, my steps, and my every movement with love.

Live It. How will you live more Second today?
Tell It. How will you share what you have learned?

🐦 Tweet using #IASlove to share your thoughts.

Day 4: Footwash

Now that I, your Lord and Teacher, have washed your feet, you also should wash one another's feet. I have set you an example that you should do as I have done for you.

—John 13:14–15

Read the whole passage in John 13:1–20, 34–35.

Never have feet been the pinnacle of beauty or cleanliness, but modern man has found ways to reduce much of the smell and dirtiness associated with biped locomotion. Socks and shoes, pavement and combustion engines have done wonders for the hygiene of the foot. But in the days before Nike and Reebok, before sidewalks and public transportation, feet were dirty things. The sharp smell of dust-caked feet and sun-baked funk scented the bottoms of every traveler and laborer, market shopper and street evangelist, wandering rabbi and following disciple. But despite the dirt and the smell and the humiliation, Jesus washed the feet of his disciples. The First became last. The Lord and Teacher became the servant. And he calls us to do the same. Whatever honor we have earned, whatever rights we have acquired, whatever prestige we hold, Jesus calls us to set those aside and become a servant, an example of love and humbleness. Where are the smelly feet in our world?

Talk with God

God, give me the humility to love without reward.

Live It. How will you live more Second today?
Tell It. How will you share what you have learned?

Tweet using #IASfootwash to share your thoughts.

Day 5: Love Defined

If I speak in the tongues of men or of angels, but do not have love, I am only a resounding gong or a clanging cymbal.

—1 Corinthians 13:1

Read the whole passage in 1 Corinthians 13:1–8.

Love is not a line on our to-do list. It is the whole list, the only goal, the only task in life. Love is God's defining attribute, his all-encompassing requirement, his only law. Mastery of words, intellect, success, power, friendship, or romance—none of these matters without love. All of life, every good deed, every noble task, if not colored and painted with love creates only an empty canvas. From the mundane to the profound, from cleaning dishes to curing cancer, nothing matters without love, and everything matters with it. Relationships are pointless and powerless without it. Love has little to do with feelings and everything to do with selfless, humble, thoughtful care for another person.

Talk with God

You loved us while we were still your enemy, you died for us while we cursed your name, and you planned our salvation knowing our rebellion and pride. We love, because you loved first.

Live It. How will you live more Second today?
Tell It. How will you share what you have learned?

🐦 Tweet using #IASlovedefined to share your thoughts.

Day 6: Unify

Make my joy complete by being like-minded, having the same love, being one in spirit and of one mind.

—Philippians 2:2

Read the whole passage in Philippians 2:1–11.

Relationships are work. Differences surface, arguments come, disagreement and fighting seem a constant threat. Being of one mind does not erase friction or conflict. It means that when differing views or desires erupt in a relationship, love wins out. Humbleness reminds us that we do not know everything and we might be wrong. Forgiveness teaches us that if Jesus forgave us for everything, then we can forgive each other for a few things. Unity calls us to remember that we are children of the same God and servants in the same kingdom. Wrapped together, practiced consistently, and held dear, these acts create love. Is love the basis of your relationships?

Talk with God

Teach me to love in such a way that makes humility, forgiveness, and unity flourish.

Live It. How will you live more Second today?
Tell It. How will you share what you have learned?

🐦 Tweet using #IASunify to share your thoughts.

Day 7: Unity

My prayer is not for them alone. I pray also for those who will believe in me through their message, that all of them may be one, Father, just as you are in me and I am in you. May they also be in us so that the world may believe that you have sent me. I have given them the glory that you gave me, that they may be one as we are one—I in them and you in me—so that they may be brought to complete unity. Then the world will know that you sent me and have loved them even as you have loved me.

—John 17:20–23

Love is the sign of our faith. Unity is the motif of our spirituality. As the Father and the Son are one, so must we be. Bitterness and resentment should have no place in our lives. Unforgiveness and prejudice should find no home in our community. Our lives and our prayers should be littered with concern for others and care for those around us.

Talk with God

Ask.

". . . that they may be one as we are one . . ."
God, I ask you to heal these relationships . . .

Tweet using #IASunity to share your prayers.

Day 1: Give

Watch the Brian Sumner Film

iamsecond.com/briansumner

What did you like, identify with, or learn from Brian's story?

But Zacchaeus stood up and said to the Lord, "Look, Lord! Here and now I give half of my possessions to the poor, and if I have cheated anybody out of anything, I will pay back four times the amount."

—Luke 19:8

Read the whole passage in Luke 19:1–10.

What It Says
1. What did you like about this passage?
2. What did you not like or find confusing about this passage?

What It Means
3. What does this passage teach about people?
4. What does this passage teach about God?

Live It. How will you live more Second today?
Tell It. How will you share what you have learned?

Practice It. Get with a friend or someone in your group. Practice or role-play your "Live and Tell" commitments.

Day 2: Ownership

At harvest time he sent a servant to the tenants so they would give him some of the fruit of the vineyard. But the tenants beat him and sent him away empty-handed.

—Luke 20:10

Read the whole passage in Luke 20:9–16.

We are the tenants of this world, the renters of this planet. We did not make it, and we do not own it. We have been given the responsibility to rule it, to care for it, and to make it prosper. But the cows on the hills, the stone in the streets, and the money in our pockets are not our own. They are his. This changes everything. No longer must we be generous with our things, but we are stewards of his things. No longer are we seekers of wealth and prosperity; we are caretakers of his interests on this planet. Making money, growing business, improving our community—all are good things but for a different reason, for his reason, for his purpose. How often do we view our wealth as a means to his end, our goods and opportunities as an avenue for God's kingdom? How often do we invest and prosper with God's goals in mind? Would this not change our budget to an investment portfolio, something to grow, to manage, and to use with purpose and foresight?

Talk with God

God, give me the wisdom to use my money and wealth with your ends in mind, with your kingdom as the goal.

Live It. How will you live more Second today?

Tell It. How will you share what you have learned?

Tweet using #IASownership to share your thoughts.

Day 3: Camels

It is easier for a camel to go through the eye of a needle than for someone who is rich to enter the kingdom of God.

—Mark 10:25

Read the whole passage in Mark 10:17–31.

Money. A little is never enough, and a lot is never much. The taste of it drives us to consume more and more until money and success and things are all we want, all we think about, all we drive toward. All without us seeing it happen; it blinds and masks our spiritual senses. Wealth gives us a sense of security and confidence, the surety that we can do it ourselves, that we can create and build and provide for ourselves. And while God lets us play in our sandboxes for a while, life will one day end and then we will face our King. Entrance into his kingdom has nothing to do with job titles or 401(k)s or manicured lawns, and everything to do with our heart, our affections, and our priorities. God will only want to know one thing. Was he First? Did the death and resurrection of his Son, the forgiveness he offered, and the faith he demanded, did it all come before our houses and our cars, our comfort and our televisions? Did we live Second, or did the things of this world consume our attention?

Talk with God

Forgive my failure to remember that you are always First.

Live It. How will you live more Second today?
Tell It. How will you share what you have learned?

Tweet using #IAScamels to share your thoughts.

Day 4: Treasure

No one can serve two masters. Either you will hate the one and love the other, or you will be devoted to the one and despise the other. You cannot serve both God and money.

—Matthew 6:24

Read the whole passage in Matthew 6:19–34.

God is not fooled. He knows our loyalty. He sees our hearts. If worries about career or cars, about retirement or stock markets, if any concern comes before his own, then God is not our master. We can serve only one. That master can be culture, comfort, money, or marriage. But if we claim to follow God, if we claim his name or call ourselves believers, then God must be our chief concern, his will our chief thought. Serving God comes with untold rewards and everlasting promises, but he demands everything in return. He will allow no other god and no other priority to take his place in our hearts.

Talk with God

I give up the gods of comfort and career to you. Nothing and no one will take your place in my life.

Live It. How will you live more Second today?
Tell It. How will you share what you have learned?

🐦 Tweet using #IAStreasure to share your thoughts.

Day 5: Vain

Yet when I surveyed all that my hands had done
and what I had toiled to achieve,
everything was meaningless, a chasing after the wind;
nothing was gained under the sun.

—Ecclesiastes 2:11

Read the whole passage in Ecclesiastes 2:1–11.

Empires fall, history forgets, and money dissipates. Success by any definition this world can offer will not breach the bounds of eternity. Nothing in this world lasts. All that our hands touch will go to dust. Only God remains. If we bank on what we can do, what we can save, what we can build or retire on, then we plan for only the seventy or eighty years we wander on earth. If we hold fast to the concerns and cares of this life, without thinking first of those of the next, then we strive in vain and we chase the wind. What might it look like to work for eternal goals, to build success for the next life, to plan for the truly long haul? What would change if nothing else but heaven really mattered?

Talk with God

Forgive me for planning for so near in the future, for seeing only the present life and not the one you have planned ahead.

Live It. How will you live more Second today?
Tell It. How will you share what you have learned?

🐦 Tweet using #IASvain to share your thoughts.

Day 6: **Naked**

Everyone comes naked from their mother's womb,
and as everyone comes, so they depart.
They take nothing from their toil
that they can carry in their hands.

—Ecclesiastes 5:15

Read the whole passage in Ecclesiastes 5:10–20.

Naked we came into this life and naked we will leave it. Nothing escapes the portal of death. Nothing passes the guard of the next life. Every earthly investment, no matter the security, no matter the long-term possibilities, is only and always a short-term investment. But what we invest in the kingdom of God, what we build in God's name, is built for the next life, for eternity. Enjoy present wealth. Enjoy work. Enjoy food and good weather, happy moments and quiet afternoons. But enjoy it not as the destination but as the rest stop along the way, as a glimpse of heaven and a coming inheritance. If we fool ourselves into thinking that what we hold in our hands matters more than what God prepares as an eternal reward, then all will be lost.

Talk with God

Give me the eyes to see what really matters in life.

Live It. How will you live more Second today?
Tell It. How will you share what you have learned?

Tweet using #IASnaked to share your thoughts.

Day 7: Enough

*Two things I ask of you, L*ORD*;*
    do not refuse me before I die:
Keep falsehood and lies far from me;
    give me neither poverty nor riches,
    but give me only my daily bread.
Otherwise, I may have too much and disown you
    *and say, "Who is the L*ORD*?"*
Or I may become poor and steal,
    and so dishonor the name of my God.

—Proverbs 30:7–9

Sometimes we approach God as if he doesn't care about our personal lives. We ask him for world peace or the universal spread of his fame but forget to ask him for next week's groceries. We ask him for the right president but not for the electric bill. The danger with this is we start to think that we paid the bills and that we earned the groceries. Our wealth makes us forget our God. Make it a habit instead to ask him for your needs and to praise him when he provides.

Talk with God

Ask.

"I ask of you . . ."
God, I need . . .

Tweet using #IASenough to share your prayers.

Day 1: **New Birth**

Watch the Tamara Jolee Film

iamsecond.com/tamarajolee

What did you like about, identify with, or learn from Tamara's story?

Very truly I tell you, no one can enter the kingdom of God unless they are born of water and the Spirit.

—John 3:5

Read the whole passage in John 3:1–21.

What It Says
    1. What did you like about this passage?
    2. What did you not like or find confusing about this passage?

What It Means
    3. What does this passage teach about people?
    4. What does this passage teach about God?

Live It. How will you live more Second today?
Tell It. How will you share what you have learned?

Practice It. Get with a friend or someone in your group. Practice or role-play your "Live and Tell" commitments.

Day 2: Branches

I am the vine; you are the branches. If you remain in me and I in you, you will bear much fruit; apart from me you can do nothing.

—John 15:5

Read the whole passage in John 15:1–11.

A vine can lose a limb and grow it back, its branches and leaves hewn apart, but still recover. But no branch, no matter its strength or maturity, can survive apart from the vine. So it is with Jesus. We may survive for a while, just as a leaf stays green for a time, but true life, life as it was meant to be, can only be experienced when connected to Jesus. How much of our lives are spent disconnected? How much of our career and family time is spent with no thought to the eternal, no care for the vine? We often wonder why our jobs drudge on, or our families struggle as they do, or our personal lives seem riddled with headache. Could it be that much of our lives are spent with no thought and no connection to the vine?

Talk with God

God, you are bigger than Sunday morning church or evening prayers. Teach me to obey and stay connected to you all day long.

Live It. How will you live more Second today?
Tell It. How will you share what you have learned?

Tweet using #IASbranches to share your thoughts.

Day 3: Friend

You are my friends if you do what I command. I no longer call you servants, because a servant does not know his master's business. Instead, I have called you friends, for everything that I learned from my Father I have made known to you.

—John 15:14–15

Read the whole passage in John 15:12–27.

A king has few friends, few people he trusts with his secrets and his plans. But the King of the universe, the Author of life, the Beginning and End, the First One, has declared us his friends. He has entrusted us with his plans, made us a part of his strategy, included us in the secrets of the kingdom. He has allowed us the opportunity to join him in his work. We are no longer mere slaves. We are counselors and ambassadors. We are sons and daughters. We are friends. At least we can be. If we deny his existence or work against his kingdom, then we are enemies. But if we choose to follow him, join his ranks, and obey his word, we become friends of the King.

Talk with God

I commit to obey and be the friend you have called me to be.

Live It. How will you live more Second today?
Tell It. How will you share what you have learned?

Tweet using #IASfriend to share your thoughts.

Day 4: Child

Yet to all who did receive him, to those who believed in his name, he gave the right to become children of God.

—John 1:12

Read the whole passage in John 1:1–18.

We tend to view God in one of two extremes. We view him as a grumpy old man in the clouds who throws lightning when angry and keeps a list of all our wrongs. Or we view him as a happy-go-lucky rich uncle who gives us whatever we want and has no rules. God is neither. He is our heavenly Father. He has rules and expectations but also a deep and unconditional love for us, his children. No good father gives his child a rock when he needs bread. No good father lets his child run amok without guidance or rules. God promises to love us as children, like no other Father could. That means blessing and relationship, answered prayers and kindness. But it also means a set of rules for our lives and discipline when we wander.

Talk with God

Thank you for loving me. Thank you for guiding my life and providing for my needs. Thank you for being my Father.

Live It. How will you live more Second today?
Tell It. How will you share what you have learned?

🐦 Tweet using #IASchild to share your thoughts.

Day 5: **Advocate**

And I will ask the Father, and he will give you another advocate to help you and be with you forever.

—John 14:16

Read the whole passage in John 14:16–21.

For those who call God their God, he grants an advocate, a lawyer who stands guard over our case, who helps in our time of need, who advocates on our behalf. This Advocate is also called Helper, Counselor, Holy Spirit. He fills God's children, gives strength to their steps, victory to their struggles, and voice to their prayers. Now let us walk with the knowledge of this Helper. Let us remember that he stands guard over those brothers and sisters we curse or argue with. He stands near when we walk into evil and befriend our old ways. He stands ready when God sends us to do his kingdom work. He helps. He guides. He remains. He is with us, whenever, wherever, forever.

Talk with God

Teach me to walk worthy of your Advocate, strengthened by his wisdom and protected by his power.

Live It. How will you live more Second today?
Tell It. How will you share what you have learned?

🐦 Tweet using #IASadvocate to share your thoughts.

Day 6: Creature

God saw all that he had made, and it was very good.

—Genesis 1:31

Read the whole passage in Genesis 1.

Stars and planets, quarks and microbes, blue birds and blue whales, they all started with God. It was his voice that made the universe, his voice that brought life from dust, light from darkness, and made something out of nothing. He knit the first family. He fathered time. He created the seen and the unseen. It was God. God was before all of it. He was and is First. We are created things, creatures made in his image, not he in ours. Life is not about us, not about our families or careers, what we accomplish or what we want. It's not even about such noble things as love, honor, or humanity. Life is about God. What would it look like if we lived like life really was all about God and less about everything else?

Talk with God

You are my Creator. I am your creature. Teach me to live never forgetting that you are First and I am not.

Live It. How will you live more Second today?

Tell It. How will you share what you have learned?

🐦 Tweet using #IAScreature to share your thoughts.

Day 7: **Known**

You have searched me, Lord,
* and you know me.*
You know when I sit and when I rise;
* you perceive my thoughts from afar.*
You discern my going out and my lying down;
* you are familiar with all my ways.*
Before a word is on my tongue,
* you, Lord, know it completely.*
You hem me in behind and before,
* and you lay your hand upon me.*
Such knowledge is too wonderful for me,
* too lofty for me to attain.*

—Psalm 139:1–6

Nothing is hidden, nothing is secret, nothing escapes God's eyes. He knows us, even better than we know ourselves. So there is no sense in trying to hide our failures or mask our complaints. Come to God knowing that he already knows. Speak with him believing he knows our words before we do. Tell him what you struggle with. Ask him your questions and give him your concerns.

Talk with God

Relationship.

"You have searched me . . ."
God, you know everything about me, including . . .

🐦 Tweet using #IASknown to share your prayers.

Session Three

Pass It On

God's economy works the reverse from the world's. Here on earth, if we want more money, we save and hoard and invest and track it. We do not let it out of our sight or away from our control. But spiritual treasure works just the opposite. If we bury it in the sand, we lose it. If we take hold of it but do not give it away, then it will be taken away. Investment is not an option but a requirement. But we invest by giving, by sacrificing, and by passing on what we learn. So as you learn more about God, remember, knowledge gained but not used will be lost; treasure that is won but not passed on to others will rot.

Day 1: Person of Peace

Watch the Stephen Baldwin Film

iamsecond.com/stephenbaldwin

What did you like about, identify with, or learn from Stephen's story?

> *When you enter a house, first say, "Peace to this house." If someone who promotes peace is there, your peace will rest on them; if not, it will return to you.*
>
> **—Luke 10:5–6**

Read the whole passage in Luke 10:1–11.

What It Says
1. What did you like about this passage?
2. What did you not like or find confusing about this passage?

What It Means
3. What does this passage teach about people?
4. What does this passage teach about God?

Live It. Who have you been telling about what you have learned about God? Make a list of people who have shown interest in spiritual things.

Tell It. How will you share what you have learned?

Practice It. Get with a friend or someone in your group. Practice or role-play your "Live and Tell" commitments.

Day 2: Village

We no longer believe just because of what you said; now we have heard for ourselves, and we know that this man really is the Savior of the world.

—John 4:42

Read the whole passage John 4:1–42.

She avoided the watchful eyes of her village and fetched water during the midday heat. Shame followed her steps. The woman in this story had five broken marriages and now a live-in boyfriend. She was well known in her village, but not for her virtue. Then she met Jesus. And meeting him sent her rushing back to the village with a story she wanted all to know. We all have our village—coworkers, neighbors, classmates, friends, and family. But do these people know the story of how we met Jesus? They may know that we go to church or pray over our meals or wear a cross around our necks. But do they know why? Have they heard our story? Have they heard the reason why God is First in our lives?

Talk with God

God, you are in charge of the harvest. Help me find the people you have prepared to hear your message.

Live It. Everyone has a village, a circle of friends and family they interact with regularly. Who is in your village?
Tell It. How will you share what you have learned?

🐦 Tweet using #IASvillage to share your thoughts.

Day 3: Ten Cities

So the man went away and began to tell in the Decapolis [Ten Cities] how much Jesus had done for him. And all the people were amazed.

—Mark 5:20

Read the whole passage Mark 5:1–20.

Crazed and naked, the man would scream into the night, running across the hillsides. But then Jesus turned the town crazy into the town preacher, and people listened. Jesus sent him to his friends and family, but the man did not stop there. The man went on to tell his story to the whole Ten Cities region. Not many of us can say God saved us from wondering naked in the hillsides, but we still have a great story to tell. God rescued each of us, changed each of us, and brought each of us from the brink of destruction. Maybe he saved you from an addiction, rescued you from a difficult childhood, or walked with you when tragedy struck. Whatever your story, there are others who need to find the hope, strength, or comfort you found in those dark moments of life.

Talk with God

God, I thank you for what you have done in my life. Please use my story to reach the people in my community.

Live It. Who in your life might relate to your story?
Tell It. How will you share what you have learned?

Tweet using #IAStencities to share your thoughts.

Day 4: Influencers

Cornelius was expecting them and had called together his relatives and close friends.

—Acts 10:24

Read the whole passage Acts 10:1–8, 23–48.

Religious people need Jesus. Influential people need Jesus. The Corneliuses of this world need the story and message of Jesus as much as anyone else. And if we give them the opportunity, many would gladly share what they learn with the people around them. Maybe you are that influencer, the person people follow, the voice people hear, or maybe you know others who are that voice. Invite them to discover Jesus and challenge them to open their networks, their relational connections to the power of God. Let each modern-day Cornelius lift his or her voice and share the message of hope the world so desperately needs. Telling God's story is not solely the task of pastors, priests, and missionaries. It is the task of every Second, every believer, every person who discovers the truth of Jesus.

Talk with God

Show me the influencers in my life who are ready to hear about you. Use my own influence, my relationships, and my connections to help make you famous.

Live It. Who are the influencers in your community who may need to hear about Jesus?

Tell It. How will you share what you have learned?

Tweet using #IASinfluencers to share your thoughts.

Day 5: **Household**

The Lord opened her heart to respond to Paul's message. When she and the members of her household were baptized, she invited us to her home.

—Acts 16:14b–15a

Read the whole passage Acts 16:11–15.

Perhaps we think too small when we share our faith. We think about the people we know who need to hear about God, about our friends and family. But we don't always think about the relationships of our friends. We don't think about their friends or their friends' friends. Maybe it's a form of selfishness that we think so small, that we think only of those we know or meet. Lydia was a traveling merchant and businesswoman. When Paul saw Lydia, he didn't just see a woman in need of Jesus. He saw dozens, hundreds, even thousands of business clients whom Paul had no access to but whom Lydia called friends. Bringing Jesus into Lydia's household meant reaching more than just a family; it meant touching the lives of family, relatives, servants, and the ancient equivalent of employees—and as time progressed, customers, clients, and business associates as well.

Talk with God

Give me the eyes to see not just the individuals in my life that need to hear about you, but also the network of relationships that each person represents.

Live It. Whom do you know who could be a gateway into a whole network of people who need to hear about God?
Tell It. How will you share what you have learned?

Tweet using #IAShousehold to share your thoughts.

Day 6: **Circles**

Believe in the Lord Jesus, and you will be saved—you and your household.

—Acts 16:31

Read the whole passage Acts 16:25–34.

Instead of talking to one person about God, what if we introduced a whole group of friends or a whole family to God? What if we found key influencers in our circles who sparked spiritual interest among a group of people rather than with just an individual? Every life is connected. Every individual affects the people around him or her. Paul did not just see a jailer in need of God. He saw the man's family as well. And Paul looked for a spiritual pathway into that family through the jailer. He wanted more than just the individual to discover Jesus. What if we did the same?

Talk with God

Give me the wisdom to see beyond just an individual to whole circles of relationships that need to hear about you.

Live It. What relational circles do you see in your life? Who are some of the key influencers in each of these circles?
Tell It. How will you share what you have learned?

🐦 Tweet using #IAScircles to share your thoughts.

Day 7: Workers

The harvest is plentiful, but the workers are few. Ask the Lord of the harvest, therefore, to send out workers into his harvest field.

—Luke 10:2

"Send out workers." Make this your daily prayer. Set your watch or phone for 10:02 every day to remind you of the Luke 10:2 prayer. The problem is not in the harvest; the harvest is ready. It's the workers; it's us. We need to get to work. We need to ask God to get others to work. The harvest is ready, but are the workers?

Talk with God

Ask.

". . . send out workers . . ."
I ask you to send workers to these local areas or people . . .
I ask you to send workers to these national industries or personalities . . .
I ask you to send workers to these international areas or people . . .

Tweet using #IASworkers to share your prayers.

Day 1: **Short Story**

Watch the Vitor Belfort Film

iamsecond.com/vitorbelfort

What did you like about, identify with, or learn from Vitor's story?

> *But whatever was to my profit I now consider loss for the sake of Christ.*
>
> **—Philippians 3:7**

Read the whole passage in Philippians 3:4–9.

What It Says
1. What did you like about this passage?
2. What did you not like or find confusing about this passage?

What It Means
3. What does this passage teach about people?
4. What does this passage teach about God?

Live It. How will you live more Second today?

Tell It. What is your story in a 140 characters or less? What were you like before your big moment(s) with God? How would you describe that moment? What were you like, or what did you learn as a result of that moment with God? Whom will you share your short story with? Use the lists you created last week for ideas.

Practice It. Get with a friend or someone in your group. Role-play telling someone your short story.

Day 2: Before

I am a Jew. . . . I studied under Gamaliel and was thoroughly trained in the law of our ancestors. I was just as zealous for God as any of you are today. I persecuted the followers [of Jesus] of this Way to their death, arresting both men and women and throwing them into prison.

—Acts 22:3–4

Read the whole passage in Acts 22:3–5.

Dedicated. Radical. Zealous. Paul saw Jesus and his followers as a threat to his country, his culture, and his God. His fury brought ruin and death to many members of the Way, the first name of the Christian faith. Paul would later become one of the church's most powerful minds, most famous missionaries, and most prolific writers. But that was later. He began as a murderer—a hate-filled persecutor of Christians. He never forgot who and what he was before he met Jesus. We all have a "before" story. For some of us, that story was before we met Jesus. For others, it was before we took our faith seriously. For others still, that story is the up-and-down journey of a long walk with God. But we all have a "before" story. What is yours?

Talk with God

God, thank you for saving me, for teaching me, for pulling me out of the mud that was my "before" life. Help me never to forget what you have done for me.

Live It. How will you live more Second today?
Tell It. We all have a "before" story. What is yours? Write it out below. Whom will you share this story with today?

Tweet using #IASbefore to share your "before" story.

Day 3: **The Moment**

About noon as I came near Damascus, suddenly a bright light from heaven flashed around me. I fell to the ground and heard a voice say to me, "Saul! Saul! Why do you persecute me?"

—Acts 22:6–7

Read the whole passage in Acts 22:6–13.

Saul, later known as Paul, realized his great mistake, the wasted life he had led. Saul had killed and imprisoned followers of Jesus, but now Jesus himself was speaking. This moment converted an anti-Christian zealot into a Jesus-following fanatic. Because of this moment, Paul would later risk his life again and again and eventually lose it all for the sake of the name he once tried to destroy. Those of us who follow Jesus have all had a moment of realization. Perhaps your moment with God was not an audible voice from heaven; maybe it was an indescribable comfort in hard times, a conversation with a believer, a televangelist, a Bible verse, a church experience, or an I am Second film. When was that moment when God became more real in your life?

Talk with God

Thank you for speaking into my life and giving me a story to tell.

Live It. How will you live more Second today?

Tell It. Describe and write out a moment or experience you had with God. This may be when you first believed in God or a later experience. Whom will you share this story with today?

🐦 Tweet using #IASthemoment to share your moment.

Day 4: **After**

You will be his witness to all people of what you have seen and heard.

—Acts 22:15

Read the whole passage in Acts 22:14–16.

Some are moved by argument and others by philosophy or rhetoric, but most just need to hear the story. The story of a changed life and a convinced believer. Often we think that we do not know enough answers to be able to share our faith with others. We claim we do not have the gift for it or have not been given the right training. But it is the simple story of what we have seen and heard that people want to hear most. People care less about proofs than a story they are told. So get out there and tell the story of what God has done in your life.

Live It. How will you live more Second today?
Tell It. Describe and write out what happened or what changed after your moment with God.

Tweet using #IASafter to share your "after" story.

Day 5: Tell It

I, Nebuchadnezzar, praise and exalt and glorify the King of heaven, because everything he does is right and all his ways are just. And those who walk in pride he is able to humble.

—Daniel 4:37

Read the whole passage in Daniel 4:1–37.

Nebuchadnezzar was king of Babylon, the pagan ruler of a pagan nation. But after an intense and real experience with the God of heaven and earth, everything changed. No longer could he boast of his accomplishments, of the kingdom he built, or the city he oversaw. He was forced to realize that all he had and all he accomplished was God's. He built his kingdom through God's power and ruled it by God's permission. And realizing this truth changed his story. He was no longer Nebuchadnezzar, the great. He was Nebuchadnezzar, the servant of the great God. We all have a unique story, a journey we have gone on with God. And it is that story and that journey that the world needs to hear about.

Talk with God

God, you have given me a story, a message to tell the world. Give me the courage and the opportunity to tell it well.

Live It. How will you live more Second today?

Tell It. Write out and practice your whole story. Talk about the moment when God became real in your life, what were you like before, what changed after. Whom will you share this story with today?

🐦 Condense your story to 120 characters and tweet using #IAStellit to share your story.

Day 6: **Dirt**

*As he was scattering the seed, some fell along the path,
and the birds came and ate it up. Some fell on rocky places,
where it did not have much soil. It sprang up quickly, because
the soil was shallow. But when the sun came up, the plants
were scorched, and they withered because they had no root.
Other seed fell among thorns, which grew up and choked
the plants, so that they did not bear grain. Still other seed fell
on good soil. It came up, grew and produced a crop, some
multiplying thirty, some sixty, some a hundred times.*

—Mark 4:4–8

Read the whole passage in Mark 4:1–20.

Not every seed will bloom. Not every soil will produce. Rejection and disappointment will greet everyone who works the garden of people's hearts. But for those unafraid to get dirty, for those undeterred by occasional failure, good soil will be the reward, soil worked and prepared by God, soil looking for and wanting the message of hope. Some will never really hear the message. Others will hear it but fall prey to discouragement and distraction. Some will be too callous to hear, too weak to last, or too distracted to stand. But some will take root. Some will multiply. And that some, that group of hungry souls, will make all the pain, all the rejection, and all the dirt under your fingernails well worth the trouble of sharing the story of Jesus and how he changed your life.

Talk with God

Father, give me the boldness to share your story, the wisdom to share your story well, and the perseverance never to stop sharing it.

Live It. How can you live more Second today?
Tell It. How will you share what you have learned?

Tweet using #IASdirt to share your thoughts.

Day 7: **Protector**

LORD, how many are my foes!
  How many rise up against me!
Many are saying of me,
  "God will not deliver him."
But you, LORD, are a shield around me,
  my glory, the One who lifts my head high.
I call out to the LORD,
  and he answers me from his holy mountain.
I lie down and sleep;
  I wake again, because the LORD sustains me.
I will not fear though tens of thousands
  assail me on every side.
Arise, LORD!
  Deliver me, my God!
Strike all my enemies on the jaw;
  break the teeth of the wicked.
From the LORD comes deliverance.
  May your blessing be on your people.

—Psalm 3

God is bigger than any danger, difficulty, or foe. If we are doing his work, we can be sure of his protection, of his careful and strong hand guiding our way. That does not guarantee an easy road or even a "successful" outcome, but it guarentees that the end he wants accomplished will come to be.

Talk with God

Protect.

"Deliver me, my God!"
God, protect me as I share what you have done in my life . . .

🐦 Tweet using #IASprotector to share your prayers.

Day 1: Basics

Watch a "How Can I Become Second?" Film

iamsecond.com/questions/
how-can-i-become-second

What did you like about, identify with, or learn from this film?

> *For what I received I passed on to you as of first importance:*
> *that Christ died for our sins according to the Scriptures, that*
> *he was buried, that he was raised on the third day according*
> *to the Scriptures.*
>
> **—1 Corinthians 15:3–4**

What It Says
1. What did you like about this passage?
2. What did you not like or find confusing about this passage?

What It Means
3. What does this passage teach about people?
4. What does this passage teach about God?

Live It. How will you live more Second today?

Tell It. We all sin, do wrong things. There is punishment for our sin. Jesus died and rose again to forgive us of our sin. This is the message we must believe and pass on. Whom will you tell this message to?

For more, see the "How Do I Become Second?" section in the back of this book or go to www.simplysharejesus.com for training.

Practice It. Get with a friend or someone in your group. Practice or role-play sharing your story and the story of Jesus with someone.

Day 2: Crime

There is no one righteous, not even one;
*   there is no one who understands;*
*   there is no one who seeks God.*
All have turned away,
*   they have together become worthless;*
there is no one who does good,
*   not even one.*

—Romans 3:10–12

Read the whole passage in Romans 3:10–18.

Following the Golden Rule does not win us heaven. Saint Peter does not guard the pearly gates to see if we are on the naughty list. The whole purpose of Jesus coming to earth was to save us because we proved incapable of saving ourselves. He said we are branches severed from the vine, seeds cast among the weeds, sheep lost in the wilderness, dead and decaying, rebellious souls. Good could not be good enough, nice or kind or loving could never be perfected in a human, and thus we could never win a spot in heaven. We are hopelessly and terribly lost, completely unable to earn the perfect goodness God demands. Quite simply, we are sinners, fallen, broken, and imperfect people. And because of that truth, we cannot save ourselves or ever hope to be good enough. We are worthless when it comes to saving our souls or earning a place in the afterlife.

Live It. How will you live more Second today?
Tell It. How could you integrate this truth into your story? Write out all or part of your "before" story and integrate the idea of Romans 3:10–12 into your story.

🐦 Tweet using #IAScrime to share your thoughts.

Day 3: Punishment

For the wages of sin is death, but the gift of God is eternal life in Christ Jesus our Lord.

—Romans 6:23

Read the whole passage in Romans 6:1–23.

We all have this sickness, this curse called sin, a degenerative disease that eats at our morals, tempts, and convinces us to do the things we do not want to do. Every time we choose stuff rather than people, people rather than God, greed over satisfaction, rudeness over kindness, hate over love—with every sinful choice we choose the disease over the healer. This disease will kill us. It will require payment for its use, and that payment is death. The world is littered with graveyards and tombs, mortuaries and cemeteries, all testifying to this: every person is a debtor to death. We were not originally created to die. We were made to live forever. But when Adam and Eve made that fateful choice in the garden, they chose the path of death, and with every vain ambition, with every selfish action, we have seconded their proposition. We have all chosen death, but God offers a gift that remedies the disease, the gift of eternal life through Jesus.

Live It. How will you live more Second today?
Tell It. How could you integrate this truth into your story? Write out all or part of your "before" story and integrate the idea of Romans 6:23 into your story.

🐦 Tweet using #IASpunishment to share your thoughts.

Day 4: **Arrest and Trial**

*"What shall I do, then, with Jesus who is called Christ?" Pilate
    asked.*
They all answered, "Crucify him!"
"Why? What crime has he committed?" asked Pilate.
But they shouted all the louder, "Crucify him!"

—Matthew 27:22–23

Read the whole passage in Matthew 27:1–31.

Jesus committed no crime and did no wrong, but still he took
our punishment. He hung on the cross in our place. It was we who
deserved the cross, we who earned his death—but it was he who
suffered for our crime. He came to this earth knowing his death
would be bloody, that his creation would ignore and reject him. But
he came out of love to offer us life and life to the fullest.

Live It. How will you live more Second today?
Tell It. How could you integrate this truth into your story?
Describe a moment or experience you had with God. This may be
when you first believed in God or a later experience. As you tell
that portion of your story, find a way to integrate how Jesus paid
for our punishment, how though he was innocent and we were
guilty, he took our place.

🐦 Tweet using #IASarrestandtrial to share your thoughts.

Day 5: Dead

When the centurion and those with him who were guarding Jesus saw the earthquake and all that had happened, they were terrified, and exclaimed, "Surely he was the Son of God!"

—Matthew 27:54

Read the whole passage in Matthew 27:32–66.

Dead. The One who created life, who gave breath to the universe, lay limp on a cross. Sacrificed and freely given, Jesus willingly and completely gave himself up for our sake. Nothing compelled him, nothing forced him to go to the cross—nothing but love for his Father and love for his fallen creatures. He could have let us wallow in our sin and suffer for our wrongs, and justice would have been upheld. But he chose grace and mercy and love. He chose us. His death blazed a path back to God and a way to eternal life, life as it was designed to be, unhindered by disease, unfettered by pain, and undeterred by death. And it all became possible through the sacrifice of Jesus. For all those willing to believe, all those ready to declare Jesus First, life can flow and forgiveness can reign.

Live It. How will you live more Second today?

Tell It. How could you integrate this truth into your story? Describe a moment or experience you had with God. This may be when you first believed in God or a later experience. As you tell that portion of your story, find a way to integrate how Jesus offers forgiveness and life for all those who believe.

🐦 Tweet using #IASdead to share your thoughts.

Day 6: Risen

*The angel said to the women, "Do not be afraid, for I know
that you are looking for Jesus, who was crucified. He is not
here; he has risen, just as he said. Come and see the place
where he lay."*

—Matthew 28:5–6

Read the whole passage in Matthew 28:1–15.

He paid the price of our sin and the debt of our wrongdoing. He
suffered and died an innocent man to secure our salvation. But the
grave could not hold him. The tomb gave up its contents, and the
Son of God rose again. This is our messege: that Jesus died for our
sins and three days later rose again. Simple as that.

Live It. How will you live more Second today?
Tell It. Jesus died and rose again to offer life and forgiveness to
all those who would believe. Write out and practice your story
and the story of Jesus, together. Talk about the moment when God
became real in your life, what you were like before, what changed
after, and what you believed about Jesus that changed everything.

Tweet using #IASrisen to share your thoughts.

Day 7: Thanks

*Shout for joy to the L*ORD*, all the earth.*
*Worship the L*ORD *with gladness;*
come before him with joyful songs.
*Know that the L*ORD *is God.*
It is he who made us, and we are his;
we are his people, the sheep of his pasture.
Enter his gates with thanksgiving
and his courts with praise;
give thanks to him and praise his name.
*For the L*ORD *is good and his love endures forever;*
his faithfulness continues through all generations.

—Psalm 100

While we may be quick to think of him when we need a job or a good grade at school, we should be even quicker to thank him for the everyday pleasures. For the green grass, for the food on our tables, for the clothes we wear, and the friends we enjoy, we should thank him and praise him for all the good things in life.

Talk with God

Worship.

"Worship the LORD . . .**"**
God, I worship you because . . .

🐦 Tweet using #IASthanks to share your prayers.

Day 1: **Chosen**

Watch the Priscilla Nicoara Film

iamsecond.com/priscillanicoara

What did you like, identify with, or learn from Priscilla's story?

> *All those the Father gives me will come to me, and whoever comes to me I will never drive away.*
>
> **—John 6:37**

Read the whole passage in John 6:35–51.

What It Says
1. What did you like about this passage?
2. What did you not like or find confusing about this passage?

What It Means
3. What does this passage teach about people?
4. What does this passage teach about God?

Live It. How will you live more Second today?
Tell It. How will you share what you have learned?

Practice It. Get with a friend or someone in your group. Practice or role-play your "Live and Tell" commitments.

Day 2: Words

My message and my preaching were not with wise and persuasive words, but with a demonstration of the Spirit's power, so that your faith might not rest on human wisdom, but on God's power.

—1 Corinthians 2:4–5

Read the whole passage in 1 Corinthians 2:1–8.

God is not impressed with our skills. And he is not afraid of our inabilities or weaknesses. He designed every limb, every tendon, every muscle, and every neuron. We are just what we need to be. And for those tasks beyond our ability and above our skill set, he provides his Spirit. Saving a lost soul is one such impossible activity. We are tasked with bringing a message meant to change a dead, sinful soul into a living, breathing servant of God, something only God can do. But he has given us a part in this miraculous event. We are the message bearers, the ambassadors of a life-giving God. But our role is more about obedience, humbleness, and diligence than wisdom and persuasion. It does not mean we purposely act like fools or search for ways to embarrass ourselves, but we do not worry when people do not respond to the message of Jesus, and we do not fret when we run out of words and shake in fear. We simply speak and let God do the rest.

Talk with God

God, give me the words to speak and bring your Spirit to the hearts of those who hear.

Live It. How can you live more Second today?
Tell It. How will you share what you have learned?

🐦 Tweet using #IASwords to share your thoughts.

Day 3: Lost Sheep

Suppose one of you has a hundred sheep and loses one of them. Doesn't he leave the ninety-nine in the open country and go after the lost sheep until he finds it?

—Luke 15:4

Read the whole passage Luke 15:1–7.

Sheep stray and wander. They separate and get lost. It is in their nature. We are all like sheep, wandering and running, losing our way. Faith and salvation are when Jesus finds us in our lostness, sins, and depravity, and he picks us up on his shoulders and carries us back. We may care deeply about our unbelieving family member or the friend who never seems ready for God, but God cares more. No matter how large our hearts, no matter how deep our feelings, Jesus loves them more. It was he who left the ninety-nine—it was he who left his throne in heaven—and came to earth in search of his lost sheep. He has not forgotten about our loved ones. Continue to pray, continue to share the message of Jesus, and trust that God wants them found even more than we do.

Talk with God

God, I ask and beg for my unbelieving friends and family. I beg that you would find them and bring them back to you.

Live It. How can you live more Second today?
Tell It. How will you share what you have learned?

Tweet using #IASlostsheep to share your thoughts.

Day 4: Lost Coin

Suppose a woman has ten silver coins and loses one. Doesn't she light a lamp, sweep the house and search carefully until she finds it?

—Luke 15:8

Read the whole passage in Luke 15:8–10.

We often forget that the King himself is on the search, that he is leading the vanguard, that all of heaven rejoices when one coin is found, when one sinner repents. God's kingdom will prevail; his way will succeed. Too often we worry about whether God can use the simple, the small, the weak. We wonder if any but the gifted few can participate in real kingdom work. But the battle is already won. Hell's gates are smoldering on the ground. Death sits defeated and impotent. We need only to join his efforts, to volunteer for his work. So let every man, woman, and child join the fray and know that the King marches ahead, that he searches for the lost, cares for our neighbors, works for our friends and family, that he searches for their souls.

Talk with God

God, I know you care and love the people in my life even more than I do, that you planned for them even before the foundation of the world. I ask that you use me, despite my weaknesses, despite my failures, to reach those yet to believe in you.

Live It. How will you live more Second today?
Tell It. How will you share what you have learned?

🐦 Tweet using #IASlostcoin to share your thoughts.

Day 5: **Conviction**

When he comes, he will prove the world to be in the wrong about sin and righteousness and judgment.

—John 16:8

Read the whole passage in John 16:1–15.

Conviction may be aided or prompted by the voice of a friend or family member, but true conviction, the kind that turns a life around, the kind that changes a heart of stone to a heart of flesh, can only happen through the Spirit. We can present our case, argue our viewpoint, and defend our position; but if God's Spirit is not at work, then no convincing will work. There will come a day, a day of judgment, when every knee will bow and every head will nod in agreement that God is right and we are not. Our only hope is in begging God for the mercy of convicting our friends and family before that day comes, that he would shake the confidence of our loved ones so that their knees will bow before God now while there is still time.

Talk with God

God, I beg you for the people in my life who do not yet believe in you. Convict them, turn their hearts, show them their need for you. Use me to bring your message of hope to hearts made hungry by you.

Live It. How will you live more Second today?
Tell It. How will you share what you have learned?

Tweet using #IASconviction to share your thoughts.

Day 6: **Authority**

All authority in heaven and on earth has been given to me.
—Matthew 28:18

Read the whole passage in Matthew 28:18–20.

Ambassadors do not merely travel as the rest of us, but they represent and speak in the name of their people and country. Jesus has given us such a task. Speaking with all authority in heaven and earth, he appointed us as ambassadors and representatives. But we do not represent a temporal kingdom with finite borders and mortal armies. We represent the kingdom of God, a kingdom without end and without rival. We are given the authority to represent and speak for the kingdom that will neither fade nor diminish. So remember, when we ask God for help, when we pray for lost souls and unbelieving friends, we ask as official representatives of his government, as royal members of his kingdom, as the hands and feet of his presence here on earth.

Talk with God

God, change the hearts and minds of those around me, speak through me, and make me a bold and effective representative for you.

Live It. How will you live more Second today?
Tell It. How will you share what you have learned?

Tweet using #IASauthority to share your thoughts.

Day 7: **All Peoples**

May God be gracious to us and bless us
and make his face shine on us—
so that your ways may be known on earth,
your salvation among all nations.
May the peoples praise you, God;
may all the peoples praise you.
May the nations be glad and sing for joy,
for you rule the peoples with equity
and guide the nations of the earth.
May the peoples praise you, God;
may all the peoples praise you.
The land yields its harvest;
God, our God, blesses us.
May God bless us still,
so that all the ends of the earth will fear him.

—Psalm 67

Though God holds all the power, though his plan is unmovable and our ability miniscule in comparison, he demands that we join him. He insists that we participate in the spreading of his kingdom. Though God does whatever he wants, he chooses to include us in his work. So if the world is to hear about him, we are to be the voice that tells them.

Talk with God

Ask.

"May the peoples praise you . . ."
God, I want these people and these groups to know you . . .

Tweet using #IASallpeoples to share your prayers.

Session Four

Grow

We need time with God, a chance to thank and praise, to recognize his rule, request his help, and beg for his forgiveness. Hard times shock us out of complacency and remind us that this world is not the sum of our lives. Community brings wisdom and correction from loving brothers and sisters, encouragement, guidance, and strength in numbers. The Bible sets a light along our paths and a mirror in front of our faces. It shows us the state of our souls and the required path for our lives. The Spirit opens our blind eyes, reminds us of long-forgotten lessons, and teaches us hard-learned truths. These are the pillars of our walk with God, the mechanisms for our growth, the food groups of our spiritual diet. Without each of them we grow anemic and sick, unbalanced and unproductive.

Day 1: How to Pray

Watch the "What's Prayer All About?" Film

iamsecond.com/
whats-prayer-all-about

What did you like about, identify with, or learn from this film?

> *Our Father in heaven,*
> *hallowed be your name,*
> *your kingdom come,*
> *your will be done,*
> *   on earth as it is in heaven.*

—Matthew 6:9–10

What It Says

1. What did you like about this passage? What are the kinds of things that Jesus tells his disciples to talk with God about?
2. What did you not like or find confusing about this passage?

What It Means

3. What does this passage teach about people?
4. What does this passage teach about God?

Live It. Take some time to talk with God as a group. Jesus' prayer had these elements: relationship, worship, surrender, ask, forgive, and protect. Talk with God now using these same topics.
Tell It. How will you share what you have learned?

Day 2: **Relationship**

You, God, are my God,
*   earnestly I seek you;*
I thirst for you,
*   my whole being longs for you,*
In a dry and parched land
*   where there is no water.*
I have seen you in the sanctuary
*   and beheld your power and your glory.*
Because your love is better than life,
*   my lips will glorify you.*
I will praise you as long as I live,
*   and in your name I will lift up my hands.*
I will be fully satisfied as with the richest of foods;
*   with singing lips my mouth will praise you.*

—Psalm 63:1–5

Relationship is what makes prayer possible. God could have chosen to not hear our prayers, to refuse us an audience, and to close off communication. But he has chosen to talk with us, us to him and him to us. Because he is the Father, he speaks to his children. Because he is our friend, he speaks with us, his friends. How has he related to you lately?

Talk with God

Relationship.

"I thirst for you . . ."
God, I love you because . . .

🐦 Tweet using #IASrelationship to share your prayers.

Day 3: Worship

I will exalt you, my God the King;
I will praise your name for ever and ever.
Every day I will praise you
and extol your name for ever and ever.
Great is the Lord and most worthy of praise;
his greatness no one can fathom.
One generation commends your works to another;
they tell of your mighty acts.
They speak of the glorious splendor of your majesty—
and I will meditate on your wonderful works.
They tell of the power of your awesome works—
and I will proclaim your great deeds.
They celebrate your abundant goodness
and joyfully sing of your righteousness.

—Psalm 145:1–7

When people speak of God we often hear uncommon words. We say things like "glory" and "splendor" and "righteous." Maybe we say these things because he is so different and so huge that we feel mundane words are too low for him. But whether you use "glory" or "hugeness," "splendor" or "brilliant," "righteous" or "good." Whether you use special words or common words, take the time to tell God how great he is.

Talk with God

Worship.

"I will praise your name . . ."
God, I worship you because . . .

Tweet using #IASworship to share your prayers.

Day 4: **Surrender**

*In you, L*ORD *my God,*
> *I put my trust.*
I trust in you;
> *do not let me be put to shame,*
> *nor let my enemies triumph over me.*
No one who hopes in you
> *will ever be put to shame,*
but shame will come on those
> *who are treacherous without cause.*
*Show me your ways, L*ORD,
> *teach me your paths.*
Guide me in your truth and teach me,
> *for you are God my Savior,*
> *and my hope is in you all day long.*
*Remember, L*ORD, *your great mercy and love,*
> *for they are from of old.*

—Psalm 25:1–7

God is First. Whether we believe it or not, he is in charge. He calls the shots. He has all the power. He makes the rules. We can try to fight him, to ignore him, or refuse him. But like trying to stop the waves or move the stars, we fight the impossibly huge. The only proper response, the only reasonable action, is to surrender to God, to make him First and ourselves Second.

Talk with God

Surrender.

"In you, LORD my God, I put my trust."
God, I surrender everything to you, including . . .

Tweet using #IASsurrender to share your prayers.

Day 5: **Ask**

Hear me, L<small>ORD</small>, and answer me,
*   for I am poor and needy.*
Guard my life, for I am faithful to you;
*   save your servant who trusts in you.*
You are my God; have mercy on me, Lord,
*   for I call to you all day long.*
Bring joy to your servant, Lord,
*   for I put my trust in you.*
You, Lord, are forgiving and good,
*   abounding in love to all who call to you.*
Hear my prayer, L<small>ORD</small>;
*   listen to my cry for mercy.*
When I am in distress, I call to you,
*   because you answer me.*

—Psalm 86:1–7

No matter how rich or secure we think we are, we need God. We are one little race on one little world, among the billions and billions of stars. We cannot tame the weather or even our own bodies. We must learn to rely on God, to ask him for our needs and beg him for our requirements.

Talk with God

Ask.

"Hear me and answer me . . ."
God, I ask for . . .

🐦 Tweet using #IASask to share your prayers.

Day 6: Forgive

Have mercy on me, O God,
*   according to your unfailing love;*
According to your great compassion
*   blot out my transgressions.*
Wash away all my iniquity
*   and cleanse me from my sin.*
For I know my transgressions,
*   and my sin is always before me.*
Against you, you only,
*   have I sinned and done what is evil in your sight;*
so you are right in your verdict
*   and justified when you judge.*
Surely I was sinful at birth,
*   sinful from the time my mother conceived me.*
Yet you desired faithfulness even in the womb;
*   you taught me wisdom in that secret place.*

—Psalm 51:1–6

Confessing our wrongs to God is an act of faith. If we believed him weak, we would continue our rebellion. If we thought him cruel, we would deny our mistakes. If we considered him unforgiving, we would plead our innocence. But because he knows all our wrongs and yet is still full of love and compassion, we can confess knowing that forgiveness is the answer and mercy is the response.

Talk with God

Forgive.

"Have mercy on me . . ."
God, forgive me for . . .

Tweet using #IASforgive to share your prayers.

Day 7: **Protect**

Whoever dwells in the shelter of the Most High
   will rest in the shadow of the Almighty.
I will say of the LORD, *"He is my refuge and my fortress,*
   my God, in whom I trust."
Surely he will save you
   from the fowler's snare
   and from the deadly pestilence.
He will cover you with his feathers,
   and under his wings you will find refuge;
   his faithfulness will be your shield and rampart.
You will not fear the terror of night,
   nor the arrow that flies by day,
Nor the pestilence that stalks in the darkness,
   nor the plague that destroys at midday.

—Psalm 91:1–6

God is bigger than our problems, bigger than our sicknesses and struggles. He outmatches our money issues and outmuscles our strongest foes. There is nowhere safer and no one stronger than our God. While difficulties may still come, nothing and no one will overcome us. While the battles may ebb and flow, the war is already won.

Talk with God

Protect.

"He will save you . . ."
God protect me from . . .

Tweet using #IASprotect to share your prayers.

Day 1: Rejected

Watch the Lee Lucas Film

iamsecond.com/leelucas

What did you like about, identify with, or learn from Lee's story?

They seized Peter and John and, because it was evening, they put them in jail until the next day. But many who heard the message believed; so the number of men who believed grew to about five thousand.

—Acts 4:3–4

Read the whole passage in Acts 4:1–31.

What It Says
1. What did you like about this passage?
2. What did you not like or find confusing about this passage?

What It Means
3. What does this passage teach about people?
4. What does this passage teach about God?

Live It. How will you live more Second today?
Tell It. How will you share what you have learned?

Practice It. Get with a friend or someone in your group. Practice or role-play your "Live and Tell" commitments.

Day 2: **Hated**

You will be hated by everyone because of me, but the one who stands firm to the end will be saved. When you are persecuted in one place, flee to another.

—Matthew 10:22–23

Read the whole passage in Matthew 10:16–42.

Jesus did not come to make everyone feel good, warm, and fuzzy, but to make us cry and squirm and wince at our state of disrepair. No doctor seeing a man dying of a curable ailment merely pumps him full of painkiller. Instead, he cuts him open, sets his bones, or showers him with radiation or any number of other painful, uncomfortable, but necessary healing practices. Likewise, Jesus came to shake us from our stupor and to wake us to our deathly separation from God. This shaking causes some to repent, some to turn to God, but it makes others turn and fight, to reject the message and lash out at those who carry it. This is our fate: to bring a message that will cause salvation and healing to some—but rejection, violence, and hatred from others.

Talk with God

Prepare me for rejection, ready me for hatred, and give me courage so that nothing may stop your message from flowing through my mouth.

Live It. How can you live more Second today?
Tell It. How will you share what you have learned?

🐦 Tweet using #IAShated to share your experiences of rejection.

Day 3: **Persecuted**

If you suffer as a Christian, do not be ashamed, but praise God that you bear that name.

—1 Peter 4:16

Read the whole passage in 1 Peter 4:12–19.

Soldiers do not feel shame for death on the battlefield. They follow their orders with utmost care and diligence and seek to survive the day. But if death stares, they do not blink. If hate flies, they do not flee. If persecution falls, they do not cry. For death and injury incurred for the sake of their country are badges of honor. So it is with God's kingdom. We do not seek persecution. We do not seek to be hated and mocked, but if it comes through no fault of our own, we welcome it. We ready our gear and arm our souls to fight the good fight. Hell's gates will not hold. Hell's walls will not stand. And if the process of gaining such victory involves our persecution, our mockery, our discomfort, or our injury, then proudly we should wear that badge.

Talk with God

I surrender my concerns and my comforts to follow your will no matter the cost.

Live It. How can you live more Second today?
Tell It. How will you share what you have learned?

🐦 Tweet using #IASpersecuted to share your experiences of rejection.

Day 4: **Vilified**

Then they secretly persuaded some men to say, "We have heard Stephen speak blasphemous words against Moses and against God."

—Acts 6:11

Read the whole passage in Acts 6:1–15.

Stephen sought only to feed the hungry, to care for the widow, and to be a light to his community. But darkness hates the light and does not recognize it as light. In the name of God, they slandered a man of God. Do not be surprised if the religious find error in your endeavors. Do not be shocked to find wolves in the church and thieves in with the sheep. Religious leaders or pious pew-sitters, all may work against you while your light shines and the lost find their way. Those efforts that best reach the lost or best impact the world are often those same methods that offend the sensibilities of the religious. Do not be too proud to consider you could be mistaken, nor too weak to know when you are right. Be ready for hardship as you preach the message of Jesus and be ready for difficulties as you spread his story. And do not be dismayed if the attack comes from behind.

Talk with God

Give me the wisdom to know how best to spread your message and the strength to withstand any attack that comes.

Live It. How will you live more Second today?
Tell It. How will you share what you have learned?

Tweet using #IASvilified to share your experiences of rejection.

Day 5: **Arrested**

Was there ever a prophet your ancestors did not persecute? They even killed those who predicted the coming of the Righteous One. And now you have betrayed and murdered him.

—Acts 7:52

Read the whole passage in Acts 7:1–53.

Prophetic voices rarely get a hearing. Those who name the disease of our planet and work to rid it from our world do not always find open arms and ready ears. Instead, resistance and reluctance greet their way. If we walk the halls of our schools or workplaces, praying for the sick and sharing Jesus with the unbeliever, we can expect stiff necks and dull ears. If we knock on the doors of our neighborhoods or visit the restaurants and bars of our communities, we can expect slow responses and unready hearts. However, this should not slow our pace or halt our mission; rather, it should sharpen our eyes for those few open minds and hearts that are ready to listen.

Talk with God

I know you have sent me to be a sheep among the wolves and a light in the darkness. I ask only that you give me the courage to venture on.

Live It. How will you live more Second today?
Tell It. How will you share what you have learned?

🐦 Tweet using #IASarrested to share your experiences of rejection.

Day 6: **Killed**

At this they covered their ears and, yelling at the top of their voices, they all rushed at him, dragged him out of the city and began to stone him.

—Acts 7:57–58

Read the whole passage in Acts 7:54–60.

None of us reading this have suffered the ultimate sacrifice of death for our faith. But from the beginning, a start set by Jesus himself on the cross, death and sacrifice have marked the history of Christianity. Even today, our brothers and sisters in Christ are murdered for claiming his name. They are stoned for spreading his message. They are tortured for his cause. They line up at death's door and await a martyr's welcome in heaven because they would not shut up, they would not be halted, and they would not cease teaching that Jesus died for our sins. The question we must ask ourselves is not will we give up a few friends or suffer some mocking or a demotion at work for sharing our faith and for living out our beliefs, but will we give up life itself for the sake of God.

Talk with God

Give me courage to suffer when I must and strength to power through when it comes.

Live It. How will you live more Second today?
Tell It. How will you share what you have learned?

🐦 Tweet using #IASkilled to share your experiences of rejection.

Day 7: **Help**

*Answer me quickly, L*ORD*;*
    my spirit fails.
Do not hide your face from me
    or I will be like those who go down to the pit.
Let the morning bring me word of your unfailing love,
    for I have put my trust in you.
Show me the way I should go,
    for to you I entrust my life.
*Rescue me from my enemies, L*ORD*,*
    for I hide myself in you.
Teach me to do your will,
    for you are my God;
may your good Spirit
    lead me on level ground.
*For your name's sake, L*ORD*, preserve my life;*
    in your righteousness, bring me out of trouble.
In your unfailing love, silence my enemies;
    destroy all my foes,
    for I am your servant.

—Psalm 143:7–12

God does not forget his servants, and he does not overlook his children. He walks with us in darkness and beside us in battle. He never leaves and never forsakes. His strength guards our weaknesses, and his grace carries us through our missteps. He hears when we call, and he listens when we ask for him.

Talk with God

Protect.

"Rescue me from my enemies . . ."
God, protect me from . . .

🐦 Tweet using #IAShelp to share your prayers.

Day 1: Gather Together

Watch the "Where Does Church Fit into All This?" Film

iamsecond.com/where-does-church-fit-into-all-of-this

What did you like about, identify with, or learn from this film?

Let us hold unswervingly to the hope we profess, for he who promised is faithful. And let us consider how we may spur one another on toward love and good deeds, not giving up meeting together, as some are in the habit of doing, but encouraging one another—and all the more as you see the Day approaching.

—Hebrews 10:23–25

What It Says
1. What did you like about this passage?
2. What did you not like or find confusing about this passage?

What It Means
3. What does this passage teach about people?
4. What does this passage teach about God?

Live It. How will you live more Second today?
Tell It. How will you share what you have learned?

Practice It. Get with a friend or someone in your group. Practice or role-play your "Live and Tell" commitments.

Day 2: The Gathering

They devoted themselves to the apostles' teaching and to fellowship, to the breaking of bread and to prayer.

—Acts 2:42

Read the whole passage in Acts 2:14–47.

The apostles were a band of unimportant people, fishermen, tax collectors, and the like. But Jesus chose these men to prove to the world his message was not reserved for the elite. It was not just for the educated or the rich. It was for everyone. These men and their associates took Jesus' teaching, his sayings and his sermons, his stories and parables, and crafted them into the twenty-seven books we call the New Testament. We follow these books not because of any brilliance or giftedness of the writers, for they were ordinary men, but because they reflect the very words and teachings of Jesus. We would be foolish to base our lives on anything less and our gatherings on anything else.

Talk with God

Teach me reliance on your Bible and faith in your teaching.

Live It. How can you live more Second today?
Tell It. How will you share what you have learned?

Tweet using #IASthegathering to share your thoughts.

Day 3: **Love Others**

"Which of these three do you think was a neighbor to the man who fell into the hands of robbers?" The expert in the law replied, "The one who had mercy on him."
Jesus told him, "Go and do likewise."

—Luke 10:36–37

Read the whole story in Luke 10:25–37.

Love is a simple but profound commandment. It shows mercy to enemies. It trades grace for wounds. It grants gifts without cause or reward. Religion may follow the rules, but love reflects God. Civic duty may encourage good deeds, but love makes those deeds good. Humanism may make man better, but love gives him value. When asked the key to eternal life, Jesus listed two commandments: love God and love others. When we believers sit around a meal or surround a living room, are we planning how we can care for the poor, reach out to the world, change a hurting neighborhood? Where does our money go? How is our time spent? Is love defining our communities? Is it defining yours?

Talk with God

Let the example of your love define our communities and our gatherings.

Live It. How can you live more Second today?
Tell It. How will you share what you have learned?

🐦 Tweet using #IASloveothers to share your thoughts.

Day 4: Encourage Others

Encourage one another and build each other up, just as in fact you are doing.

—1 Thessalonians 5:11

Read the whole passage in 1 Thessalonians 5:1–15.

Life is short. The day of Jesus' return is coming, a day of judgment and reckoning. He will call us to give an account of our time, of our opportunities, and of our effort. Believers do not gather just for fun and fellowship, though that naturally occurs, but they join together for encouragement and equipping. We push each other toward greatness. We help each other remember the battle surrounding us and the mission before us. We join together to encourage soberness in the face of apathy and discipline in the depth of darkness. We meet to inspire a revolution of Second. So let us rethink the mode of our gatherings and the spirit of our communities. Do we meet for fun or for God's strategic planning? Do we rally out of obligation or to prepare for battle? Do we convene for a purpose or merely for a get-together?

Talk with God

Wake us from our slumber and motivate us to be more than just a gathering and to instead be a mustering of your forces.

Live It. How will you live more Second today?
Tell It. How will you share what you have learned?

🐦 Tweet using #IASencourageothers to share your thoughts.

Day 5: **Help Others**

God's grace was so powerfully at work in them all that there were no needy persons among them. For from time to time those who owned land or houses sold them, brought the money from the sales and put it at the apostles' feet, and it was distributed to anyone who had need.

—Acts 4:33–35

Read the whole passage in Acts 4:32–5:11.

We may build buildings or programs or personalities, but are we building a people who care for the poor, who look out for the needy, and who sacrifice for their brothers and sisters? The early Christian community had no needy persons; they had the poor, and they had widows and orphans, but no one went hungry or was in need. Can we say the same? If someone in our meeting could not pay rent, would we drain our savings to meet the need? If someone in our group wrecked their car, would we give them ours? Would we really dare to view our things as their things as well?

Talk with God

Give us success at work, in business, and with our money so that we could help those around us.

Live It. How will you live more Second today?
Tell It. How will you share what you have learned?

🐦 Tweet using #IAShelpothers to share your thoughts.

Day 6: Teach Others

And the things you have heard me say in the presence of many witnesses entrust to reliable people who will also be qualified to teach others.

—2 Timothy 2:2

Read the whole passage in 2 Timothy 2:1–10.

We have each been entrusted with a valuable and powerful message. As members of the believing community and as members of God's family, we are compelled to share what we learn with others. We do not merely sit on what we learn or self-reflect on what we discover. We are compelled to share it, to teach others, and to find faithful people who will teach it to others. This life is too short and this world too fragile to wait around with the truth in our pockets. Find ready learners and faithful teachers. It has nothing to do with a person's ability to speak or talent in a classroom but everything to do with the willingness and eagerness to simply and clearly pass on what is learned to those ready to do the same.

Talk with God

Show me the faithful people in my life. Help me find those people I can pour my life into and teach to do the same for others.

Live It. How will you live more Second today?
Tell It. How will you share what you have learned?

🐦 Tweet using #IASteachothers to share your thoughts.

Day 7: **Chosen**

Praise be to the God and Father of our Lord Jesus Christ, who has blessed us in the heavenly realms with every spiritual blessing in Christ. For he chose us in him before the creation of the world to be holy and blameless in his sight. In love he predestined us for adoption to sonship through Jesus Christ, in accordance with his pleasure and will— to the praise of his glorious grace, which he has freely given us in the One he loves. In him we have redemption through his blood, the forgiveness of sins, in accordance with the riches of God's grace that he lavished on us. With all wisdom and understanding, he made known to us the mystery of his will according to his good pleasure, which he purposed in Christ, to be put into effect when the times reach their fulfillment—to bring unity to all things in heaven and on earth under Christ.

—Ephesians 1:3–10

God redeemed us to be a family. He saved us to be brothers and sisters. We are bonded by his blood and held together by his Spirit. Let us remember this truth when we are tempted to squabble or are drawn to disagreement. Let us remember our family in our prayers and their needs when we tell God about ours.

Talk with God

Ask.

"**. . . he** predestined us for adoption . . ."
God, teach me to love these people better . . .

Tweet using #IASchosen to share your prayers.

Day 1: Perfect

Watch the "What's So Great about the Bible?" Film

iamsecond.com/
whats-so-great-about-the-bible

What did you like about, identify with, or learn from this film?

> *The law of the LORD is perfect,*
> *   refreshing the soul.*
> *The statutes of the LORD are trustworthy,*
> *   making wise the simple.*

—Psalm 19:7

Read the whole passage in Psalm 19:1–14.

What It Says
1. What did you like about this passage?
2. What did you not like or find confusing about this passage?

What It Means
3. What does this passage teach about people?
4. What does this passage teach about God?

Live It. How will you live more Second today?
Tell It. How will you share what you have learned?

Practice It. Get with a friend or someone in your group. Practice or role-play your "Live and Tell" commitments.

Day 2: **Obey**

Blessed are those who keep his statutes
*   and seek him with all their heart—*
they do no wrong
*   but follow his ways.*
You have laid down precepts
*   that are to be fully obeyed.*

—Psalm 119:2–4

Read the whole passage in Psalm 119:1–8.

The Bible is not a book of suggestions. It is the guidebook and law of God. While we may attempt to twist its meaning or bend its teachings to tickle our ears, God allows no such subjective luxury. We do not get to mold it to our desires or cut it down to the parts we find inoffensive. We have only two choices. We can accept it as truth, as the perfect testimony of his work and as our guidebook for life. We can accept it and become God's children and heirs to his throne. Or we can abandon it all, create our own little gods in our own little images, and find death our greeter and emptiness our end. That is the choice before us. Accept and obey the Bible, or walk away. He gives us no other option.

Talk with God

There are passages in the Bible I do not understand and commands I do not enjoy, but, God, I choose you and I choose your way.

Live It. How can you live more Second today?
Tell It. How will you share what you have learned?

Tweet using #IASobey to share your thoughts.

Day 3: **Remember**

I meditate on your precepts
*   and consider your ways.*
I delight in your decrees;
*   I will not neglect your word.*

—Psalm 119:15–16

Read the whole passage in Psalm 119:9–16.

Reading without reflection cannot bring the kind of life change God desires. He does not want us to read and forget but to remember and reflect. The Bible is meant to change our behavior and alter our mind, two tasks that require constant attention and consistent care. True meditation is not emptying one's mind; it is filling it with the words and thoughts of God. Not thoughts we create or rules we invent but rather the precepts of God, the decrees of his will, and the example of his love. Maybe we read our Bibles, but do we reflect and mediate on it? Maybe we do Bible studies, but do we think about the lessons learned throughout our days and weeks? Does God's Word fill our thoughts beyond those few brief moments of study?

Talk with God

Remind me of your teaching, of your word, and of the way you wish me to lead my life.

Live It. How can you live more Second today?
Tell It. How will you share what you have learned?

🐦 Tweet using #IASremember to share your thoughts.

Day 4: **Different**

Though rulers sit together and slander me,
*   your servant will meditate on your decrees.*
Your statutes are my delight;
*   they are my counselors.*

—Psalm 119:23–24

Read the whole passage in Psalm 119:17–24.

Some may value the Golden Rule or the promises of hope and heaven, but only the true believer finds value in every verse in every book of the Bible. There may be stories we do not understand or teachings we find difficult or hard to live out. There may even be lessons we do not like. But we love God more than ourselves, and so we put him and the Bible First despite our feelings. God is different from us, and so his Bible contrasts with many of our beliefs and traditions. But putting God First means that when the Bible differs from us—and it will—we bow our knees rather than the other way around.

Talk with God

I do not always understand your Bible nor find your commands easy, but when we differ, I submit to you.

Live It. How will you live more Second today?
Tell It. How will you share what you have learned?

🐦 Tweet using #IASdifferent to share your thoughts.

Day 5: **Strength**

My soul is weary with sorrow;
strengthen me according to your word.

—Psalm 119:28

Read the whole passage in Psalm 119:25–32.

The Bible contains hope for a future beyond this world. It tells the story of struggling saints and of persecuted brothers and sisters, people who can relate to our feelings and understand our predicaments. But while the stories, sayings, and poems of the Bible by themselves can bring strength and hope, they are more than just literature, more than stories of fabled hope or wished-for rescue. They are true utterances of God through his saints. They will never fade and never fail. His Bible will always stand and always ring true as a testimony to God's nature and a picture of his work in this world.

Talk with God

God, use your Bible to give me strength in times of doubt and courage in times of fear.

Live It. How will you live more Second today?
Tell It. How will you share what you have learned?

Tweet using #IASstrength to share your thoughts.

Day 6: **Director**

Direct me in the path of your commands,
for there I find delight.
Turn my heart toward your statutes
and not toward selfish gain.

—Psalm 119:35–36

Read the whole passage in Psalm 119:33–40.

God gave us a guidebook and a director for our lives. He gave us the Bible, a collection of sixty-six books from dozens of authors spanning nearly fifteen hundred years of history. While no authors survived into the modern time, their issues and themes speak into even the most urbanized ears. Their world may have been different, the names of their cities and countries foreign and strange. But the struggles these authors faced and the issues they grappled with speak truth into modern problems and contexts better than any best seller. If we let the Bible teach us and guide us, direct our paths and light our way, we will find life works better. While the ultimate reward awaits us in heaven, the principles of the Bible, when lived out here and now, have immediate benefit to our lives. Whether it be about improving our relationships or bringing sanity to our finances, the Bible lays out God's playbook for life.

Talk with God

Guide me through your Bible and teach me your principles.

Live It. How will you live more Second today?
Tell It. How will you share what you have learned?

Tweet using #IASdirector to share your thoughts.

Day 7: **Unfailing**

May your unfailing love come to me, LORD,
your salvation, according to your promise;
Then I can answer anyone who taunts me,
for I trust in your word.
Never take your word of truth from my mouth,
for I have put my hope in your laws.
I will always obey your law,
for ever and ever.
I will walk about in freedom,
for I have sought out your precepts.
I will speak of your statutes before kings
and will not be put to shame,
For I delight in your commands
because I love them.
I reach out for your commands, which I love,
that I may meditate on your decrees.

—Psalm 119:41–48

God is different from us. For him goodness is natural; love is second-nature. Wisdom is a limitless resource for him but a scarce novelty for us. When we read the Bible, we are sure to find commands and teachings that differ from our own habits and understandings. When we find these differences, we have a choice. We can either claim superiority and refuse the Bible's teaching, call it archaic or passé, or we can surrender and let God be God. The choice is ours.

Talk with God

Surrender.

"I will always obey your law . . ."
God, I commit to obey your Bible . . .

Tweet using #IASunfailing to share your prayers.

Day 1: Filled

Watch the Sean Little Film

iamsecond.com/seanlittle

What did you like about, identify with, or learn from Sean's story?

> Then Peter, filled with the Holy Spirit, said to them: ". . .
> It is by the name of Jesus Christ of Nazareth, whom you
> crucified but whom God raised from the dead, that this man
> stands before you healed."
>
> **—Acts 4:8, 10**

Read the whole passage in Acts 4:1–14.

What It Says
1. What did you like about this passage?
2. What did you not like or find confusing about this passage?

What It Means
3. What does this passage teach about people?
4. What does this passage teach about God?

Live It. How will you live more Second today?
Tell It. How will you share what you have learned?

Practice It. Get with a friend or someone in your group. Practice or role-play your "Live and Tell" commitments.

Day 2: **Poured Out**

I will pour out my Spirit on all people.
Your sons and daughters will prophesy,
your old men will dream dreams,
your young men will see visions.

—Joel 2:28

Read the whole passage in Joel 2:28–32.

Science is the standard for truth in our culture. If we cannot touch, see, and test it, it does not exist. But some things cannot be quantified. Some things cannot be validated by the scientific method. God exists outside our universe and thus does not bend to its laws or submit to its limitations. This does not mean that every dream, every vision, or every "experience" is a touch of God, but it makes such things possible. God can speak to us. God can communicate, if he so chooses. He is not compelled or obligated, but he is capable. The wisdom of others, the teachings of the faith, and above all the truth of the Bible will be the guides and the judges of those experiences. But when he speaks, God must not be ignored or rationalized away.

Talk with God

God, forgive any reluctance to believe or slowness to accept that you indeed can speak. I ask that you do speak, that you do guide my life through your Spirit.

Live It. How can you live more Second today?
Tell It. How will you share what you have learned?

🐦 Tweet using #IASpouredout to share your thoughts.

Day 3: Baptism

I baptize you with water for repentance. . . . He will baptize you with the Holy Spirit and fire.

—Matthew 3:11

Read the whole passage in Matthew 3:1–17.

Never before has God lived in his people. He, in the days before Jesus, spoke to his people, empowered them in times of need. But with the coming of Jesus, with his death and resurrection, came something new, something different from anything in the past. Now God surrounds and covers us with his Holy Spirit. We may not always feel him, and we often do not realize it. But the small, quiet voice that speaks when we disobey, the nagging force that pushes us toward a path in life, those words that flow when we speak in his name, the prayer that reaches the heavens, all of it comes from the Holy Spirit, who lives within us. We offend the Holy Spirit when we ignore God's commands. We speak through him when we speak with God, and we walk in him when we tell others of Jesus and live out the love we were called to share. His presence should both encourage us and sober us.

Talk with God

God, thank you for promising never to leave me, never to forsake me, and to always live with me through your Spirit.

Live It. How can you live more Second today?
Tell It. How will you share what you have learned?

🐦 Tweet using #IASbaptism to share your thoughts.

Day 4: Teacher

*But the Advocate, the Holy Spirit, whom the Father will send
in my name, will teach you all things and will remind you of
everything I have said to you.*

—John 14:26

Read the whole passage in John 14:15–31.

Father. Son. Holy Spirit. One God, three persons, different, distinct, but still one. The Holy Spirit is that person of God who dwells within us, serves as our conscience, reminds us of our mission, and recalls for us the message and teaching of our Savior. Rarely is he seen, but he is there—moving and reminding us, guiding and teaching us. We never need to worry about prayers not being heard, about missions being impossible, for we walk with God at our side, with the Spirit in our words. Be encouraged when life seems to crumble around us, when God seems far and removed. Be strengthened that he mourns at our heartaches and cheers at our victories. Whether it is a hard day at work, a lonely walk down school hallways, or a difficult journey through divorce, death, or disappointment, God is with us to remind us of all that he said and all that he promises.

Talk with God

Guide my daily steps, strengthen my weaknesses, comfort my pains, and teach me what I have yet to learn about you.

Live It. How will you live more Second today?
Tell It. How will you share what you have learned?

Tweet using #IASteacher to share your thoughts.

Day 5: Tongues

They saw what seemed to be tongues of fire that separated and came to rest on each of them. All of them were filled with the Holy Spirit and began to speak in other tongues as the Spirit enabled them.

—Acts 2:3–4

Read the whole passage in Acts 2:1–33.

God did not need linguists or translators. He did not need educated or gifted people. He empowered the people on that day to speak in languages never practiced, tongues never known by their mouths. We should ready our stories and practice telling the story of Jesus, be ready in season and out of season to share the message of God. No matter our speaking ability or lack thereof, God is not at the mercy of our weaknesses. He can say what he wants and speak how he wills. So let us charge forward in boldness knowing that the God who knows all knows what we need to say. Let us shout his story knowing that the God who has all the power can change the hearts and minds of anyone he chooses. Let us be emboldened to share his message with his help and with his power.

Talk with God

God, use me, speak through me, and change the lives around me through your Spirit.

Live It. How will you live more Second today?
Tell It. How will you share what you have learned?

🐦 Tweet using #IAStongues to share your thoughts.

Day 6: **Dwelling**

And if the Spirit of him who raised Jesus from the dead is living in you, he who raised Christ from the dead will also give life to your mortal bodies because of his Spirit who lives in you.

—Romans 8:11

Read the whole passage in Romans 8:1–11.

Every person on earth is mortal. We live and then we die. There are no exceptions. Some live for only a moment; others survive to see the rise and fall of empires. But in the end all die—the good, the bad, the wise, and the fool. Jesus broke that endless reign of death by his resurrection. While our bodies will still suffer death, death will not keep its hold. As Jesus died and rose again, so will we through his Spirit rise from death and live forever after. The same Spirit who gave Jesus life will grant us immortality. How small our worries become, how insignificant the sacrifices God asks us, how petty our arguments and our complaints, our wealth and our careers. How puny everything becomes when the Spirit of God promises a life without end.

Talk with God

God, so often I am distracted by the small things of this world. Teach me to remember the future you have promised us.

Live It. How will you live more Second today?
Tell It. How will you share what you have learned?

🐦 Tweet using #IASdwelling to share your thoughts.

Day 7: **Present**

Where can I go from your Spirit?
Where can I flee from your presence?
If I go up to the heavens, you are there;
if I make my bed in the depths, you are there.
If I rise on the wings of the dawn,
if I settle on the far side of the sea,
even there your hand will guide me,
your right hand will hold me fast.
If I say, "Surely the darkness will hide me
and the light become night around me,"
even the darkness will not be dark to you;
the night will shine like the day,
for darkness is as light to you.

—Psalm 139:7–12

God is always there. We cannot run from him and we cannot escape from him. He lives within his people and dwells among his children. He is always there to comfort us, to guide us, to empower and instruct us. There is no escaping his love or avoiding his strength.

Talk with God

Relationship.

"**. . . you** are there . . ."
God, thank you for always being there when . . .

🐦 Tweet using #IASpresent to share your prayers.

Session Five

Jesus Says

Jesus' teachings can be summarized into a few short principles. This session focuses on four of those teachings. The first is a warning to obey the others. Jesus tells us to listen to his wisdom and apply the truth to our lives. *Repent, believe,* and *follow* are three ways of saying the same thing. Jesus does not expect us to clean ourselves before coming to him or to save ourselves before we beg his forgiveness. That his role. Ours is to repent, to feel remorse for our failures and ask for forgiveness, to believe that he can forgive, and to follow him in grateful response to that forgiveness. The next command is to be baptized. We must present ourselves to the believing community and declare our faith in Jesus and our identification with his sacrifice. The last command sums up all others. Love. We are to love God with all our strength, mind, and heart and to love others as ourselves. The rest of life is just details.

Day 1: **If You Love**

Watch the Clayton Kershaw Film

 iamsecond.com/claytonkershaw

What did you like about, identify with, or learn from Clayton's story?

If you love me, keep my commands.

—John 14:15

Read the whole passage in John 14:15–21.

What It Says
    1. What did you like about this passage?
    2. What did you not like or find confusing about this passage?

What It Means
    3. What does this passage teach about people?
    4. What does this passage teach about God?

Live It. How will you live more Second today?
Tell It. How will you share what you have learned?

Practice It. Get with a friend or someone in your group. Practice or role-play your "Live and Tell" commitments.

Day 2: **Faithful**

Well done, good and faithful servant! You have been faithful with a few things; I will put you in charge of many things. Come and share your master's happiness!

—Matthew 25:23

Read the whole passage in Matthew 25:13–40.

Jesus will return to this earth. He came the first time as a baby, born in a manger. He preached forgiveness and a way back to God. He died on a cross and rose again three days later to bring us life. The second time he will come as King and Judge. The time for mercy will be over; second chances will expire. We do not know the time of his return or the day of his coming. But he will come. To the faithful, he promises happiness and eternal peace. To the wicked, to the unbeliever, to the unfaithful, he promises judgment and hell. Will you be ready when he comes?

Talk with God

Teach me to serve you faithfully and remember you always.

Live It. How can you live more Second today?
Tell It. How will you share what you have learned?

🐦 Tweet using #IASfaithful to share your thoughts.

Day 3: Hypocrite

Woe to you, teachers of the law and Pharisees, you hypocrites! You are like whitewashed tombs, which look beautiful on the outside but on the inside are full of the bones of the dead and everything unclean.

—Matthew 23:27

Read the whole passage in Matthew 23:1–39.

Jesus pronounced curses and fashioned whips. He stirred arguments and challenged authorities. But never do we see him raging against the sinner or against the pagan. Never do we see him crying foul when the drunk drinks or the prostitute sells her body. No, it was the religious people who stirred his rage. It was the temple clerks who felt the sting of his whip. Religious teachers, temple priests, and biblical scholars suffered his condemnation and judgment. What sinner does not recognize his sin? What addict does not crave healing? What lost, confused soul does not seek redemption? The tax collectors and wayward women panted for his forgiveness, but it was the religious who hung him on a cross. So often we pride ourselves on our goodness or our religiosity, but dare we put ourselves with those who know the good yet refuse its call? Let Jesus' words bring sobriety to our religious boasting. Let Jesus' condemnation force a review of our lives and a reality check of our obedience to his call.

Talk with God

Father, am I one of the Pharisees? Am I religious without sincere obedience? Humble me to see the truth of my condition.

Live It. How can you live more Second today?
Tell It. How will you share what you have learned?

🐦 Tweet using #IAShypocrite to share your thoughts.

Day 4: Tradition

Going on from that place, he went into their synagogue, and a man with a shriveled hand was there. Looking for a reason to bring charges against Jesus, they asked him, "Is it lawful to heal on the Sabbath?"

—Matthew 12:9–10

Read the whole passage in Matthew 12:1–14.

God's law is less a list of rules than it is an orientation of the heart. Israel had one day set aside each week as holy, a day without work and without distraction to remember and worship God. They called it Sabbath. If you plowed fields for a living, on Sabbath you let your land rest. If you cut rock or built homes, on Sabbath you set down your tools. The people built a wall around this law, a layer of protection to guard its importance. They devised new and greater methods of obedience. This wall grew till even healing the injured on this holy day became a crime, a transgression against God and his people. How often have we done the same? If drinking has its dangers, then we outlaw it. If dancing has its temptations, then we forbid it. If music or movies or culture have their deceptions, then we run from them. But to obey our version of God's law, have we let the injured, the hurting, and the lost go without the healing of the message we carry?

Talk with God

God, give me the wisdom to know and obey your law rather than the one we invent.

Live It. How will you live more Second today?
Tell It. How will you share what you have learned?

Tweet using #IAStradition to share your thoughts.

Day 5: Religion

He has shown you, O mortal, what is good. And what does the Lᴏʀᴅ require of you? To act justly and to love mercy and to walk humbly with your God.

—Micah 6:6–8

Read the whole passage in Micah 6:1–16.

Micah lived in a time when following God meant bloody sacrifices and burnt offerings. Religion had the scent of charred meat and oil. God demanded that his people, the nation of Israel, produce physical signs of repentance. He wanted bulls and rams, sheep, grain, and oil, given in confession of sin and in thanks for his blessings. But even in that day, God wanted the heart, not the religion. He wanted bulls, but only as a sign of a life lived justly. He wanted oil, but only from a heart full of mercy that saw fellow humans as objects of love and care, not judgment and condemnation. And above all, God wanted his people to walk humbly before him, not in arrogance boasting in their goodness, not in pride rejoicing over their sinful escapades, but in humbleness. Does justice define your life? Or has the temptation to cheat on taxes or break confidences marred your integrity? Does mercy rule your way? Or has gossip and apathy found a home in your heart? Do you walk humbly with your God?

Talk with God

Show me the injustices in my life and the lack of mercy in my heart. Teach me to live humbly with you.

Live It. How will you live more Second today?
Tell It. How will you share what you have learned?

🐦 Tweet using #IASreligion to share your thoughts.

Day 6: **Doers**

Do not merely listen to the word, and so deceive yourselves.
Do what it says.

—James 1:22

Read the whole passage in James 1:19–27.

The Bible works as a mirror. It convicts and confronts. It shows us the way to lead our lives and the way we have failed to do that leading. It defines the purpose and goal of our existence. It lays out the manner in which we are to pursue life's goal. Love, mercy, justice, humbleness, kindness, and integrity, to name but a few. The Bible sets a standard, a line to balance upon, and a road on which to walk. To look at this standard and refuse its wisdom is like seeing our wild morning hair, our crusty eyes, and stained teeth in the mirror and doing nothing about it. We deceive ourselves into thinking nobody will notice, nobody will care. But God sees everything. He gave us this mirror of his Word, and he expects us to use it.

Talk with God

I commit to obey what I learn, to live out what I discover in your Word.

Live It. How will you live more Second today?
Tell It. How will you share what you have learned?

🐦 Tweet using #IASdoers to share your thoughts.

Day 7: **Decrees**

You are my portion, L<small>ORD</small>;
*   I have promised to obey your words.*
I have sought your face with all my heart;
*   be gracious to me according to your promise.*
I have considered my ways
*   and have turned my steps to your statutes.*
I will hasten and not delay
*   to obey your commands.*
Though the wicked bind me with ropes,
*   I will not forget your law.*
At midnight I rise to give you thanks
*   for your righteous laws.*
I am a friend to all who fear you,
*   to all who follow your precepts.*
The earth is filled with your love, L<small>ORD</small>;
*   teach me your decrees.*

—Psalm 119:57–64

There is something about making a commitment and about confessing intentions. When we draw a line in the sand, it somehow makes it harder to cross that line. When we declare our allegiance, it somehow makes us more loyal. So what is your commitment? What have you dedicated to God? Tell God now where you stand with him.

Talk with God

Surrender.

"I have promised to obey . . ."
God, I will follow and obey you in this . . .

Tweet using #IASdecrees to share your prayers.

Day 1: Good News

Watch the Josh Hamilton Film

iamsecond.com/joshhamilton

What did you like, identify with, or learn from Josh's story?

> *"The time has come," he said. "The kingdom of God has come near. Repent and believe the good news!"*
>
> **—Mark 1:15**

Read the whole passage in Mark 1:1–20.

What It Says
1. What did you like about this passage?
2. What did you not like or find confusing about this passage?

What It Means
3. What does this passage teach about people?
4. What does this passage teach about God?

Live It. How will you live more Second today?
Tell It. How will you share what you have learned?

Practice It. Get with a friend or someone in your group. Practice or role-play your "Live and Tell" commitments.

Day 2: **Doctor**

It is not the healthy who need a doctor, but the sick.

—Matthew 9:12

Read the whole passage in Matthew 9:9–13.

No one is unmarred by sin or unhindered by the struggles of humanity. But despite our obvious failings, many of us will convince ourselves that we are all right, that we are not as bad as the guy next to us. We think that if we could just get ahead of the curve, tip the scales of goodness in our favor, then the pearly gates will swing wide their welcome. But whether we have only a few mild symptoms or a host of ailments, we are all sick. And the sickness of sin, if left untended, will spare none of our lives. Jesus asks only that we come to him in recognition that we need a doctor. He does not need us pretending we can heal ourselves or that we have somehow escaped this world unscathed by evil. He knows our plight and freely offers his remedy.

Talk with God

God, I know I need a doctor. I know I fail your standard and fall prey to temptation. Forgive me and give me strength today.

Live It. How will you live more Second today?
Tell It. How will you share what you have learned?

🐦 Tweet using #IASdoctor to share your thoughts.

Day 3: **Faith**

For it is by grace you have been saved, through faith—and this is not from yourselves, it is the gift of God—not by works, so that no one can boast.

—Ephesians 2:8–9

Read the whole passage in Ephesians 2:1–10.

We can do nothing to earn or deserve salvation. We receive it all by grace, by unearned, undeserved favor. Never can we boast that it was we who accomplished it. All we can do is believe, believe that God is God, that he will give us life that never ends, a heaven that never mourns, and a place in his family that never ceases. Sometimes we get this idea that if we are good enough, if we accomplish enough, if we prove our worth, God will love us more or owe us something. But his love for us is already perfect, and his plan for us is already beyond what we could imagine. He offers a gift, free and clear, simple and undeserved. All we have to do is take it, to accept the gift of salvation in faith.

Talk with God

Thank you for the gift of your love and the grace of your salvation.

Live It. How can you live more Second today?
Tell It. How will you share what you have learned?

Tweet using #IASfaith to share your thoughts.

Day 4: Obey

Why do you call me, "Lord, Lord," and do not do what I say?

—Luke 6:46

Read the whole passage in Luke 6:43–49.

We become God's children and enter his kingdom by faith, but it is a faith tied to repentance, the admission that nothing we do is good enough to save ourselves and nothing we say meets his perfect standard. It is the kind of faith that motivates action and inspires effort and change. God does not ask us merely to acknowledge his existence, for even Satan and his demons admit that. God wants the kind of faith that stirs us to love and honor him, to follow his voice and listen to his call. Jesus challenges us to repent, believe, and follow. Are we merely sorry for our mistakes? Do we merely believe in his existence? Or are our faith and our repentance of such a quality that our lives are different and our outlook on life altered?

Talk with God

I know my obedience is incomplete and often delayed, but I commit to change, to fight the good fight, and to continue to follow you daily.

Live It. How can you live more Second today?
Tell It. How will you share what you have learned?

Tweet using #IASobey to share your thoughts.

Day 5: Leave

Go from your country, your people and your father's
household to the land I will show you.
    I will make you into a great nation.

—Genesis 12:1–2

Read the whole passage in Genesis 12:1–9.

Abram did nothing to earn God's promise, nothing to deserve it, nothing to make God his debtor. God simply appeared and promised to make Abram's descendants a great nation. Abram responded with immediate and radical obedience. When God called him to leave his family, his home—everything he knew—and trek to an unknown land, Abram obeyed. Favors can't be earned with God. His grace is not for sale. God expects absolute obedience, complete surrender. But it is not a trade or barter, obedience for favor. It's an absolute. God is the creator and owner of the universe. Nothing we possess could add to his wealth. Nothing we do could impress or obligate God. His gifts are simply gifts, and our obedience is a demand, not a request.

Talk with God

I am your servant. Send me where you will and use me how you wish.

Live It. How will you live more Second today?
Tell It. How will you share what you have learned?

🐦 Tweet using #IASleave to share your thoughts.

Day 6: Faith History

Now faith is confidence in what we hope for and assurance about what we do not see. This is what the ancients were commended for.

—Hebrews 11:1–2

Read the whole passage in Hebrews 11:1–40.

Faith is the hallmark of our legacy. The heroes of the Bible never thought they could earn their way to God or force their way to heaven. They only hoped for it. They trusted God for it but knew it was nothing they deserved or had a right to. They trusted God when he promised his blessings and had faith in his words that no matter the wait and no matter the delay, God would fulfill what he said. They saw the fulfillment from a distance, hoped for it from afar. But they never touched it while in this life. They died never having seen his promises come true. They were mocked, ridiculed, beaten, tortured, or even killed for their reckless faith. But they never stopped hoping, never quit believing. Why? Because they knew that God could be trusted and that despite any hardship, regardless of any delay, God would come through in ways more amazing than they ever could imagine, ways that made all the waiting worth the hardship.

Talk with God

God, sometimes I just wish to see the end of your plan and enjoy your promises now. But I will wait. I will trust you and keep hold of hope.

Live It. How will you live more Second today?
Tell It. How will you share what you have learned?

🐦 Tweet using #IASfaithhistory to share your thoughts.

Day 7: **Stronghold**

The Lord is my light and my salvation—
whom shall I fear?
The Lord is the stronghold of my life—
of whom shall I be afraid? . . .
Hear my voice when I call, Lord;
be merciful to me and answer me.
My heart says of you, "Seek his face!"
Your face, Lord, I will seek.
Do not hide your face from me,
do not turn your servant away in anger;
you have been my helper.
Do not reject me or forsake me,
God my Savior.

—Psalm 27:1, 7–9

We do not live in an ideal world. Friends are not as friendly as they should be. Neighbors are not as neighborly as they could be. And enemies are not as easily reconciled as we wish they would be. Bad things happen to good people and good people are not as good as we might imagine. Therefore, asking God for his protection is not a pleasantry we can take lightly but a necessity we must take seriously.

Talk with God

Protect.

"Do not hide your face . . ."
God, protect me from . . .

🐦 Tweet using #IASstronghold to share your prayers.

Day 1: Faith and Water

Then Philip began with that very passage of Scripture and told him the good news about Jesus. As they traveled along the road, they came to some water and the eunuch said, "Look, here is water. What can stand in the way of my being baptized?"

—Acts 8:35–36

Read the whole passage in Acts 8:26–38.

What It Says
1. What did you like about this passage?
2. What did you not like or find confusing about this passage?

What It Means
3. What does this passage teach about people?
4. What does this passage teach about God?

Live It. How will you live more Second today? Do you or anyone in your group need to make plans to get baptized?
Tell It. How will you share what you have learned?

Practice It. Get with a friend or someone in your group. Practice or role-play your "Live and Tell" commitments.

Day 2: **The Baptist**

I baptize you with water for repentance.

—Matthew 3:11

Read the whole passage in Matthew 3:1–11.

John came to prepare the way, to ready the road for Jesus. He taught people to turn from their sin, to repent of their wrongs, and to be washed clean from the stain of their failures. John represented this repentance and cleansing through being dunked or baptized in the Jordan River and washed clean with its waters. People streamed to hear him speak and wandered out to his desert dwelling to practice his repentance. His crowds grew, and his popularity soared to such a point where he became known as John the Baptist. But he also talked of another man, one who would take away the sins of the world, one who would wash us clean and dunk us into a greater baptism—a baptism of the Holy Spirit. John prepared the people to hear the message of Jesus, a message of repentance, of turning away from evil, and of making God first.

Talk with God

Father, I am a broken and sinful person. I constantly need your forgiveness and your grace. Cleanse my heart and wash clean my mind.

Live It. How can you live more Second today? If you have not yet been baptized, talk to your pastor, priest, or mentor to make plans for baptism.

Tell It. How will you share what you have learned?

Tweet using #IASthebaptist to share your thoughts.

Day 3: **The Jordan**

As soon as Jesus was baptized, he went up out of the water.
At that moment heaven was opened, and he saw the Spirit
of God descending like a dove and alighting on him.

—Matthew 3:16

Read the whole passage in Matthew 3:13–17.

Despite living a perfect life and having no need for repentance, Jesus set an example. An example that we must all walk humbly before our God, admit our need for him, and follow his commands. Jesus had no need for forgiveness, but he still submitted to his Father's plan and was baptized in the Jordan River. We all have those places in our lives, those hidden rooms, and those stubborn areas where we do what we want. It is our time, our place, our little pleasure. But God wants every area of our lives, every corner of our hearts. He calls for humble confession and honest repenting. He wants all of us, even the hidden things.

Talk with God

God, I confess my need for forgiveness and my failure to always put you First.

Live It. How can you live more Second today?
Tell It. How will you share what you have learned?

Tweet using #IASthejordan to share your thoughts.

Day 4: In the Name

All authority in heaven and on earth has been given to me. Therefore go and make disciples of all nations, baptizing them in the name of the Father and of the Son and of the Holy Spirit, and teaching them to obey everything I have commanded you. And surely I am with you always, to the very end of the age.

—Matthew 28:18–20

Read the whole passage in Matthew 28:16–20.

Making disciples is comprised of two main elements: baptizing and teaching. The first is an initiatory step, a rite of passage into the family. This is the first act of obedience for every disciple. It displays a heart of sorrow for wrongs made and a commitment to follow and obey moving forward. But it also displays a certain and basic understanding of God. God is one, but that one God is three persons, distinct and different, but all still one God. God is Father, Son, and Holy Spirit. The Father is God. The Son is God. The Spirit is God. There is not three gods but only one.

Talk with God

I confess I believe in one God—Father, Son, and Holy Spirit.

Live It. How will you live more Second today?
Tell It. How will you share what you have learned?

🐦 Tweet using #IASinthename to share your thoughts.

Day 5: Immediate

Then they spoke the word of the Lord to him and to all the others in his house. At that hour of the night the jailer took them and washed their wounds; then immediately he and all his household were baptized.

—Acts 16:32–33

Read the whole passage in Acts 16:16–34.

No delay. No hesitation. The jailer witnessed the faith of Paul and Silas, heard their message, and believed. And immediately afterward, he was baptized into the faith, along with all his household. As Jesus died, was buried, and raised again to life, so baptism symbolizes a believer's identification with Jesus in being "buried" in water and rising again with new life. It holds no special power over our souls, but it draws a picture of our salvation and makes public our commitment to Jesus. It works to solidify our decision to obey our new King and follow him in life and death. The jailor gladly and immediately committed this act of obedience. Have you done the same? Have you made public your commitment?

Talk with God

God, thank you for the sacrifice of your Son and the opportunity to share his story with others.

Live It. How will you live more Second today?
Tell It. How will you share what you have learned?

Tweet using #IASimmediate to share your thoughts.

Day 6: Picture

We were therefore buried with him through baptism into death in order that, just as Christ was raised from the dead through the glory of the Father, we too may live a new life.

—Romans 6:4

Read the whole passage in Romans 6:1–14.

There is a price for our selfishness, for our pride, for our dependence on things and self. The debt we owe is our lives. We owe our own blood for the choice of sin. But unwilling to let death win and his creation fall to ruin, Jesus came and paid our debt. He died in our stead, and three days later he rose again and offered us a new life. Baptism is a picture of Jesus' sacrifice and our response to it. We fall, buried in death for our sin, but through Jesus we rise from the water a new creature, a new person. The old is gone, and the new has come. The water has no magical powers, but it pictures a miraculous event. Baptism itself may have no mystical workings, but it is an image of salvation and a demonstration of Jesus' sacrifice.

Talk with God

I confess my helplessness to save myself, my inability to pay my debt. Thank you for the sacrifice of your Son. Help me live a life of grateful response.

Live It. How will you live more Second today?
Tell It. How will you share what you have learned?

🐦 Tweet using #IASpicture to share your thoughts.

Day 7: Covered

Blessed is the one
  whose transgressions are forgiven,
  whose sins are covered.
Blessed is the one
  whose sin the LORD does not count against them
  and in whose spirit is no deceit.
When I kept silent,
  my bones wasted away
  through my groaning all day long.
For day and night
  your hand was heavy on me;
my strength was sapped
  as in the heat of summer.
Then I acknowledged my sin to you
  and did not cover up my iniquity.
I said, "I will confess
  my transgressions to the LORD."
And you forgave
  the guilt of my sin.

—Psalm 32:1–5

He grants it freely. He gives it generously. He offers it universally. Forgiveness is available to all who ask for it. No sin is too great. No life is too tarnished. God will forgive anyone of anything so long as they ask for it. So let us make confession our habit and forgiveness our daily request.

Talk with God

Forgive.

"Blessed is the one . . . whose sins are covered."
God, forgive me for my sins, including . . .

🐦 Tweet using #IAScovered to share your prayers.

Day 1: Love Story

Watch the Darrell Waltrip Film

iamsecond.com/darrellwaltrip

What did you like about, identify with, or learn from Darrell's story?

"Love the Lord your God with all your heart and with all your soul and with all your strength and with all your mind;" and, "Love your neighbor as yourself."

—Luke 10:27

Read the whole passage in Luke 10:25–37.

What It Says
1. What did you like about this passage?
2. What did you not like or find confusing about this passage?

What It Means
3. What does this passage teach about people?
4. What does this passage teach about God?

Live It. How will you live more Second today?
Tell It. How will you share what you have learned?

Practice It. Get with a friend or someone in your group. Practice or role-play your "Live and Tell" commitments.

Day 2: Lone God

*The L*ORD *our God, the L*ORD *is one. Love the L*ORD *your God with all your heart and with all your soul and with all your strength.*

—Deuteronomy 6:4–5

Read the whole passage in Deuteronomy 6:1–9.

There is only one God. No other name, no other idol, and no other loyalty will be accepted. God wants all our hearts, every corner of our souls, and every ounce of our strength. He promises riches and peace, eternity and strength. But he demands in return our complete and undivided love. We may not always feel warm and fuzzy at his memory, but we must remain loyal. We may not always sense his presence, but we must trust his promise to never leave or forsake. We may feel tired and worn, tempted and stressed, but our love for him demands we stay strong. He knows our weakness; he sees all our failures, past, present, and future. But he asks that our affections never falter, that our apologies follow quickly after our failures, and that our commitments renew with every stumble. He asks for our love; imperfect as it is, he wants all of it.

Talk with God

God, you have my love. Though I am weak and forgetful, I commit to always love you and follow your voice.

Live It. How can you live more Second today?
Tell It. How will you share what you have learned?

Tweet using #IASlonegod to share your thoughts.

Day 3: Original love

Dear friends, let us love one another, for love comes from God. Everyone who loves has been born of God and knows God. Whoever does not love does not know God, because God is love.

—1 John 4:7–8

Read the whole passage in 1 John 7–12.

God loved first. He has always loved, and he always will love. He defines and embodies love. Not the romanticized emotion we see displayed in our movies but the self-sacrificing, all-forgiving, never-ending love displayed by God. We know love only because he showed love to us. He created us, not out of need, but out of love. He saved us, not out of drudgery, but out of impassioned care for his people. His love can never be doubted, and his heart will never change. Let us mimic this love in our own lives and demonstrate it to the people surrounding us.

Talk with God

God, I love you because you loved me first. Teach me to love others as you have loved me.

Live It. How can you live more Second today?
Tell It. How will you share what you have learned?

Tweet using #IASoriginallove to share your thoughts.

Day 4: **Jealous**

I gave you my solemn oath and entered into a covenant with you, declares the Sovereign LORD, and you became mine.

—Ezekiel 16:8

Read the whole passage in Ezekiel 16:1–22.

God gave us his covenant and promise. We are his people and he is our God. He takes this oath seriously and will not stand for betrayal on our part. God is a jealous God. He hates divided loyalties and disdains unfaithfulness. He loved us in our sins, cared for us while we wallowed in our misery and hopelessness, and now he demands our undivided love. He lavished us with his kindness and guaranteed us eternal bliss and forever life. Now he asks for our hearts. Nothing stirs his vengeance more or reaps his wrath like spurned love and forgotten grace. Let the history of his kindness and the memory of his grace motivate us toward a life of unbroken love for him.

Talk with God

Father, I thank and love you for caring for me, for saving me when no one else could.

Live It. How will you live more Second today?
Tell It. How will you share what you have learned?

Tweet using #IASjealous to share your thoughts.

Day 5: **Feet**

*When he had finished washing their feet, he put on his
clothes and returned to his place. "Do you understand what
I have done for you?" he asked them.*

—John 13:12

Read the whole passage in John 13:1–17.

Follow Jesus' example of love. He had the right to demand
service, but he chose to serve. He had the authority to order submission, but he chose to submit to his Father. He had the ability
to call a legion of angels to ease his misery, but he chose suffering.
He could have required that his feet be cleaned, but he took off his
robe, bent to the floor, and washed the feet of twelve men, eleven
who loved and followed him and one who would soon betray him.
His command is to love unconditionally, without hope for reward
and without promise of returned favors. He washed the feet of
friend and traitor, of ally and enemy. Even terrorists and murderers
love their friends and family, but only those following the example
of Jesus will love their enemy and their betrayer.

Talk with God

God, mirror my heart after yours. Help me love friend and foe.

Live It. How will you live more Second today?
Tell It. How will you share what you have learned?

Tweet using #IASfeet to share your thoughts.

Day 6: Least of These

Truly I tell you, whatever you did not do for one of the least of these, you did not do for me.

—Matthew 25:45

Read the whole passage in Matthew 25:31–46.

God takes our hoarding personally. We live in carpeted homes and work in paneled offices. We drive shiny cars and walk in padded shoes. Meanwhile, a billion people suffer without clean, drinkable water. Thousands of children die every day from preventable disease. Millions of our brothers and sisters in Christ suffer untold persecution and hardship for their faith. What will God say about the way we invest our money? What will he think about our obsession with more, while the least of these suffer and die? What have we done to alleviate their suffering or aid in their empowerment? What we do or fail to do is taken personally by the God who created all, rich and poor, strong and weak.

Talk with God

Forgive me for my failure to love the least of these as I should. Show me how best to love those in need.

Live It. How will you live more Second today?
Tell It. How will you share what you have learned?

🐦 Tweet using #IASleastofthese to share your thoughts.

Day 7: **Love Abounds**

I love you, LORD, my strength.
The LORD is my rock, my fortress and my deliverer;
my God is my rock, in whom I take refuge,
my shield and the horn of my salvation, my stronghold. . . .
He reached down from on high and took hold of me;
he drew me out of deep waters.
He rescued me from my powerful enemy,
from my foes, who were too strong for me.
They confronted me in the day of my disaster,
but the LORD was my support.
He brought me out into a spacious place;
he rescued me because he delighted in me.

—Psalm 18:1–2, 16–19

What is your history with God? When you look back on your life, where do you see God intervening? How has he protected you, guided you, or comforted you? What enemy has he battled in your stead? Take a moment, today, to think back at the journey you have had with God and the record of his love for you through the years.

Talk with God

Ask.

"I love you, LORD, my strength."
God, I love you because . . .

🐦 Tweet using #IASloveabounds to share your prayers.

Jesus Also Says

Weeks 23–26
Week 23: Talk with God
Week 24: Remember
Week 25: Give
Week 26: Pass It On

Conversing with God is not an optional activity for his children or an elective for his servants. If we claim to follow God, then we must listen for his voice and ask him for his help.

As baptism is a sign of our conversion, of our identification with Jesus' sacrifice, so are bread and wine a remembrance of that sacrifice. As believers we are commanded not to forget the body that was broken and the blood that was spilled to ensure our entrance into heaven. We are commanded to commemorate Jesus' sacrifice with the sharing of bread and the drinking of wine.

The command to give means more than adding a new item to our budget. It means living a lifestyle of generosity and demonstrating a habit of grateful reflection—as we are given so we give to others.

The last command completes the circle. We are given this basic set of commands by our Lord, and we are commanded to pass them on to others and to teach others to do the same, each generation obeying his commands, passing them on and teaching others to do likewise.

Day 1: How to Pray

Our Father in heaven,
hallowed be your name,
your kingdom come,
your will be done,
*   on earth as it is in heaven.*
Give us today our daily bread.
And forgive us our debts,
*   as we also have forgiven our debtors.*
And lead us not into temptation,
*   but deliver us from the evil one.*

—Matthew 6:9–13

What It Says

1. What did you like about this passage? What are the kinds of things that Jesus tells his disciples to talk with God about?
2. What did you not like or find confusing about this passage?

What It Means

3. What does this passage teach about people?
4. What does this passage teach about God?

Live It. Take some time and talk with God as a group. Use Jesus' model prayer as a guide to your own prayer.

Tell It. How will you share what you have learned?

Practice It. Get with a friend or someone in your group. Practice or role-play your "Live and Tell" commitments.

Day 2: Relationship

*I love the L*ORD*, for he heard my voice;*
*   he heard my cry for mercy.*
Because he turned his ear to me,
*   I will call on him as long as I live.*
The cords of death entangled me,
*   the anguish of the grave came over me;*
*   I was overcome by distress and sorrow.*
*Then I called on the name of the L*ORD*:*
*   "L*ORD*, save me!"*
*The L*ORD *is gracious and righteous;*
*   our God is full of compassion.*
*The L*ORD *protects the unwary;*
*   when I was brought low, he saved me.*

—Psalm 116:1–6

The Lord hears us. We are not just creatures wandering across a small planet. We are not just blips in the cosmic vastness. We are children of God, guests of the King, and friends of the Creator. We are heard. And that fact alone should be enough to turn our hearts forever to him and our minds forever to his will.

Talk with God

Relationship.

"I love the Lord . . ."
God, I love you because . . .

🐦 Tweet using #IASrelationship to share your prayers.

Day 3: Worship

Come, let us sing for joy to the LORD;
*   let us shout aloud to the Rock of our salvation.*
Let us come before him with thanksgiving
*   and extol him with music and song.*
For the LORD is the great God,
*   the great King above all gods.*
In his hand are the depths of the earth,
*   and the mountain peaks belong to him.*
The sea is his, for he made it,
*   and his hands formed the dry land.*
Come, let us bow down in worship,
*   let us kneel before the LORD our Maker;*
for he is our God
*   and we are the people of his pasture,*
*   the flock under his care.*

—Psalm 95:1–7

We praise our fellow humans for their accomplishments in science, for their beauty through art, or for their strength in athletics. But how often do we praise the God who made it all possible, who wrote the rules of science, created our sense of beauty, and designed our bodies? Take some time today and every day to praise the God who made it all possible.

Talk with God

Worship.

"For the LORD is the great God . . ."
God, I worship you because . . .

Tweet using #IASworship to share your prayers.

Day 4: Surrender

I will sing of your love and justice;
to you, LORD, I will sing praise.
I will be careful to lead a blameless life—
when will you come to me?
I will conduct the affairs of my house
with a blameless heart.
I will not look with approval
on anything that is vile.
I hate what faithless people do;
I will have no part in it.
The perverse of heart shall be far from me;
I will have nothing to do with what is evil.
Whoever slanders their neighbor in secret,
I will put to silence;
Whoever has haughty eyes and a proud heart,
I will not tolerate.

—Psalm 101:1–5

God's love should inspire our commitment and his justice remind us of the danger of disobedience. He is both loving and just. We must not forget either quality of God. He is quick to love, to forgive, to extend patience, but he also holds the power to judge and correct. Let the vastness of his love move us to obedience and the sureness of his justice keep us steady when tempted.

Talk with God

Surrender.

"I will lead a blameless life . . ."
God, I surrender everything to you, including . . .

Tweet using #IASsurrender to share your prayers.

Day 5: Ask

You, LORD, showed favor to your land;
you restored the fortunes of Jacob.
You forgave the iniquity of your people
and covered all their sins.
You set aside all your wrath
and turned from your fierce anger.
Restore us again, God our Savior,
and put away your displeasure toward us.
Will you be angry with us forever?
Will you prolong your anger through all generations?
Will you not revive us again,
that your people may rejoice in you?
Show us your unfailing love, LORD,
and grant us your salvation.

—Psalm 85:1–7

God cares about our well-being and understands our predicaments. He gives out of his love and forgives out of his patience. He is the good Father and the kind Master. He will provide what we need and grant us what is best for us, but he wants us to ask him for it.

Talk with God

Ask.

"You, LORD, showed favor to your land . . ."
God, I ask for . . .

🐦 Tweet using #IASask to share your prayers.

Day 6: Forgive

*Good and upright is the L*ORD*;*
therefore he instructs sinners in his ways.
He guides the humble in what is right
and teaches them his way.
*All the ways of the L*ORD *are loving and faithful*
toward those who keep the demands of his covenant.
*For the sake of your name, L*ORD*,*
forgive my iniquity, though it is great.
*Who, then, are those who fear the L*ORD*?*
He will instruct them in the ways they should choose.
They will spend their days in prosperity,
and their descendants will inherit the land.
*The L*ORD *confides in those who fear him;*
he makes his covenant known to them.
*My eyes are ever on the L*ORD*,*
for only he will release my feet from the snare.

—Psalm 25:8–15

Sin is a trap, a snare that keeps us from where we should go. It dulls our senses and hardens our hearts. Each misstep makes the next both more grievous and more likely. God's conviction helps snap us back to our senses. His voice brings a fresh dose of reality. But he will not call forever if we persist in ignoring his words.

Talk with God

Forgive.

". . . forgive my iniquity . . ."
God, forgive me for . . .

🐦 Tweet using #IASforgive to share your prayers.

Day 7: Protect

"They have greatly oppressed me from my youth,"
let Israel say;
"They have greatly oppressed me from my youth,
but they have not gained the victory over me.
Plowmen have plowed my back
and made their furrows long.
*But the L*ord *is righteous;*
he has cut me free from the cords of the wicked."
May all who hate Zion
be turned back in shame.
May they be like grass on the roof,
which withers before it can grow;
A reaper cannot fill his hands with it,
nor one who gathers fill his arms.
May those who pass by not say to them,
*"The blessing of the L*ord *be on you;*
*we bless you in the name of the L*ord*."*

—Psalm 129

This world is dangerous. Temptations put our spiritual health at risk. Disease and violence threaten our physical well-being. Peril approaches from every corner, but no matter the size of the threat or the shape of the danger, God is not dismayed. He is not surprised or scared. Ask him for help; ask him for protection.

Talk with God

Protect.

"Plowmen have plowed my back . . ."
God, protect me from . . .

🐦 Tweet using #IASprotect to share your prayers.

Day 1: Commemorate

Watch the Janelle Hail Film

iamsecond.com/janellehail

What did you like about, identify with, or learn from Janelle's story?

> *And he took bread, gave thanks and broke it, and gave it to them, saying, "This is my body given for you; do this in remembrance of me." In the same way, after the supper he took the cup, saying, "This cup is the new covenant in my blood, which is poured out for you."*
>
> **—Luke 22:19–20**

Read the whole passage in Luke 22:1–23.

What It Says
1. What did you like about this passage?
2. What did you not like or find confusing about this passage?

What It Means
3. What does this passage teach about people?
4. What does this passage teach about God?

Live It. How will you live more Second today? How will you or your group obey this command to remember Jesus through the taking of bread and wine?

Tell It. How will you share what you have learned?

Practice It. Get with a friend or someone in your group. Practice or role-play your "Live and Tell" commitments.

Day 2: Greatest

For who is greater, the one who is at the table or the one who serves? Is it not the one who is at the table? But I am among you as one who serves.

—Luke 22:27

Read the whole passage in Luke 22:24–34.

God could rule with unmitigated justice, with unrelenting might, and unguarded fairness. But he has chosen to season justice with mercy, power with gentleness, and fairness with grace. Jesus could have come with legions of wrathful angels, with vengeance and judgment. But he came meek and gentle. He came to serve and not to be served. He chose to set aside his rights as the Son of God, to sacrifice his life on our behalf, and become the servant of all. If the Son of God chose humility over pride, how could we do otherwise? If he chose kindness and forgiveness, how could we hold grudges and bitterness? If he chose to serve all, why do we strive for leadership, position, and honor? Why must we call it *servant leadership*, when he simply called it service?

Talk with God

Part of me always wants to be first, to be the greatest, but your sacrifice reminds me that it is only in service to others that I find greatness.

Live It. How can you live more Second today?
Tell It. How will you share what you have learned?

🐦 Tweet using #IASgreatest to share your thoughts.

Day 3: Cup

Father, if you are willing, take this cup from me; yet not my will, but yours be done.

—Luke 22:42

Read the whole passage in Luke 22:39–46.

The death and resurrection of Jesus is the single greatest event of the human race and an event we are rightfully called to remember every time we gather together and share bread and wine. It serves as the foundation of our faith and the basis for our salvation. But, perhaps, there is another reason we are called to remember this sacrifice. We are driven to self-preservation and programmed to think of ourselves first. We obsess over our importance and our pride. But Jesus is the only man ever qualified to boast and yet the only one who never did. He gave up his rights, sacrificed his pride, and demonstrated with clear and unquestionable humility that none of us has anything to boast about. So every time we eat from that loaf of bread and sip that glass of wine, we are reminded of the bankruptcy of our arrogance. We are reminded of our need for humility.

Talk with God

God, forgive my pride and my constant need for attention. Teach me the humility that your Son so perfectly demonstrated.

Live It. How can you live more Second today?
Tell It. How will you share what you have learned?

🐦 Tweet using #IAScup to share your thoughts.

Day 4: **Disowned**

The Lord turned and looked straight at Peter. Then Peter remembered the word the Lord had spoken to him: "Before the rooster crows today, you will disown me three times." And he went outside and wept bitterly.

—Luke 22:61–62

Read the whole passage in Luke 22:47–62.

Peter never thought it would happen. It never crossed his mind that one day he would betray the one he loved. He promised never to leave and never to forsake his Lord, to die at his side if need be. But only Jesus has kept that promise. The rest of us betray our Savior with every failure to share his story, to stick up for his name, with every wicked thought and unfaithful desire. The bread and wine remind us of our sins and of our need for a Savior, one to pay the bloody cost of our failures. We could only pay our debt through our death, but Jesus conquered death and provided forgiveness through his broken body.

Talk with God

God, I praise you for sending your Son to pay my debt.

Live It. How will you live more Second today?
Tell It. How will you share what you have learned?

🐦 Tweet using #IASdisowned to share your thoughts.

Day 5: **Division**

So then, when you come together, it is not the Lord's
Supper you eat, for when you are eating, some of you go
ahead with your own private suppers. As a result, one
person remains hungry and another gets drunk. Don't you
have homes to eat and drink in? Or do you despise the
church of God by humiliating those who have nothing?

—1 Corinthians 11:20–22

Read the whole passage in 1 Corinthians 11:17–22.

God's family has no room for division or favoritism. Each of his sons and daughters holds equal rights, equal value, and deserves equal treatment. The cost for our adoption was the same as everyone else's. Our sin was no less costly, our redemption no less expensive. We each cost the life of God's Son. The arrogance of belittling our fellow brothers or sisters, of excluding them from the commemoration of his sacrifice, of allowing petty differences or shallow materialism to separate us, all profane the beauty of God's grace. Jesus is the great equalizer. Compared to him we are all filthy rags, through him we all find forgiveness, and in him we all live forever and ever. Let the bread and wine be a reminder of our equality and unity.

Talk with God

Make me quick to forgive, swift to show mercy, and sure to promote peace and unity.

Live It. How will you live more Second today?
Tell It. How will you share what you have learned?

🐦 Tweet using #IASdivision to share your thoughts.

Day 6: Guilty

So then, whoever eats the bread or drinks the cup of the
Lord in an unworthy manner will be guilty of sinning against
the body and blood of the Lord.

—1 Corinthians 11:27

Read the whole passage in 1 Corinthians 11:23–34.

God hates duplicity and hypocrisy. When we eat the bread and drink the wine with fellow believers, we profess to be members of God's family, to be united as one in Jesus through his sacrifice for all. But if we harbor unforgiveness against a brother or sister, if we foster division and separatism while participating in communion, then we ignore its meaning and violate its purpose. In doing so, we announce our unity while practicing our disunity. God has no patience for such behavior. The bread and the wine offer a symbol of the single sacrifice that brought all of us together into one family and one church. To eat the elements without first making amends with our neighbor or getting right with a fellow believer invites God's anger.

Talk with God

God, you were so quick to forgive me, and yet I am so slow to forgive those around me. Teach me your forgiveness.

Live It. How will you live more Second today?
Tell It. How will you share what you have learned?

Tweet using #IASguilty to share your thoughts.

Day 7: **Redeemed**

Why should I fear when evil days come,
when wicked deceivers surround me—
Those who trust in their wealth
and boast of their great riches?
No one can redeem the life of another
or give to God a ransom for them—
The ransom for a life is costly,
no payment is ever enough—
So that they should live on forever
and not see decay.
For all can see that the wise die,
that the foolish and the senseless also perish,
leaving their wealth to others.
Their tombs will remain their houses forever,
their dwellings for endless generations,
though they had named lands after themselves. . . .
But God will redeem me from the realm of the dead;
he will surely take me to himself.

—Psalm 49:5–11, 15

We will all die. This is the one sure thing of the world. It is the cost of our separation from God, the price of our disobedience. But for those who ask for his forgiveness, God promises resurrection. For those who commit to follow God and to love his name, he promises to redeem from the grave.

Talk with God

Worship.

"God will redeem me from the realm of the dead . . ."
God, thank you for you promises . . .

🐦 Tweet using #IASredeemed to share your prayers.

Day 1: Share

Watch the Blake Mankin Film

iamsecond.com/blakemankin

What did you like about, identify with, or learn from Blake's story?

> *In everything I did, I showed you that by this kind of hard work we must help the weak, remembering the words the Lord Jesus himself said: "It is more blessed to give than to receive."*
>
> **—Acts 20:35**

Read the whole passage in Acts 4:32–37.

What It Says
1. What did you like about this passage?
2. What did you not like or find confusing about this passage?

What It Means
3. What does this passage teach about people?
4. What does this passage teach about God?

Live It. How will you live more Second today?
Tell It. How will you share what you have learned?

Practice It. Get with a friend or someone in your group. Practice or role-play your "Live and Tell" commitments.

Day 2: **Everything**

When Jesus heard this, he said to him, "You still lack one thing. Sell everything you have and give to the poor, and you will have treasure in heaven. Then come, follow me."

—Luke 18:22

Read the whole passage in Luke 18:18–30.

Do we give out of our plenty or out of our need? Do we give with a smile or give till it hurts? Maybe the question instead should be: how much do we love God? If we really loved God with all our hearts, minds, and souls, then we would know that our lives are not our own, that our time, money, and other resources are for him, not us. With that in mind, generosity becomes a way of life. If we loved God with our whole being, then we would give him everything. That doesn't mean we suddenly become destitute, but it means we ask ourselves, how will my stuff serve God? How will my car or my job opportunities make God more famous? How can I best use my time to make him known? We become stewards of his money and resources. We are not giving anything away. We are simply investing what is already God's in the first place.

Talk with God

God, I give you my life, my money, my wealth, and all the things I hold dear.

Live It. How can you live more Second today?
Tell It. How will you share what you have learned?

🐦 Tweet using #IASeverything to share your thoughts.

Day 3: **From Poverty**

Truly I tell you, this poor widow has put more into the treasury than all the others. They all gave out of their wealth; but she, out of her poverty, put in everything—all she had to live on.

—**Mark 12:43–44**

Read the whole passage in Mark 12:41–44.

Most of the world's saints are never named, never known by the history books, and never recorded by our scribes. They live simple, meager lives. They give when it makes no sense. They sacrifice when others only donate. They throw themselves headlong into the kingdom of God, knowing nothing they could possess and nothing they could hold in this world could ever rival the rewards of God. They give in secret and die in obscurity. But their reward will come. Their recognition will be given and their valor made known. The God of heaven and earth never forgets a generous heart and always rewards his faithful servants.

Talk with God

Teach me to live a faithful, generous life, one that wins rewards in heaven and not here on earth.

Live It. How can you live more Second today?
Tell It. How will you share what you have learned?

🐦 Tweet using #IASfrompoverty to share your thoughts.

Day 4: **Lies**

Peter said to her, "How could you conspire to test the Spirit of the Lord? Listen! The feet of the men who buried your husband are at the door, and they will carry you out also."

—Acts 5:9

Read the whole passage in Acts 5:1–11.

God has not changed. The same God who flooded the earth in Genesis demands our allegiance today. The same God who sent Israel into exile still walks with us now. He is patient, though not ignorant of our sins. He is kind, though not easy on our pride. He will not hesitate to call us home if defection is our intent. He will not wink to bring us low if lies and hypocrisy become our lives. Our donations should not be given in order to win praise from others. Giving is for God, to God, and in honor of God.

Talk with God

Teach me to give and to give humbly without need for recognition.

Live It. How will you live more Second today?
Tell It. How will you share what you have learned?

Tweet using #IASlies to share your thoughts.

Day 5: Love of Money

For the love of money is a root of all kinds of evil. Some people, eager for money, have wandered from the faith and pierced themselves with many griefs.

—1 Timothy 6:10

Read the whole passage in 1 Timothy 6:6–10.

The god of money offers no permanence and no insurance; it is fickle and cold. It may bring pleasure for a while, security for a season, but in the end money always disappoints. War and famine, market swings, or the unforeseen—if nothing else, then death—will take it all away. Whatever the outcome, however great the financial planning, money will eventually cease to exist and cease to matter. The best bet and the most solid investment is in the God who does not change and cannot fail. The love of money brings heartache and disappointment. But God brings promises of reward and an eternity of wealth. We must train our eyes to see beyond the fading wealth of this world to the everlasting wealth of the next.

Talk with God

I praise you for the heavenly reward you promise and the security you guarantee.

Live It. How will you live more Second today?
Tell It. How will you share what you have learned?

🐦 Tweet using #IASloveofmoney to share your thoughts.

Day 6: Flour and Oil

*"As surely as the L*ORD* your God lives," she replied, "I don't have any bread—only a handful of flour in a jar and a little olive oil in a jug. I am gathering a few sticks to take home and make a meal for myself and my son, that we may eat it—and die."*

—1 Kings 17:12

Read the whole passage in 1 Kings 17:7–16.

Generosity is an expression of our faith, an outlet for our trust in God. This widow had food for one last meal. A beggar's portion of flour and oil, enough to satiate hunger for one more hour, to slow the bloating stomach of her son for one moment longer, and then they would die. With no government aid, no food drives, or Red Cross, this widow had no means to survive and no safety net to rely on. But despite her dire circumstance, when God called on her to give away the one thing that kept death at bay, the one thing that kept the cries of her starving son quiet, she trusted God and relied on his promise to provide. If we measured our faith in the dollars we donated, in the currency we gave away, would we still be rich? Would the wealth of our generosity shout our dependence on God, or our doubts? Would our faith prove poor and desperate or wealthy and strong?

Talk with God

Grow my faith through my consistent gifts and my generous wallet.

Live It. How will you live more Second today?
Tell It. How will you share what you have learned?

🐦 Tweet using #IASflourandoil to share your thoughts.

Day 7: **Generous**

Surely the righteous will never be shaken;
they will be remembered forever.
They will have no fear of bad news;
their hearts are steadfast, trusting in the Lord.
Their hearts are secure, they will have no fear;
in the end they will look in triumph on their foes.
They have freely scattered their gifts to the poor,
their righteousness endures forever;
their horn will be lifted high in honor.
The wicked will see and be vexed,
they will gnash their teeth and waste away;
the longings of the wicked will come to nothing.

—Psalm 112:6–10

Our life here on earth will echo in eternity. What we do here matters. If we squander the opportunities God gives us or hoard the wealth he blesses us with, he will remember our wickedness. But if we give freely, love completely, and live righteously, then that too will be remembered forever.

Talk with God

Worship.

"The righteous will never be shaken . . ."
God, thank you for all your gifts, including . . .

Tweet using #IASgenerous to share your prayers.

Day 1: Make Disciples

Watch the Michael W. Smith Film

iamsecond.com/michaelwsmith

What did you like about, identify with, or learn from Michael's story?

> *All authority in heaven and on earth has been given to me. Therefore go and make disciples of all nations, baptizing them in the name of the Father and of the Son and of the Holy Spirit, and teaching them to obey everything I have commanded you. And surely I am with you always, to the very end of the age.*
>
> **—Matthew 28:18–20**

What It Says
1. What did you like about this passage?
2. What did you not like or find confusing about this passage?

What It Means
3. What does this passage teach about people?
4. What does this passage teach about God?

Live It. How will you live more Second today?
Tell It. How will you share what you have learned?

Practice It. Get with a friend or someone in your group. Practice or role-play your "Live and Tell" commitments.

Day 2: True

They got up and returned at once to Jerusalem. There they found the Eleven and those with them, assembled together and saying, "It is true! The Lord has risen and has appeared to Simon."

—Luke 24:33–34

Read the whole passage in Luke 24:13–34.

Jesus is alive. That is the message we bring, the banner we carry. Our Prophet is not dead, our Savior is not absent, and our God is not gone. He came and lived among us; he preached a message of love and forgiveness, of hope and eternal life. But then like all people and all preachers of the past, he died. But unlike all of them, unlike every other religious leader, Jesus rose from the dead. He proved himself more than a mere man. He showed himself to be the Son of God, the Eternal One, the only victor over death and only way to the Father. When discouraged by rejection or saddened by life's struggles, let the truth of his resurrection and the fact of his victory bring new blood to our hearts and new strength to our muscles. Let the reliability of his power and the sureness of our message give hope for a better future.

Talk with God

Encourage me when doubts surface, strengthen me when the storms come, and help me when I cannot see past the fog.

Live It. How can you live more Second today?
Tell It. How will you share what you have learned?

🐦 Tweet using #IAStrue to share your thoughts.

Day 3: All Nations

The Messiah will suffer and rise from the dead on the third day, and repentance for the forgiveness of sins will be preached in his name to all nations, beginning at Jerusalem. You are witnesses of these things.

—Luke 24:46–48

Read the whole passage in Luke 24:36–53.

God wants no borders for his kingdom. And while he could step down from heaven and force every heart to his will or poke his finger through the sky and rain down wrath on all who oppose him, he grants us the honor of ambassadors. He has made us his witnesses, his representatives to the world. If people die without hearing his name, it is our fault. If nations fall never hearing his story, we carry their blood. We are watchmen for this world, heralds of God's truth. Though he could send the angels in their legions or make the rocks cry out his name, he has chosen us to bring him to all the nations. It is not just our pastor's job, the job of radio or television preachers, or the responsibility of professional Christian workers; it is the job of each and every believer. We are all his missionaries.

Talk with God

Fill my mouth with your story as I work, go to school, or walk down my street.

Live It. How can you live more Second today?
Tell It. How will you share what you have learned?

Tweet using #IASallnations to share your thoughts.

Day 4: Witnesses

But you will receive power when the Holy Spirit comes on you; and you will be my witnesses in Jerusalem, and in all Judea and Samaria, and to the ends of the earth.

—Acts 1:8

Read the whole passage in Acts 1:1–11.

God is not dependent on our skills or held captive by our weaknesses—rather, just the opposite. He made Moses, a stuttering murderer, into the greatest lawgiver of earth. He made David, a simple shepherd boy, into the greatest songwriter and king of our history. He made Peter, an uneducated fisherman, the rock upon which the church was built. God turned hearts through the speech of idiots and the writings of fools. When we speak about God to others, we do not need to worry about our lack of skill or fret over our inabilities, for it is through his Spirit that we witness and in his power that we proclaim his story. God has no patience for our excuses and sees no reason for our reluctance, because it is not through our power that we speak, but through his.

Talk with God

Teach me the habit of relying on you for my words and trusting in your Spirit when I give witness of you.

Live It. How will you live more Second today?
Tell It. How will you share what you have learned?

🐦 Tweet using #IASwitnesses to share your thoughts.

Day 5: **Reason**

Always be prepared to give an answer to everyone who asks you to give the reason for the hope that you have. But do this with gentleness and respect.

—1 Peter 3:15

Read the whole passage in 1 Peter 3:13–22.

We often confuse the need to be ready with the failure to practice that readiness. We study, read books, fill our heads with facts and proofs, but we forget to put it to good use. Following Jesus is more than knowing things or memorizing verses; it is about living out and telling others about what we learn. Being ready to give answers means continuing to grow in our knowledge of God, but it also means actually sharing those insights and displaying that wisdom when the time arrives. The soldier who trains to shoot but runs from battle makes his training useless. The employee who punches his time card but does not work his task proves his training useless. True preparedness is the habit of learning from God and then passing on that learning to others.

Talk with God

Prepare me to talk with those you have put in my life about the story you have worked in my life.

Live It. How will you live more Second today?
Tell It. How will you share what you have learned?

Tweet using #IASreason to share your thoughts.

Day 6: **Preacher**

For Christ did not send me to baptize, but to preach the gospel—not with wisdom and eloquence, lest the cross of Christ be emptied of its power.

—1 Corinthians 1:17

Read the whole passage in 1 Corinthians 1:10–17.

We are not doers of religion or followers of pious men. We are worshipers of the one true God. We are messengers of his story and heralds of his message. It is not about who gets credit, who gets more web hits, or who fills bigger auditoriums. It is about passing on the pure and simple story of Jesus, the story of his coming to die for our sins and rising from the dead. Dividing into factions and separating into competing parties only furthers the schemes of the enemy. Let us push aside our pride, forget our petty differences, and work to let the power of Jesus' sacrifice shine in this world through our unity and love for one another. Let us stop the message-board bickering and the water-cooler backbiting and set to work on telling the story we were sent to tell.

Talk with God

Teach me to love my brothers and sisters in Christ and to work in unison with my believing family.

Live It. How will you live more Second today?
Tell It. How will you share what you have learned?

🐦 Tweet using #IASpreacher to share your thoughts.

Day 7: **Praise**

Praise the Lᵃᵒᵃ from the earth,
you great sea creatures and all ocean depths,
Lightning and hail, snow and clouds,
stormy winds that do his bidding,
You mountains and all hills,
fruit trees and all cedars,
Wild animals and all cattle,
small creatures and flying birds,
Kings of the earth and all nations,
you princes and all rulers on earth,
Young men and women,
old men and children.
Let them praise the name of the Lᵃᵒᵃ,
for his name alone is exalted;
his splendor is above the earth and the heavens.
And he has raised up for his people a horn,
the praise of all his faithful servants,
of Israel, the people close to his heart.

—Psalm 148:7–14

Worship fulfills two purposes. The first and most obvious is to give God the credit and respect he deserves. But we also praise God as a witness to those who have yet to hear of his greatness. The reason believers are not just swept into heaven at the moment of faith is so we can show the world what a life dedicated to worshiping God looks like, so the world can hear of God's greatness and love.

Talk with God

Worship.

"Praise the Lord . . ."
God, I praise you because . . .

Tweet using #IASpraise to share your prayers.

Follow As I Follow

Weeks 27–30
Week 27: Search
Week 28: Make Disciples
Week 29: Way of Life
Week 30: Persecution

We were never told to make converts, proselytize, or push heavenly sales numbers. We were called to make disciples, to teach others to follow Jesus as we follow Jesus. We search for ready ears and hungry souls, knowing not everyone will listen but being prepared to teach anyone. We pass on a way of life not just a set of rules, a pattern of living not a form of legalism, an affection for our God and a love for his law. Despite the hardships that come and the difficulties that befall us, we push on, knowing that God is in charge, that he still rules the world, and that in the end he wins.

Day 1: Deposit

Watch the Natalie Sebastian Film

iamsecond.com/nataliesebastian

What did you like about, identify with, or learn from Natalie's story?

> *What you heard from me, keep as the pattern of sound teaching, with faith and love in Christ Jesus. Guard the good deposit that was entrusted to you—guard it with the help of the Holy Spirit who lives in us.*
>
> **—2 Timothy 1:13–14**

Read the whole passage in 2 Timothy 1:1–18.

What It Says
1. What did you like about this passage?
2. What did you not like or find confusing about this passage?

What It Means
3. What does this passage teach about people?
4. What does this passage teach about God?

Live It. How will you live more Second today?

Tell It. How will you share what you have learned?

Practice It. Get with a friend or someone in your group. Practice or role-play your "Live and Tell" commitments.

Day 2: **New**

This man is my chosen instrument to proclaim my name to
the Gentiles and their kings and to the people of Israel.

—Acts 9:15

Read the whole passage in Acts 9:1–19.

Saul was a new believer and still reeking of his former life when he ran into the streets telling people about Jesus. Too often we wait for someone to dress like us, talk like us, or act and preach like us before we let them do anything useful for God. We put them through long classes or tell them to sit in our churches for years before they can go out and share their newfound faith. But it is precisely in that short but potent time just after someone makes Jesus First in their lives when they have the biggest opportunity to witness into their community. So rather than waiting for someone to finish some yearlong training course, recite the gospel of John, or finish seminary, let's send them out. Let's train brand-new believers, even that very same day, to go and make disciples of others by telling the story of Jesus.

Talk with God

Give me the passion to share your story and the ability to inspire that passion in others.

Live It. How can you live more Second today?
Tell It. How will you share what you have learned?

🐦 Tweet using #IASnew to share your thoughts.

Day 3: **Changed**

At once he began to preach in the synagogues that Jesus is the Son of God. All those who heard him were astonished and asked, "Isn't he the man who raised havoc in Jerusalem among those who call on this name?"

—Acts 9:21–22

Read the whole passage in Acts 9:19–22.

Immediate, radical obedience. The converted Saul saw no reason for delay, no cause for postponement. His life needed to change and change immediately. He once sought to kill those who promoted Jesus. Now he went to those same synagogues where he once hunted his prey and became the prey himself. He wreaked havoc in Jerusalem, but in Damascus he would raise Jesus. This is the sign of a disciple. This is the sign of a person serious about their faith and genuine about their decision. Search for those like Saul. Maybe the steps of obedience are smaller, maybe they are less dangerous—but immediate, radical obedience is the sign that a person is ready to follow God and multiply disciples.

Talk with God

God, I know you have no interest in reproducing mediocrity. Teach me immediate, radical obedience and help me teach others the same.

Live It. How can you live more Second today?
Tell It. How will you share what you have learned?

🐦 Tweet using #IASchanged to share your thoughts.

Day 4: Faithful

He told them how Saul on his journey had seen the Lord and that the Lord had spoken to him, and how in Damascus he had preached fearlessly in the name of Jesus.

—Acts 9:27

Read the whole passage in Acts 9:23–31.

Saul was a believer for a matter of hours, a disciple for a matter of moments, when he acted on that new faith. He knew Jesus was real and the message he preached was genuine. Jesus came and died for the sins of the world, offering forgiveness to all who would believe. That was all Saul knew. But he was faithful with that one lesson and immediately went out and told others what he had learned. The mark of faithfulness is not in the quantity of knowledge or quality of skill, but in the immediacy of obedience. How faithful are we with the truths that God gives us and the lessons that he teaches? How faithful are we to pass them on and to teach others to do the same? Are we the kind of disciples whom God multiplies? Or are we the kind who grow fat with our unused knowledge?

Talk with God

Keep me far from mediocrity and complacency. Make me the faithful disciple you designed me to be.

Live It. How will you live more Second today?
Tell It. How will you share what you have learned?

🐦 Tweet using #IASfaithful to share your thoughts.

Day 5: **Available**

She had a sister called Mary, who sat at the Lord's feet listening to what he said. But Martha was distracted by all the preparation that had to be made.

—Luke 10:39–40

Read the whole passage in Luke 10:38–42.

One week consists of 168 hours. Never more, never less. Subtract eight hours a night for sleep, and all we have left is 112 hours. This is our available time—the time for work, society, family, recreation, and anything else we might wish to do. Schedules may fluctuate and shift, but that 112 hours each week is ours to manage, ours to spend. An available disciple sees those 112 hours as opportunity, a chance to bring God into the workplace, to tell of Jesus at school and to friends or family. We do not need to work at a church to work for God. He has given each of us the same amount of time and calls us to view that block of 112 hours as available for his use. What will you do with that time?

Talk with God

I am your worker. Show me how you want me to spend my 112 hours each week.

Live It. How will you live more Second today?
Tell It. How will you share what you have learned?

Tweet using #IASavailable to share your thoughts.

Day 6: Teachable

Barnabas they called Zeus, and Paul they called Hermes because he was the chief speaker.

—Acts 14:12

Read the whole passage in Acts 14:8–20.

We often think of Paul as a pioneer, a leader who championed the faith. And he was, but he was also a follower, a learner, and a disciple. In this story, we see that Paul proves himself a gifted and moving speaker, so much so that the local population confuses him with Hermes, the messenger god of the Greek pantheon. However, Paul's humility and teachability are so obvious that even though he speaks like the gods, the crowd still clearly sees Barnabas as the leader. Great leaders are great followers. Even someone of Paul's caliber knew how to follow, how to listen, and how to let someone else be the teacher.

Talk with God

Father, give me Paul's humility. Make me teachable, willing to listen, and able to learn.

Live It. How will you live more Second today?
Tell It. How will you share what you have learned?

Tweet using #IASteachable to share your thoughts.

Day 7: For Rome

To all in Rome who are loved by God and called to be his holy people: Grace and peace to you from God our Father and from the Lord Jesus Christ.

First, I thank my God through Jesus Christ for all of you, because your faith is being reported all over the world. God, whom I serve in my spirit in preaching the gospel of his Son, is my witness how constantly I remember you in my prayers at all times; and I pray that now at last by God's will the way may be opened for me to come to you.

—Romans 1:7–10

Paul was a gifted leader, organizer, and strategist, but he also was a man of great prayer. He remembered his brothers and sisters when he talked with God. He thanked God for their witness and begged God for their continued growth. Can we say the same?

Talk with God

Ask.

"I remember you in my prayers . . ."
God, I pray for those I am influencing . . .

Tweet using #IASforrome to share your prayers.

Day 1: **Teach Others**

Watch the Colt McCoy Film

iamsecond.com/coltmccoy

What did you like about, identify with, or learn from Colt's story?

And the things you have heard me say in the presence of many witnesses entrust to reliable people who will also be qualified to teach others.

—2 Timothy 2:2

Read the whole passage in 2 Timothy 2:1–26.

What It Says
1. What did you like about this passage?
2. What did you not like or find confusing about this passage?

What It Means
3. What does this passage teach about people?
4. What does this passage teach about God?

Live It. How will you live more Second today?
Tell It. How will you share what you have learned?

Practice It. Get with a friend or someone in your group. Practice or role-play your "Live and Tell" commitments.

Day 2: Endure

Join with me in suffering, like a good soldier of Christ Jesus.

—2 Timothy 2:3

Roses and butterflies do not pave the roads we walk. Those who say Jesus makes all our problems go away do a disservice to the faith. The evil one has little reason to attack those in self-destruct mode. The rich who pride themselves in their own self-importance, the do-gooders who boast of their own goodness, the pleasure seekers and the utterly lost ruin their own lives just fine without his help. But those earnestly seeking to honor God, those who strive to further his kingdom, they become a threat, a target for Satan's armies. Those who follow God most closely know suffering most personally. Challenging new disciples to soldier on, to endure, to join in the suffering is not mere metaphor but a genuine call to prepare oneself for the battle that is ahead for true followers.

Talk with God

God, prepare me for what lies ahead. Keep me from temptation. Keep me out of the enemy's reach.

Live It. How can you live more Second today?
Tell It. How will you share what you have learned?

Tweet using #IASendure to share your thoughts.

Day 3: **Remember**

This is my gospel, for which I am suffering even to the point of being chained like a criminal. But God's Word is not chained. Therefore I endure everything for the sake of the elect, that they too may obtain the salvation that is in Christ Jesus, with eternal glory.

—2 Timothy 2:8–10

Though suffering may come, though hardships may follow, we fight for a worthy and eternal cause. Our struggle goes beyond empires and nations that build on soldiers' blood. Our war pushes further than the pangs of hunger and disease. We endure not only for the temporal and physical but for the spiritual and the eternal. Remember, the gospel, the good news that Jesus paid for our sins and purchased our forgiveness, is a message that brings the weary strength, the sick to health, and the dead to life. Whether suffering like criminals or enduring through mockery and injustice, these discomforts are the price we pay to bring the message of salvation to lost souls. And it is a price well worth the cost.

Talk with God

When persecution floods into my life, I ask that you give me the strength to endure and the memory to recall the reason for the struggle.

Live It. How can you live more Second today?
Tell It. How will you share what you have learned?

🐦 Tweet using #IASremember to share your thoughts.

Day 4: Worker

Do your best to present yourself to God as one approved, a worker who does not need to be ashamed and who correctly handles the word of truth.

—2 Timothy 2:15

We are workers, not just learners or listeners, but people who go out and do things, accomplish goals, and tackle problems. Making disciples is more than teaching someone a set of rules or talking through a list of books or curriculum. Disciple making involves real-life, hands-on, in-the-game kind of mentoring. There will be no multiple choice tests in heaven, no essay or short-answer exam, only a review of our lives, of the work we were given to accomplish. The question we must answer and we must prepare our disciples to answer is this: did we accomplish the work and correctly handle the message entrusted to us?

Talk with God

Help me be a master trainer, someone who helps make disciples who will work for your kingdom and change your world.

Live It. How will you live more Second today?
Tell It. How will you share what you have learned?

Tweet using #IASworker to share your thoughts.

Day 5: **Useful**

*Those who cleanse themselves from the latter will be
instruments for special purposes, made holy, useful to the
Master and prepared to do any good work.*

—2 Timothy 2:21

"They might fail," some will say. And surely they will. But certain
things can only be learned through failure. "But this is important
work," others will argue. But if disciples are never given important
work, they become proficient in only the menial and unnecessary.
Too often we restrict what a person can do for God's kingdom;
we limit what we think God could accomplish through someone.
But God is not looking for certifications, talent, or charisma; he
is looking for obedient and holy followers. If someone is obedient,
willing to listen and follow God, then God can use that person to
accomplish great things. We need to train our eyes to see potential
as God sees it, as something marked more by obedience than by
talent.

Talk with God

God, give me the wisdom to train others and the humility to let
them use that training.

Live It. How will you live more Second today?
Tell It. How will you share what you have learned?

Tweet using #IASuseful to share your thoughts.

Day 6: **Warn**

*Flee the evil desires of youth and pursue righteousness,
faith, love and peace, along with those who call on the Lord
out of a pure heart.*

—**2 Timothy 2:22**

We each face our own set of temptations. We each face our own giants. These struggles may be inherited from our families or learned through experience and exposure, but every temptation possesses the possibility of disaster. Each struggle and each temptation threatens to disarm us of our effectiveness and slow us from our mission. Making disciples means delving into the personal and messy areas of another person's life. Go forward knowing dirt will be found. Dig deeper knowing messiness and struggles will be laid bare. Make disciples in the full knowledge that we all struggle, we all need mercy, and we all need the voices of others to warn us of danger and to encourage us to right living.

Talk with God

Give me the boldness to correct and warn when needed and the humility to accept the same in my life.

Live It. How will you live more Second today?
Tell It. How will you share what you have learned?

🐦 Tweet using #IASwarn to share your thoughts.

Day 7: For Corinth

Grace and peace to you from God our Father and the Lord Jesus Christ.

I always thank my God for you because of his grace given you in Christ Jesus. For in him you have been enriched in every way—with all kinds of speech and with all knowledge—God thus confirming our testimony about Christ among you. Therefore you do not lack any spiritual gift as you eagerly wait for our Lord Jesus Christ to be revealed. He will also keep you firm to the end, so that you will be blameless on the day of our Lord Jesus Christ. God is faithful, who has called you into fellowship with his Son, Jesus Christ our Lord.

—1 Corinthians 1:3–9

The most powerful thing in our arsenal is prayer. Our words can only do so much. Our actions and plans can only go so far. But prayer taps into the power of God. It calls in heavenly reinforcements and invokes irresistible strength. In our endeavors to make disciples, let us never forget the power of prayer.

Talk with God

Protect.

". . . firm until the end . . ."
God, protect and guard those whom I am teaching . . .

🐦 Tweet using #IASforcorinth to share your prayers.

Day 1: Life

Watch the Jack Graham Film

iamsecond.com/jackgraham

What did you like about, identify with, or learn from Jack's story?

> *You, however, know all about my teaching, my way of life, my purpose, faith, patience, love, endurance, persecutions, sufferings—what kinds of things happened to me in Antioch, Iconium and Lystra, the persecutions I endured.*
>
> **—2 Timothy 3:10–11**

Read the whole passage in 2 Timothy 3:1–17.

What It Says
1. What did you like about this passage?
2. What did you not like or find confusing about this passage?

What It Means
3. What does this passage teach about people?
4. What does this passage teach about God?

Live It. How will you live more Second today?
Tell It. How will you share what you have learned?

Practice It. Get with a friend or someone in your group. Practice or role-play your "Live and Tell" commitments.

Day 2: **Constant**

Impress them on your children. Talk about them when you sit at home and when you walk along the road, when you lie down and when you get up. Tie them as symbols on your hands and bind them on your foreheads. Write them on the doorframes of your houses and on your gates.

—Deuteronomy 6:7–9

Read the whole passage in Deuteronomy 6:1–12.

Church is not a Sunday activity. Discipleship is not a coffeehouse meeting. Leadership development is not a class or a degree. Teaching others to follow Jesus is a daily endeavor, an ongoing lifestyle. We teach our children as we cook dinner or mow the lawn. We guide our friends as we make jokes or tell stories. We instruct fellow believers as we eat our meals, get dressed, and go to work. Every activity is a teaching moment and every moment a discipleship opportunity. God calls for our constant attention to his mission and our continued effort to pass on his truth.

Talk with God

Remind me, every moment of every day, to inspire the life of Second.

Live It. How can you live more Second today?
Tell It. How will you share what you have learned?

🐦 Tweet using #IASconstant to share your thoughts.

Day 3: Hands-On

I am sending you out like sheep among wolves. Therefore be as shrewd as snakes and as innocent as doves.

—Matthew 10:16

Read the whole passage in Matthew 10:1–23.

Jesus did not coddle his disciples. He did not worry over their potential failures or run from the messy process of leadership development. He threw them into the water and made them swim. He dropped them into the fray and inspired them to fight. He sent them out like sheep to battle the wolves. He knew they would fall, they would disappoint and grow weary, but he also knew they would learn. They would see their mistakes and grow because of them. They would stumble along and, through it, learn to run. How often does our spiritual leadership look more like micromanaging? How often does our training or mentoring look like classroom management? It's time to let believers get their hands dirty, to inspire real-life, hands-on discipleship, the kind that goes beyond books and curriculum, beyond pep talks and sermons. Let's walk the hard road, ask the tough questions, and challenge people to do big things for God.

Talk with God

Show me how to inspire the kind of hands-on leadership development that you have called all of us to participate in.

Live It. How can you live more Second today?
Tell It. How will you share what you have learned?

🐦 Tweet using #IAShandson to share your thoughts.

Day 4: Demanding

Foxes have dens and birds have nests, but the Son of Man has no place to lay his head.

—Luke 9:58

Read the whole passage in Luke 9:57–62.

Jesus wandered this earth a homeless preacher, and while few of us are called to that exact profession, our commission is no less difficult. It is right to talk about the blessings of God and the pleasures that await us in heaven, but it is equally important to talk of the challenges of our faith and the demand God places on our life. We do a disservice when we sugarcoat the reality of discipleship. We are not saved to sit on our couches and eat popcorn. We are rescued to do a task, to fulfill a mission. Discipleship, no matter the specifics, is always costly. It means battling addiction and character flaws. It requires speaking up about our faith and telling our story to an unreceptive world. It means having difficult conversations and facing stiff resistance. And while the walk is always worth the destination, we deceive people if we do not make clear the traps and dangers that clutter the path.

Talk with God

God, I pray for the struggles and difficulties these people are dealing with . . .

Live It. How will you live more Second today?
Tell It. How will you share what you have learned?

🐦 Tweet using #IASdemanding to share your thoughts.

Day 5: Visual

Seeing a fig tree by the road, he went up to it but found nothing on it except leaves. Then he said to it, "May you never bear fruit again!" Immediately the tree withered.

—Matthew 21:19

Read the whole passage in Matthew 21:18–22.

When Jesus saw a grain of salt, a fish in the sea, or a fig tree along the road, he saw opportunity to teach. He used simple stories of farmers or widows, pictures from the world around him, to convey God's truth. We often think that if we make something convoluted or complicated, if we have fancy charts or PowerPoint presentations, then we are great teachers. But Jesus had none of those things. He spoke profound truth through simple stories and common items. We fail our students when we make lessons only we can teach or sermons only we can preach. Great mentors use the tools, words, and visuals that everyone can access and reproduce. They use the fig trees of this world to teach truth.

Talk with God

Give me the wisdom to speak simply and the humility to keep things accessible.

Live It. How will you live more Second today?
Tell It. How will you share what you have learned?

🐦 Tweet using #IASvisual to share your thoughts.

Day 6: Challenged

*Immediately Jesus reached out his hand and caught him.
"You of little faith," he said, "why did you doubt?"*

—Matthew 14:31

Read the whole passage in Matthew 14:22–33.

Correction is a dirty word, constructive criticism a forgotten concept. But Jesus did not flee from such teaching tools. He scolded when it was necessary and challenged when appropriate. He was not a bitter, unpleasable crank, but he also was not afraid to make clear his disappointment when necessary. He reached out his hand in love, but he still did not fail to correct. How often would we rather let a brother lose himself in sin or a sister self-destruct through her poor choices than risk hurting friendship or feelings? How often do we hide our selfishness behind an inept definition of love? Love is not always polite and quite often is downright blunt. This is not a call to be rude or hateful people but rather a reminder that Jesus sometimes made people mad in order to make them better.

Talk with God

God, teach me to face confrontation boldly and lovingly.

Live It. How will you live more Second today?
Tell It. How will you share what you have learned?

Tweet using #IASchallenged to share your thoughts.

Day 7: For Ephesus

For this reason, ever since I heard about your faith in the Lord Jesus and your love for all God's people, I have not stopped giving thanks for you, remembering you in my prayers. I keep asking that the God of our Lord Jesus Christ, the glorious Father, may give you the Spirit of wisdom and revelation, so that you may know him better. I pray that the eyes of your heart may be enlightened in order that you may know the hope to which he has called you, the riches of his glorious inheritance in his holy people, and his incomparably great power for us who believe. That power is the same as the mighty strength he exerted when he raised Christ from the dead and seated him at his right hand in the heavenly realms, far above all rule and authority, power and dominion, and every name that is invoked, not only in the present age but also in the one to come. And God placed all things under his feet and appointed him to be head over everything for the church, which is his body, the fullness of him who fills everything in every way.

—Ephesians 1:15–23

We are designed to be a family, a group of people who love unconditionally, forgive unfailingly, and pray unceasingly. When we talk with God on behalf of our fellow brothers and sisters, we perform a necessary task and an eternally significant duty. So let us follow the example of Paul and pray for our fellow believers.

Talk with God

Ask.

". . . that you may know him better . . ."
God, I ask that you would help these people know you better . . .

Tweet using #IASforephesus to share your prayers.

Day 1: Prepared

Watch the Scott Hamilton Film

    iamsecond.com/scotthamilton

What did you like about, identify with, or learn from Scott's story?

> *Preach the word; be prepared in season and out of season; correct, rebuke and encourage—with great patience and careful instruction. For the time will come when people will not put up with sound doctrine. Instead, to suit their own desires, they will gather around them a great number of teachers to say what their itching ears want to hear.*
>
> **—2 Timothy 4:2–3**

Read the whole passage in 2 Timothy 4:1–22.

What It Says
1. What did you like about this passage?
2. What did you not like or find confusing about this passage?

What It Means
3. What does this passage teach about people?
4. What does this passage teach about God?

Live It. How will you live more Second today?

Tell It. How will you share what you have learned?

Practice It. Get with a friend or someone in your group. Practice or role-play your "Live and Tell" commitments.

Day 2: Trials

In all this you greatly rejoice, though now for a little while you may have had to suffer grief in all kinds of trials. These have come so that the proven genuineness of your faith—of greater worth than gold, which perishes even though refined by fire—may result in praise, glory and honor when Jesus Christ is revealed.

—1 Peter 1:6–7

Read the whole passage in 1 Peter 1:1–25.

When metal hits the fire, it weakens and melts but only for a time. The impurities are sifted away, and the ugliness is separated. A stronger, purer metal emerges. A new shape is pounded into place, and something more beautiful and more perfect is created. Like metal refined in the furnace, we endure to be purified and perfected. Our trials serve a purpose. We do not suffer in vain. God knows what character flaws need ironing, where our faith needs to grow, and where our trust in him needs to strengthen. He sees the bigger picture and is preparing us for an eternity with him. So while we suffer for a time, he allows it so that we may become a stronger tool and purer metal.

Talk with God

God, I don't always understand why things happen as they do in my life, but I trust that you have a plan.

Live It. How can you live more Second today?
Tell It. How will you share what you have learned?

Tweet using #IAStrials to share your thoughts.

Day 3: **Strangers**

I urge you, as foreigners and exiles, to abstain from sinful desires, which wage war against your soul.

—1 Peter 2:11

Read the whole passage in 1 Peter 2:1–25.

We once lived as the world did because we too were a part of the world. But now we belong to another kingdom, another nation, one ruled by a holy God with a different set of rules. Though we still live in this world, he expects us to live as citizens of his kingdom and not this one. The habits of our old life may fade slowly; few will ever die before we enter eternity. But we are called to abstain nonetheless, to battle our demons and to wage war against our weaknesses. Maybe that means ditching our computer or joining a support group. For some it will require cutting up credit cards or buying some running shoes. We each have our difficulties, and we each must activate our battle plans.

Talk with God

Make me a good citizen of your heavenly kingdom. Give me strength in the face of temptation.

Live It. How can you live more Second today?
Tell It. How will you share what you have learned?

🐦 Tweet using #IASstrangers to share your thoughts.

Day 4: **Answers**

Always be prepared to give an answer to everyone who asks you to give the reason for the hope that you have. But do this with gentleness and respect, keeping a clear conscience, so that those who speak maliciously against your good behavior in Christ may be ashamed of their slander.

—1 Peter 3:15–16

Read the whole passage in 1 Peter 3:1–22.

While we may never silence our critics, our character and our love may at least prove our sincerity. If held long enough, integrity speaks for itself. If shown brightly enough, love breaks into even the darkest corner. When our message is rejected or questioned, we should give an answer and a defense but in humility and with respect. Granting these to someone does not mean we abandon our principles; rather, it means we value their humanity. It means we avoid heated rhetoric and ugly mudslinging. We let the other person speak, and we avoid personal attacks. We stay on message, on the message of Jesus. Our lives are the only Jesus many will ever see and the only gospel many will hear. And while speaking the gospel in deed alone will never be completely sufficient, it can win us an audience and at least muffle the voices of those who speak against us.

Talk with God

God, help me to respond to my critics with gentleness and respect.

Live It. How will you live more Second today?
Tell It. How will you share what you have learned?

🐦 Tweet using #IASanswers to share your thoughts.

Day 5: **Unsurprised**

*Do not be surprised at the fiery ordeal that has come on you
to test you, as though something strange were happening
to you. But rejoice inasmuch as you participate in the
sufferings of Christ, so that you may be overjoyed when his
glory is revealed.*

—1 Peter 4:12–13

Read the whole passage in 1 Peter 4:1–19.

We all like to ponder the happy promises of God, his words of sweet reward and happy futures. But there are also the darker promises. The promise that this world will not accept or understand us. The promise that suffering will come, that fiery ordeals will befall us. We do not fit in this world. We believe in a God above science, in a life beyond death, in absolute truths and divine intervention. Our loyalties fall first to God and second to country, to family, to friends, and to everything else in this world. We are square pegs on a round globe and strangers in a foreign land. But there is some small comfort in knowing that we journey this strange land together, a family of believers and participants in the same kind of rejection faced by Jesus himself.

Talk with God

Give me the strength to make it through each day and to remember that I am not alone.

Live It. How will you live more Second today?
Tell It. How will you share what you have learned?

🐦 Tweet using #IASunsurprised to share your thoughts.

Day 6: Lion

*Be alert and of sober mind. Your enemy the devil prowls
around like a roaring lion looking for someone to devour.
Resist him, standing firm in the faith, because you know that
the family of believers throughout the world is undergoing
the same kind of sufferings.*

—1 Peter 5:8–9

Read the whole passage in 1 Peter 5:1–14.

We have an enemy. He does not carry a pitchfork or wear a
red suit. He is not the fairy-tale character we see on television. He
is real, and he is prowling around looking for his next victim. He
rules this world and runs free across its surface. Therefore, we must
be alert, be ready for his temptations, and be sober-minded as we
move about in his realm. He cannot touch even the hair on our
head without permission from God, but God often allows our testing, a check on our spiritual alertness. So let us keep God close in
our thoughts, be frequently in his presence in our prayers, and read
his Bible often so that we may be ready when the challenge comes.

Talk with God

God keep me spiritually alert and ready to face the dangers that
await me in this world.

Live It. How will you live more Second today?
Tell It. How will you share what you have learned?

Tweet using #IASlion to share your thoughts.

Day 7: **Fortress**

Who will rise up for me against the wicked?
Who will take a stand for me against evildoers?
Unless the LORD had given me help,
I would soon have dwelt in the silence of death.
When I said, "My foot is slipping,"
your unfailing love, LORD, supported me.
When anxiety was great within me,
your consolation brought me joy.
Can a corrupt throne be allied with you—
a throne that brings on misery by its decrees?
The wicked band together against the righteous
and condemn the innocent to death.
But the LORD has become my fortress,
and my God the rock in whom I take refuge.
He will repay them for their sins
and destroy them for their wickedness;
the LORD our God will destroy them.

—Psalm 94:16–23

Do not pretend your self-reliance. God is not impressed with our posturing or our boasting. He knows our weaknesses, and he understands our frailty. He offers his aid and lends his strength to all who ask. He may not sweep away the trouble, but he will always walk alongside us.

Talk with God

Protect.

"My foot is slipping . . ."
God, give me the strength to persevere and the courage to help others do the same . . .

Tweet using #IASfortress to share your prayers.

Session Eight

Multiply

Weeks 31–34
Week 31: Viral
Week 32: Gather Together
Week 33: Person of Peace
Week 34: Who's Ready?

All living things multiply; believers are no exception. God expects his gift of our spiritual awakening to reproduce in a viral reaction, that our new life would result in a dedication to pass that life on to others. And his plan is not only that we multiply disciples but that we multiply groups of disciples, that our gatherings spawn other gatherings, each with a new set of leaders and a new mission in their community. The gatekeepers of our world and social networkers of our communities hold the key to this multiplication. They may not look like us or fit in with our group, but they lead an unofficial group of their own, a network of relationships. These are the apartment managers of our cities, the business owners, the socialites, and the leaders. They connect and lead, and if they catch our virus, catch wind of our message, spiritual multiplication will be the natural result.

Day 1: Openness

Watch the NASCAR Drivers Film

iamsecond.com/nascar

What did you like about, identify with, or learn from the story?

> *When you enter a house, first say, "Peace to this house." If someone who promotes peace is there, your peace will rest on them; if not, it will return to you.*
>
> **—Luke 10:5–6**

Read the whole passage in Luke 10:1–11.

What It Says
1. What did you like about this passage?
2. What did you not like or find confusing about this passage?

What It Means
3. What does this passage teach about people?
4. What does this passage teach about God?

Live It. How will you live more Second today?

Tell It. How will you share what you have learned?

Practice It. Get with a friend or someone in your group. Practice or role-play your "Live and Tell" commitments.

Day 2: **Soldier**

When Jesus heard this, he was amazed at him, and turning to the crowd following him, he said, "I tell you, I have not found such great faith even in Israel."

—Luke 7:9

Read the whole passage in Luke 7:1–10.

Too often we feel we have to bludgeon someone into heaven or fight them out of hell. We spend untold amounts of energy, sweat, and tears on those unwilling or unready to listen. Meanwhile, there are people, like the centurion Jesus spoke to in the story above, who need no convincing, no proofs, no grand arguments or big miracles. They would gladly welcome the message and person of Jesus, if only someone would point him out. We are called to share with the world the great story of our God and search for those open hearts who are waiting for Jesus to come to their town. We need not worry about those who refuse to listen, those who slam their doors or close their hearts. While we may know people who are ready to argue, it's our mission to find those who are ready to believe.

Talk with God

Bring me people ready to hear about you and persons hungry for your message.

Live It. How can you live more Second today?
Tell It. How will you share what you have learned?

🐦 Tweet using #IASsoldier to share your thoughts.

Day 3: Matthew

While Jesus was having dinner at Matthew's house, many tax collectors and sinners came and ate with him and his disciples.

—Matthew 9:10

Read the whole passage in Matthew 9:9–13.

Jesus gave his followers a mission, a commission: go and make disciples of all the nations. He demands that, through us, his kingdom grows and multiplies. He will not accept mediocrity and will not be content with stagnation. He wants multiplication. He wants growth. And this kind of growth requires a certain viral element to our plans. Billions of people will die without hearing the message of Jesus. And every one of them has a face and a family, hopes and aspirations. We are called to search for the Matthews, the people who respond to the gospel and reach others, who spiritually multiply. They hear and pass on the "virus." They possess forward momentum and ready obedience to the mission that Jesus gave us. They make reaching the billions and fulfilling Jesus' commission a possibility.

Talk with God

Give me the vision to work toward the completion of your great mission and the desire to see it realized.

Live It. How can you live more Second today?
Tell It. How will you share what you have learned?

🐦 Tweet using #IASmatthew to share your thoughts.

Day 4: Saul

*At once he began to preach in the synagogues that Jesus is
the Son of God.*

—Acts 9:20

Read the whole passage in Acts 9:19–31.

One of the world's greatest missionaries was once one of
Christianity's greatest critics. Saul of Tarsus hated and persecuted
those who claimed Jesus as their Messiah. He brought havoc to the
early church and carried death and destruction to early believers.
But when the tide turned and God reshaped Saul into the apostle
Paul, all his passion, fire, and energy came pouring out into his new
faith. The same drive he once had to persecute believers, he now
threw toward reaching the lost. The same commitment he once had
to persecute Jesus followers, he now used to fuel his preaching in
the synagogues, marketplaces, and street corners of ancient Rome.
Saul is not meant to be the exception to the faith but the norm,
the accepted standard for passion and dedication. We are called to
be inexplicably, uncontrollably, and undoubtedly sold out for the
cause of Jesus.

Talk with God

Make me an agent of change for my community and my world.

Live It. How will you live more Second today?
Tell It. How will you share what you have learned?

Tweet using #IASsaul to share your thoughts.

Day 5: Lydia

When she and the members of her household were baptized, she invited us to her home.

—Acts 16:15

Read the whole passage in Acts 16:11–15.

Every social group has a gatekeeper, a person who is officially or unofficially responsible for leading the group. This is true of cliques at school or groups at work, of families, neighborhoods, or countries. These gatekeepers are the guards of traditions and the voices of change. They provide wisdom or chaos, peace or hostility. Whether good or bad, these people influence those around them. Lydia was one such person. When she shared the story of Jesus, everyone listened. No one is more capable than these gatekeepers of bringing the message of Jesus to their friends and family. If only we noticed their unnamed leadership and promoted their natural influence for the kingdom of God, we could again see whole households, not just individuals, come to Jesus.

Talk with God

Help me spot the gatekeepers, the leaders among my peers, so I can share with them the story of Jesus.

Live It. How will you live more Second today?
Tell It. How will you share what you have learned?

🐦 Tweet using #IASlydia to share your thoughts.

Day 6: Growing Pains

"These men who have caused trouble all over the world have now come here, and Jason has welcomed them into his house. They are all defying Caesar's decrees, saying that there is another king, one called Jesus."

—**Acts 17:6–7**

Read the whole passage in Acts 17:1–15.

Word was getting out. The message of Jesus was spreading from one end of the Roman Empire to the other. Rumors began to swirl, and misunderstandings swept in about who this *Jesus* was. Was he an insurrectionist? A Jewish healer and teacher? Soon these young believers found themselves at the mercy of mobs and vigilante courtrooms. But while we must always strive for clarity in our message and innocence in our dealings, as the message of Jesus spreads, prejudices and troubles will surface. The faster the movement travels, the faster trouble will follow in its wake. Be ready.

Talk with God

God, give me the wisdom to invest my time well and the strength to persevere in hard times.

Live It. How will you live more Second today?
Tell It. How will you share what you have learned?

🐦 Tweet using #IASgrowingpains to share your thoughts.

Day 7: **Contagious**

For this reason, since the day we heard about you, we have not stopped praying for you. We continually ask God to fill you with the knowledge of his will through all the wisdom and understanding that the Spirit gives, so that you may live a life worthy of the Lord and please him in every way: bearing fruit in every good work, growing in the knowledge of God, being strengthened with all power according to his glorious might so that you may have great endurance and patience, and giving joyful thanks to the Father, who has qualified you to share in the inheritance of his holy people in the kingdom of light. For he has rescued us from the dominion of darkness and brought us into the kingdom of the Son he loves, in whom we have redemption, the forgiveness of sins.

—Colossians 1:9–14

Ceaseless prayer is when we turn our worried thoughts into requests of God. It is when we capture our stress or our daydreaming or our wandering thoughts and focus them on God. Whenever Paul thought of his brothers and sisters at Colossae, his thoughts turned to prayers, his worries to requests of God, and his dreams to earnest intercession.

Talk with God

Ask.

"**. . . we** have not stopped praying for you . . ."
God, give us the knowledge, wisdom, and understanding to bear much fruit . . .

🐦 Tweet using #IAScontagious to share your prayers.

Day 1: Devoted

Watch the Lee Yih Film

iamsecond.com/leeyih

What did you like about, identify with, or learn from Lee's story?

They devoted themselves to the apostles' teaching and to fellowship, to the breaking of bread and to prayer.

—Acts 2:42

Read the whole passage in Acts 2:14–47.

What It Says
1. What did you like about this passage?
2. What did you not like or find confusing about this passage?

What It Means
3. What does this passage teach about people?
4. What does this passage teach about God?

Live It. How will you live more Second today?
Tell It. How will you share what you have learned?

Practice It. Get with a friend or someone in your group. Practice or role-play your "Live and Tell" commitments.

Day 2: Teachings

All Scripture is God-breathed and is useful for teaching, rebuking, correcting and training in righteousness, so that the servant of God may be thoroughly equipped for every good work.

—2 Timothy 3:16–17

Read the whole passage in 2 Timothy 3:10–17.

Followers of Jesus meet and congregate; we gather together. But we do so with a centerpiece, a foundation, an agreed-upon constitution: the Bible. Without God's message to humanity, we would be lost in the smallness of our subjectivity and the vastness of our own ignorance. We can know little without it and hope for less with anything else. We may ask it questions, but never question it. We may present it with our doubts, but never disbelieve it. We may dislike the hard words it contains, but never hate it for telling the truth with those words. We may read other books and find truth in other writings, but never may we allow anything else trump the God-breathed, perfect, and unerring book of God. The Bible alone is the complete and unfailing training manual for every good work God gave us to do.

Talk with God

Remind us that your Bible is the teacher of our gatherings and your Spirit the guide to its interpretation.

Live It. How can you live more Second today?
Tell It. How will you share what you have learned?

🐦 Tweet using #IASteachings to share your thoughts.

Day 3: Fellowship

Consequently, you are no longer foreigners and strangers, but fellow citizens with God's people and also members of his household, built on the foundation of the apostles and prophets, with Christ Jesus himself as the chief cornerstone.

—Ephesians 2:19–20

Read the whole passage in Ephesians 2:19–3:12.

Fellowship is more than pizza parties and bowling trips, but a commitment to forgive when injured and a desire to serve rather than be served. Fellowship means irrevocable love and irreplaceable care. It means when one falls, the other picks up. When one stumbles, the other lends his shoulder. It means team play, not individual showmanship. If we ignore the unpopular when we gather, then we do not truly gather. If we fight and bicker, then we do not really have fellowship. If we stoke unforgiveness, gossip, or destructive speech, then we do not understand the essence of our meetings. We are family, fellow citizens, pieces of one house, parts of one body. Let our meetings reflect that reality, our gatherings be a picture of that truth—a truth purchased with Jesus' blood.

Talk with God

Make our gatherings a picture of your love and a reflection of your goodness.

Live It. How can you live more Second today?
Tell It. How will you share what you have learned?

🐦 Tweet using #IASfellowship to share your thoughts.

Day 4: Body

Now you are the body of Christ, and each one of you is a part of it.

—1 Corinthians 12:27

Read the whole passage in 1 Corinthians 12:12–27.

In a healthy body, damaged cells are either repaired or removed. Cancer occurs when those unhealthy cells are allowed to continue and multiply. They perform no healthy bodily function and aid in no helpful physical activity. They merely multiply their ineptitude and reproduce their wastefulness, until the body ceases to function. How cancerous is the body of Christ? How many of his cells refuse to perform their duties or his body parts reject his medical attention? How many of us think that our role in the body is to sit and do nothing or, worse, encourage others to do the same? How many of us view church activities as something for priests and pastors, the gifted few or the anointed select? How many of us are cancer in the church, cells that do nothing but complain, cause pain, and pursue our own goals without thought of others around us? How many of us need to submit to repair or to prepare for removal?

Talk with God

I want to be a healthy and active part of your body. Show me my role and give me strength for my task.

Live It. How will you live more Second today?
Tell It. How will you share what you have learned?

🐦 Tweet using #IASbody to share your thoughts.

Day 5: **Breaking Bread**

For whenever you eat this bread and drink this cup, you proclaim the Lord's death until he comes.

—1 Corinthians 11:26

Read the whole passage in 1 Corinthians 11:17–34.

We must never forget that this family, this new life, this relationship with God, and our role in his kingdom all exist because of the sacrifice of Jesus. We do not gather for padded seats or a Christian rock show. We do not meet for witty performances or moving speeches. We do not do church to get the "kids of the street" or to find a "healthier, wealthier" life. We meet to commemorate Jesus' death, burial, and resurrection and to encourage each other to live in reflection of this sacrifice. The sharing of a loaf of bread and a glass of wine reminds us that his body was broken and his blood spilled that our lives be saved and our forgiveness made possible. We unite behind one story of one Savior, the death of Jesus and the resurrection of the same. We gather to remember and live out this truth—nothing more and nothing less.

Talk with God

Help the manner of our gatherings and the goal of meetings be to shout the truth of your sacrifice with our lives.

Live It. How will you live more Second today? How will you commemorate Jesus' death when you gather with other believers?
Tell It. How will you share what you have learned?

🐦 Tweet using #IASbreakingbread to share your thoughts.

Day 6: **Prayer**

And pray in the Spirit on all occasions with all kinds of prayers and requests. With this in mind, be alert and always keep on praying for all the Lord's people.

—Ephesians 6:18

Read the whole passage in Ephesians 6:10–20.

We battle in a dangerous land, and we fight unseen forces. But communication with our homeland is not cut off—reinforcements are near, and help is at hand. We are more than slaves, more than servants. We are royalty, children of the King, ambassadors of his kingdom. When we speak, our King hears. When we cry, he sends his response. When we shout our needs and beg his help, he answers our call. We each carry a radio tuned to his channel, but how often do we use it? How often do we take seriously the prayer requests we receive? How often do we realize our daily tasks and our frequent troubles do not have to be tackled alone, that we have armies and guards from heaven itself? Let our conversations with God reflect not just the trivialities of life but the seriousness of our privileged position with God and the reality of the strength he offers.

Talk with God

God, I ask you to make your will happen in my life, that you answer my cries for protection and my requests for help.

Live It. How will you live more Second today?
Tell It. How will you share what you have learned?

🐦 Tweet using #IASprayer to share your thoughts.

Day 7: **Rooted**

For this reason I kneel before the Father, from whom every family in heaven and on earth derives its name. I pray that out of his glorious riches he may strengthen you with power through his Spirit in your inner being, so that Christ may dwell in your hearts through faith. And I pray that you, being rooted and established in love, may have power, together with all the Lord's holy people, to grasp how wide and long and high and deep is the love of Christ, and to know this love that surpasses knowledge—that you may be filled to the measure of all the fullness of God.

Now to him who is able to do immeasurably more than all we ask or imagine, according to his power that is at work within us, to him be glory in the church and in Christ Jesus throughout all generations, for ever and ever! Amen.

—Ephesians 3:14–21

As our lives should be molded around the one goal of love, so also our prayers should reflect the unity of our vision. Love is the greatest end of our lives and the only care of our God. How often are our prayers rooted in the simple goal of love? How often are we distracted, even in our prayers, by materialism, selfishness, and trivialities?

Talk with God

Ask.

". . . to grasp how wide and long and deep is the love of Christ . . ."
God, teach us to love each other as you have loved us . . .

Tweet using #IASrooted to share your prayers.

Day 1: Messenger

Watch the Matt Barkley Film

iamsecond.com/mattbarkley

What did you like about, identify with, or learn from Matt's story?

> *So the man went away and began to tell in the Decapolis how much Jesus had done for him. And all the people were amazed.*
>
> **—Mark 5:20**

Read the whole passage in Mark 5:1–20.

What It Says
1. What did you like about this passage?
2. What did you not like or find confusing about this passage?

What It Means
3. What does this passage teach about people?
4. What does this passage teach about God?

Live It. How will you live more Second today?
Tell It. How will you share what you have learned?

Practice It. Get with a friend or someone in your group. Practice or role-play your "Live and Tell" commitments.

Day 2: **Reputation**

At Caesarea there was a man named Cornelius, a centurion in what was known as the Italian Regiment. He and all his family were devout and God-fearing; he gave generously to those in need and prayed to God regularly.

—Acts 10:1–2

Read the whole passage in Acts 10:1–8.

Multiplication requires a multiplier, a person willing to take the movement forward. Cornelius was one such person. But he did not become a multiplier when Peter arrived at his home. He was already one long before then, a person with influence and followers. His reputation brought respect and earned an audience. When Cornelius spoke, people listened. When he invited, people came. He was a leader in his community both by title and by practice. Sometimes we ignore these types of people when we plan for multiplication. We hope to reach our workplace but forget to involve the boss or manager. We try to get the word out in our neighborhood, but we neglect the homeowner associations, apartment managers, or local businesses. If we want to multiply, to see our world infiltrated with the message of Jesus, we have to identify and pursue the influencers, the movers and shakers, the people with a reputation in the community.

Talk with God

God, go ahead of me and prepare the hearts of the leaders in my community. Get them ready to hear your message.

Live It. How can you live more Second today?
Tell It. How will you share what you have learned?

🐦 Tweet using #IASreputation to share your thoughts.

Day 3: Barriers

"Surely not, Lord!" Peter replied. "I have never eaten anything impure or unclean."

—**Acts 10:14**

Read the whole passage in Acts 10:9–16.

Jesus asks for everything. He demands to be first above all else. His call is difficult enough without us adding our own set of barriers and requirements. Some would try to require a certain length of hair to come to church, a certain manner of religious speech to talk with God, a certain taste in music—all these are barriers we build to prevent someone from coming into our community. Persons of peace, multipliers, and agents of change may not fit our mold. They may not speak "Christianese" or color their language with "holy" substitutes. Their friends may not be "mother approved" or be sober enough to invite to church. Their hangouts may not be the same as those in the Christian community, but none of that matters. What matters is whether they consistently obey what they learn and readily pass on what they believe. That is what makes them agents of change. The moment we try to make them like us, take them out of their circle of friends, or change their environment, we sever their ability to change the very people we most wish to reach.

Talk with God

Give me the wisdom to know which are my own prejudices, rules, and made-up requirements and which are yours.

Live It. How can you live more Second today?
Tell It. How will you share what you have learned?

🐦 Tweet using #IASbarriers to share your thoughts.

Day 4: **Supernatural**

We have come from Cornelius the centurion. He is a righteous and God-fearing man, who is respected by all the Jewish people. A holy angel told him to ask you to come to his house so that he could hear what you have to say."

—**Acts 10:22**

Read the whole passage in Acts 10:17–23.

God does not need us, but he is determined to use us. He does not require our aid, but he insists on our participation. We bring nothing to the table, but he calls us forward anyway. Despite our weaknesses, regardless of our failures, God is stubbornly, insistently, absolutely determined to include us in his plans. He had no need of Peter and required nothing from Cornelius, but still he arranged their supernatural meeting. God is at work. His plan moves forward with or without us. But he screams for our involvement and cries for our cooperation. We must train our ears to hear his call when unexpected spiritual conversations occur. We must open our eyes when serendipitous meetings happen. We must ready our attention when God brings persons of peace to our doorstep, across our Facebook page, or interrupting our daily plans.

Talk with God

God, send them my way. I volunteer. I will make disciples. I will look for those ready persons and hungry hearts, ready to learn about you. Send them my way and use me to reach them.

Live It. How will you live more Second today?
Tell It. How will you share what you have learned?

🐦 Tweet using #IASsupernatural to share your thoughts.

Day 5: Gatherer

The following day he arrived in Caesarea. Cornelius was expecting them and had called together his relatives and close friends.

—Acts 10:24

Read the whole passage in Acts 10:23–29.

Persons of peace are gatherers. They are people magnets, group glue, and social stickies. They do everything with others. They show up to parties with friends and to family reunions with unrelated strangers. They cannot help but involve others in everything they do. They may have just a few friends who never leave their sides or twenty who rotate constantly, but they are always surrounded by others. What would happen if we made these magnets point true north? What would happen if their glue was glued to God and their stickiness stuck on God? What would happen if we taught the social butterflies and the network gatekeepers to spread the message of God? What would happen if we tapped into the gathering strength of those we introduce to Jesus?

Talk with God

Show me the gatekeepers in my community, the people who make the connections and create the social network. Move their hearts and ready their souls for your message.

Live It. How will you live more Second today?
Tell It. How will you share what you have learned?

🐦 Tweet using #IASgatherer to share your thoughts.

Day 6: **Ready**

Now we are all here in the presence of God to listen to everything the Lord has commanded you to tell us.

—Acts 10:33

Read the whole passage in Acts 10:16–40.

Not everyone is ready. This is the sad truth of our message. Few will accept it, and fewer will follow it. Many will like it, many will admire and appreciate it, but few will throw their lives in the service of it. Our mission is to tell the story, to shout it with our lives, and to speak it with our words—but the convincing is up to God. He alone can change a heart, and he alone can reshape a soul. Those he prepares will answer his call. Our job is to make the invitation known, but the answering is God's job. So be encouraged when our message greets blank faces or empty smiles. Be comforted knowing that our abilities and our talents, or lack thereof, do not tip the balance of a person's eternal destination. We are called simply to share Jesus and tell about what he has done in our lives. The rest is up to God.

Talk with God

God, I am frustrated that these people have yet to believe in you. But I trust you know what you are doing.

Live It. How will you live more Second today?
Tell It. How will you share what you have learned?

Tweet using #IASready to share your thoughts.

Day 7: Delivered

No king is saved by the size of his army;
no warrior escapes by his great strength.
A horse is a vain hope for deliverance;
despite all its great strength it cannot save.
But the eyes of the L<small>ORD</small> *are on those who fear him,*
on those whose hope is in his unfailing love,
To deliver them from death
and keep them alive in famine.
We wait in hope for the L<small>ORD</small>*;*
he is our help and our shield.
In him our hearts rejoice,
for we trust in his holy name.
May your unfailing love be with us, L<small>ORD</small>*,*
even as we put our hope in you.

—Psalm 33:16–22

God wants our country to know him, so ask him to bring the nation to faith. God wants your city to experience his grace, so beg him to make that grace irresistible. God desires that your friends and family follow him, so ask him to turn their hearts.

Talk with God

Ask.

"May your unfailing love be with us . . ."
God, help my country, my city, my community make you their God . . .

🐦 Tweet using #IASdelivered to share your prayers.

Day 1: Good Soil

Watch the Lisa Luby Ryan Film

iamsecond.com/lisalubyryan

What did you like about, identify with, or learn from Lisa's story?

> *Still other seed fell on good soil, where it produced a crop—a hundred, sixty or thirty times what was sown.*
>
> **—Matthew 13:8**

Read the whole passage in Matthew 13:1–9.

What It Says

1. What did you like about this passage?
2. What did you not like or find confusing about this passage?

What It Means

3. What does this passage teach about people?
4. What does this passage teach about God?

Live It. How will you live more Second today?

Tell It. How will you share what you have learned?

Practice It. Get with a friend or someone in your group. Practice or role-play your "Live and Tell" commitments.

Day 2: Multiplier

But the seed falling on good soil refers to someone who hears the word and understands it. This is the one who produces a crop, yielding a hundred, sixty or thirty times what was sown.

—Matthew 13:23

Read the whole passage in Matthew 13:10–23.

All living things reproduce. Spiritual life is no different. We are not given eternal life to sit on our hands. We are not given healing from sin and answers to life's questions without responsibility. We are given to give to others. We are blessed to be a blessing. A sign of a ready disciple, of a person of peace and an agent of change, is the desire to multiply. They do not need cajoling or threats. They do not need fifteen-step action plans or twenty-three principles for multiplication; they just do it. Training hones their abilities. Encouragement improves their results. Guidance brings longevity to their efforts. But spiritual multiplication is natural for them. They cannot help but tell others of what they learn. They share their story and consistently talk about God. They live out and tell others what they learn. They are multipliers. They reproduce because they are spiritually alive. Are you a multiplier? Are you pouring yourself into others who do the same?

Talk with God

Make me a spiritual multiplier. Make me a multiplier of multipliers. God, use me to produce a crop of thousands.

Live It. How can you live more Second today?
Tell It. How will you share what you have learned?

🐦 Tweet using #IASmultiplier to share your thoughts.

Day 3: **Weeds**

The kingdom of heaven is like a man who sowed good seed in his field. But while everyone was sleeping, his enemy came and sowed weeds among the wheat, and went away.

—**Matthew 13:24–25**

Read the whole passage in Matthew 13:24–30.

Weeds will mingle with the wheat. Some will do so knowingly. They attend our meetings because it lets them check off the "religion" box or please their parents or spouse. Many never think themselves the imposter. They do good deeds thinking our faith is just a do-gooder-club. They attend our gatherings thinking our God is a social calendar event or a civic duty. But regardless of their reason for joining us, we will rarely succeed in separating them from the wheat. We may invent new rules to enforce, new classes to complete, or new standards to meet, all in the hopes of finding those who do not fit. But all these things only uproot the good with the bad. They confuse entrance requirements into our community with the discipleship process of our community. Making and growing disciples will always involve the occasional Judas. We are called only to keep working the field and to let the Lord of the harvest worry about the fruit.

Talk with God

Give me the humbleness to accept confession when offered, remorse when presented, and repentance when evidenced, without attempting to judge the things beyond my capacity.

Live It. How can you live more Second today?
Tell It. How will you share what you have learned?

🐦 Tweet using #IASweeds to share your thoughts.

Day 4: At His Word

"Go," Jesus replied, "your son will live."
The man took Jesus at his word and departed.

—John 4:50

Read the whole passage in John 4:46–53.

This man needed no convincing. He needed no arguing or urging. He was ready. When Jesus spoke, he believed. When Jesus healed, he had no reservations. Sharing Jesus with others is a fishing expedition. We cast our lines and throw our nets and hope the fish bite. We go when they are hungry, and we wait when they are not. We use lures to entice them and bait to attract them. But it is not our job to make them hungry, to dive in after them, or to teach them to walk on land. We simply present what we are given as best we know how and wait for them to bite. We are fishers of men, not hunters or salesmen or orators. We are called to faithfully tell about Jesus and disciple those who believe our word and accept the message we carry.

Talk with God

Give me the patience to keep sharing Jesus, knowing that most fish will never bite.

Live It. How will you live more Second today?
Tell It. How will you share what you have learned?

Tweet using #IASathisword to share your thoughts.

Day 5: **Blind Faith**

*He answered, "I have told you already and you did not listen.
Why do you want to hear it again? Do you want to become
his disciples too?"*

—John 9:27

Read the whole passage in John 9:1–34.

    This formerly blind man opened his eyes to an unseeing world.
He knew one simple truth: Jesus had healed him. He did not know
why or how, only that once he was blind and now he could see. He
did not understand religious politics or power-hungry leaders. He
did not care about reputation or position. He could not fathom why
anyone would care about who gets credit or who is in charge. He
only thought about looking for people willing to pass on the story
of his healing and the message of his Healer. Ready disciples are
blind to the cares of this world. Their faith has distorted their ability to participate in pride or prestige or position. They do not worry
about repercussions or rocking the boat, only that the story of their
Healer be told as loud and as far their voice will carry. So when we
look at our lives, which do we find: the one who only risks when he
knows there is no risk—or the one who steps out in faith not caring
how we are perceived?

Talk with God

Make me a blind-faith disciple, a risky follower, and a daring messenger. Teach me to multiply in others the same blind faith.

Live It. How will you live more Second today?
Tell It. How will you share what you have learned?

Tweet using #IASblindfaith to share your thoughts.

Day 6: Eager

"Who is he, sir?" the man asked. "Tell me so that I may believe in him."

—John 9:36

Read the whole passage in John 9:35–41.

A hungry person does not care whether you feed him steak or cabbage, rutabaga or lobster. He only cares that you feed him. Some require that the mountains move and the sky fall before they trust God, and even then they wonder if nature could provide explanation. But if someone is searching for God, looking for his sign, praying for his healing and for his forgiveness, he will recognize God when you share his story. He will ask for more when you tell him about Jesus. Not everyone will answer God's call, but the harvest is still ripe, and the fields still calling for more workers. Our task is not to make fruit out of the rocks or trees out of the grass but to find the eager and willing fruit that hangs on the branches.

Talk with God

Father, prepare a harvest in my workplace, my school, my neighborhood, and my family.

Live It. How will you live more Second today?
Tell It. How will you share what you have learned?

🐦 Tweet using #IASeager to share your thoughts.

Day 7: **Fruit**

Blessed is the one
who does not walk in step with the wicked
Or stand in the way that sinners take
or sit in the company of mockers,
But whose delight is in the law of the Lord,
and who meditates on his law day and night.
That person is like a tree planted by streams of water,
which yields its fruit in season
And whose leaf does not wither—
whatever they do prospers.
Not so the wicked!
They are like chaff
that the wind blows away.
Therefore the wicked will not stand in the judgment,
nor sinners in the assembly of the righteous.
For the Lord watches over the way of the righteous,
but the way of the wicked leads to destruction.

—Psalm 1

When we do God's will, we have the full power of his kingdom behind us. When we are working his mission, we have heaven's host at our backs. He watches over his faithful servants and empowers his honest laborers. If we obey his command, then all we need do is ask, and he hears us.

Talk with God

Protect.

"The Lord watches over . . ."
God, protect me as I teach others what you have taught me . . .

Tweet using #IASfruit to share your prayers.

Lead

Weeks 35–39
Week 35: Model (Like This)
Week 36: Model (Not This)
Week 37: Assist
Week 38: Watch
Week 39: Leave

It takes no special talent to ride a bike, only a bit of guidance and some practice. It begins with modeling. We watch as someone else takes flight down the street. We do not need long hours in the film room or meticulous study of the masters, only a quick glance and then we are eager to try it ourselves.

At first, our knuckles are white with fear and our steering choppy and unsure. But with Dad holding the back of our shirt, we soon find ourselves riding our bikes, with some assistance.

But Dad must eventually free us to fall, to scrape our knees, and to bump our heads. Not because he wants us to get hurt, but because failure and pain are the best teachers.

But soon that too will end, and Dad will have to let us go. Eventually he must release us to explore city streets and dirt roads. He teaches us the rules of the road, but eventually the time comes when he leaves, and we are on our own.

Model. Assist. Watch. Leave. It is how we learned to ride our bikes and how we are to teach others to follow Jesus. It is the process of teaching that Jesus exemplified, that his disciples passed on, and that Paul illustrated. It is the process by which we are to teach all that Jesus has taught us.

Day 1: Servant

Watch the Wayne Huizenga Film

iamsecond.com/waynehuizenga

What did you like about, identify with, or learn from Wayne's story?

> *I have set you an example that you should do as I have done for you.*
>
> **—John 13:15**

Read the whole passage in John 13:1–30.

What It Says
1. What did you like about this passage?
2. What did you not like or find confusing about this passage?

What It Means
3. What does this passage teach about people?
4. What does this passage teach about God?

Live It. How will you live more Second today?
Tell It. How will you share what you have learned?

Practice It. Get with a friend or someone in your group. Practice or role-play your "Live and Tell" commitments.

Day 2: Tough

*Then Moses cried out to the L*ord*, "What am I to do with these people? They are almost ready to stone me."*

—Exodus 17:4

Read the whole passage in Exodus 17:1–7.

Moses showed his people the art of prayer and demonstrated the power of faith. He brought them out of the land of Egypt, out of the terrors of slavery, and to the brink of a new country. He wrote down the law of God and spoke to them the truth of his Word. He lived dedicated to God and upright before his Maker. But rarely did they care, and rarely did the people learn from his example. They complained and argued. They threatened his life and challenged his position. They talked about returning to slavery in Egypt rather than continuing under his leadership. God called them a stubborn and stiff-necked people and punished their disobedience with forty years of wandering in the desert. Leadership is filled with difficult tasks and even more difficult people. Mentoring requires tough skin and tougher determination. Despite your best example, people will not always follow.

Talk with God

Give me the patience and the endurance to lead and mentor others successfully.

Live It. How can you live more Second today?
Tell It. How will you share what you have learned?

🐦 Tweet using #IAStough to share your thoughts.

Day 3: Courageous

Then Caleb silenced the people before Moses and said, "We should go up and take possession of the land, for we can certainly do it."

—**Numbers 13:30**

Read the whole passage in Numbers 13–14.

The Israelites were newly released slaves. They were not an army. They had few weapons, no training, and no experience on the battlefield. They spied out a rich and well-equipped land, complete with tall walls and chariots and men trained for war. Everyone said it could not be done. They could not walk into battle and hope for victory. Running away was their only logical course of action. But Caleb stood apart. He saw the same dangers and the same impossibilities, but he also saw that God was on their side, that God marched ahead of them. He let courage be his guide and faith be his motivation, and he voted to march forward into war. Courage is strength in the face of opposition and faith in the wake of the impossible. Leaders must see what others cannot and believe possible what others call foolishness. Do we live safe lives, or do we try the impossible for God?

Talk with God

God, give me the courage to pursue your mission boldly.

Live It. How can you live more Second today?
Tell It. How will you share what you have learned?

🐦 Tweet using #IAScourageous to share your thoughts.

Day 4: **Spiritual**

Lord, let your ear be attentive to the prayer of this your servant and to the prayer of your servants who delight in revering your name. Give your servant success today by granting him favor in the presence of this man.

—Nehemiah 1:11

Read the whole passage in Nehemiah 1:1–11.

Nehemiah learned of a problem and moved to fix that problem. But before he stepped out on his own, he talked with God. He asked for God's hand to aid him and his grace to surround him. Nehemiah knew his goals were too big to accomplish alone and too risky to attempt without God. Leaders are bold, but they are bold knowing that God walks beside them. They ask for his help and beg for his protection. They are crazy enough to try the impossible and faithful enough to trust that God can make it happen. They are risky enough to do what others refuse and smart enough to know that the spiritual world is as real and dangerous as the physical. Prayer and God's intervention are essential elements of their plans and crucial aspects of their leadership. Modeling a life of godly leadership means remembering God hears our prayers.

Talk with God

Make me into a person worth following and a leader worth multiplying.

Live It. How will you live more Second today?
Tell It. How will you share what you have learned?

🐦 Tweet using #IASspiritual to share your thoughts.

Day 5: Planner

"And may I have a letter to Asaph, keeper of the royal park, so he will give me timber to make beams for the gates of the citadel by the temple and for the city wall and for the residence I will occupy?" And because the gracious hand of my God was on me, the king granted my requests.

—Nehemiah 2:8

Read the whole passage in Nehemiah 2:1–20.

Nehemiah prayed and relied on God, but he also planned. He was ready and organized. He saw the dangers that lay ahead and prepared accordingly. He knew the supplies required, the relationships necessary, and the risks involved in his task. We tend to waver between always planning but never doing and always doing without ever preparing. Nehemiah knew the balance between the two. He thought ahead about the relationships and resources required to complete his task, but he also boldly stepped out when the time ripened. Leaders prepare. They see both things and people as crucial resources for every goal and work to acquire them both.

Talk with God

Give me the wisdom to know how best to plan and the faith to execute the plans you provide.

Live It. How will you live more Second today?
Tell It. How will you share what you have learned?

🐦 Tweet using #IASplanner to share your thoughts.

Day 6: **Recruiter**

When he came to Jerusalem, he tried to join the disciples, but they were all afraid of him, not believing that he really was a disciple. But Barnabas took him and brought him to the apostles.

—Acts 9:26–27

Read the whole passage in Acts 9:1–31.

Leaders believe in untapped potential and find talent in unusual places. They see possibilities in people that few recognize and fewer act on. They take risks, not just with money or with goals, but with people because they understand that people are the world's most valuable resource and a team's most treasured asset. They look past the doubts and worries of others and dig deep for the raw materials that make the leaders of the next generation. Leaders attract passion and energy, and they search for others who do the same. They are not afraid of mentoring those who will soon outpace them or quickly surpass them. Instead, they find such opportunity a welcome challenge and a happy exercise. They would rather become less so that others may become more, step down so others may step up. Leaders lead, but only long enough to develop the potential around them.

Talk with God

Give me the humility to make other leaders, not just more followers.

Live It. How will you live more Second today?
Tell It. How will you share what you have learned?

Tweet using #IASrecruiter to share your thoughts.

Day 7: Bold

Lᴏʀᴅ, the God of heaven, the great and awesome God, who keeps his covenant of love with those who love him and keep his commandments, let your ear be attentive and your eyes open to hear the prayer your servant is praying before you day and night for your servants, the people of Israel. I confess the sins we Israelites, including myself and my father's family, have committed against you. We have acted very wickedly toward you. We have not obeyed the commands, decrees and laws you gave your servant Moses. . . .

Lord, let your ear be attentive to the prayer of this your servant and to the prayer of your servants who delight in revering your name. Give your servant success today by granting him favor in the presence of this man.

—Nehemiah 1:5–7, 11

Nehemiah praised God, confessed sins, and spoke with humbleness and respect, but he also asked for big and bold things. He was not afraid to ask that God keep his promises, that God answer his prayers and use him to do great things. May our prayers be as bold.

Talk with God

Ask.

"Give your servant success . . ."
God, give me boldness to pursue your plans and grant me success as I step into leadership . . .

🐦 Tweet using #IASbold to share your prayers.

Day 1: First

Watch the Daniel Sepulveda Film

iamsecond.com/danielsepulveda

What did you like about, identify with, or learn from Daniel's story?

I wrote to the church, but Diotrephes, who loves to be first, will not welcome us.

—3 John 9

Read the whole passage in 3 John 1–14.

What It Says
1. What did you like about this passage?
2. What did you not like or find confusing about this passage?

What It Means
3. What does this passage teach about people?
4. What does this passage teach about God?

Live It. How will you live more Second today?
Tell It. How will you share what you have learned?

Practice It. Get with a friend or someone in your group. Practice or role-play your "Live and Tell" commitments.

Day 2: **Passive**

Barak said to her, "If you go with me, I will go; but if you don't go with me, I won't go."

—Judges 4:8

Read the whole passage in Judges 4:1–24.

Deborah looked across her country and found one thing lacking: leadership. No one stood against evil. No one raised the banner for good. No one charged forward to inspire greatness. Leaders were absent in the face of difficulty and unready on the dawn of opportunity. Fear and ineptitude ruled, while godliness and courage grew unpopular and unfamiliar. Barak had potential, opportunity, experience, and now a mission from God, but he too refused to face the task before him. Modeling leadership means living it, not just talking about it or preaching on it. Leadership is action, bold living in motion. To make great leaders, we must be great leaders. So let us rise together to be the leaders our world needs, to demonstrate the kind of bold, humble, and diligent servants our communities deserve.

Talk with God

Make me into the person and the leader you desire me to be.

Live It. How can you live more Second today?
Tell It. How will you share what you have learned?

🐦 Tweet using #IASpassive to share your thoughts.

Day 3: Unfaithful

Gideon made the gold into an ephod, which he placed in Ophrah, his town. All Israel prostituted themselves by worshiping it there, and it became a snare to Gideon and his family.

—Judges 8:27

Read the whole passage in Judges 8:22–28.

A vastly superior army invaded the land of Israel. But Gideon stood in the gap and marched a puny force to route the enemy in the name of God. But his career as a leader ended a dismal failure. He brought Israel from unbelief and confusion to faith in God. But he ended back where he started, and all of Israel prostituted itself by worshiping other gods. This is the price of unfaithfulness, of failing to finish the race, of stumbling along the way. We are all leaders. We lead our friends, our families, our coworkers, and our communities. Some of us have titles and official responsibilities to remind us of our role, but we all have a role. Leadership is influence, and all of us have it. All of us persuade and dissuade, encourage and discourage. We help and we hurt. We build and we tear down. We all lead. The question we must answer is, will we be faithful in the role we have been given?

Talk with God

Teach me to model faithful, consistent, and deliberate obedience to you.

Live It. How can you live more Second today?
Tell It. How will you share what you have learned?

🐦 Tweet using #IASunfaithful to share your thoughts.

Day 4: **Evil**

Thus God repaid the wickedness that Abimelek had done to his father by murdering his seventy brothers.

—Judges 9:56

Read the whole passage in Judges 9:1–57.

We all aim for good, for love and justice, for peace and harmony, but we somehow ruin it. We aim to enjoy a meal but end in gluttonous obsession. We dream of loving deeply but find ourselves bickering over triviality and cheating with wandering thoughts of discontent and unfaithfulness. Every action and every good deed are tainted with conflicting desires and uneven intentions. Great leaders do not ignore this native weakness in our hearts or the evil caged in our heads. We tame it and subdue. We refuse to bow our knee to it, to let it run wild through our minds or in our actions. We do not trust ourselves but the Spirit who resides within us. We do not listen to the lies in our heads but rather to the truth of the Bible. We follow Jesus and not our own desires.

Talk with God

Tame the evil in my heart. Turn my mind into a holy place and my heart into a sacred space. Make my actions reflect your goodness.

Live It. How will you live more Second today?
Tell It. How will you share what you have learned?

🐦 Tweet using #IASevil to share your thoughts.

Day 5: **Rash**

When he saw her, he tore his clothes and cried, "Oh no, my daughter! You have brought me down and I am devastated. I have made a vow to the LORD that I cannot break."

—**Judges 11:35**

Read the whole passage in Judges 11:1–40.

Boldness attempts great things for God. Rashness attempts great things on a whim. Courage jumps into the unknown with a goal in mind and a purpose at hand. Idiocy jumps into the unknown thinking it knows it all. God expects us to attempt the impossible but not without wisdom, the difficult but not without a willingness to learn and a readiness to adjust and grow. Too often we commit ourselves, our time, and our energy without first asking if God has a better plan, if he has a bigger goal. How often do we plan but not include the author of all plans? How often do we work without including the worker of all things? How often do we charge ahead never checking our progress, never measuring the results, and never learning from our mistakes?

Talk with God

God, help me learn from the rash decisions I have made in the past.

Live It. How will you live more Second today?
Tell It. How will you share what you have learned?

🐦 Tweet using #IASrash to share your thoughts.

Day 6: **Deceived**

So Delilah said to Samson, "Tell me the secret of your great strength and how you can be tied up and subdued."

—Judges 16:6

Read the whole passage in Judges 16:4–20.

Samson tinkered at greatness but indulged in decadence. His strength could slay armies and tear down enemy gates. He could have rescued his people from oppression and their enemies, but instead he thought of himself, of women and food and comfort. He thought about what he wanted and forgot about the plan that God had given. How easily we are deceived by the offerings of this world. We see a pretty face or smell tasty food or step into a beautiful house, and we forget that God offers so much more. Leaders must see past money, past titles and career, beyond the pleasures of this world, to a greater goal and a bigger promise. What we do matters, where we go people follow, how we live is copied by others, and the model we set will mark the lives of everyone around us, for good or ill. Let us set an example worthy of following.

Talk with God

God, keep me from being deceived by the pleasure that this world offers.

Live It. How will you live more Second today?
Tell It. How will you share what you have learned?

Tweet using #IASdeceived to share your thoughts.

Day 7: **Unguarded**

In the days of Shamgar son of Anath,
in the days of Jael, the highways were abandoned;
travelers took to winding paths.
Villagers in Israel would not fight;
they held back until I, Deborah, arose,
until I arose, a mother in Israel.
God chose new leaders
when war came to the city gates,
But not a shield or spear was seen
among forty thousand in Israel.
My heart is with Israel's princes,
with the willing volunteers among the people.
Praise the LORD!

—Judges 5:6–9

God is looking for ready volunteers, people ready to step into the unknown and sign up for his grand plan. It may not always be easy and the path may not always be clear, but one thing is sure: God is big enough and smart enough to make it all turn out in the end. Will you trust him?

Talk with God

Forgive.

"But not a shield or spear was seen . . ."
God, forgive me for my failures in leadership . . .

🐦 Tweet using #IASunguarded to share your prayers.

Day 1: Opportunity

Watch the Joe Gibbs Film

iamsecond.com/joegibbs

What did you like about, identify with, or learn from Joe's story?

Jesus was in the stern, sleeping on a cushion. The disciples woke him and said to him, "Teacher, don't you care if we drown?"

—Mark 4:38

Read the whole passage in Mark 4:35–41.

What It Says
1. What did you like about this passage?
2. What did you not like or find confusing about this passage?

What It Means
3. What does this passage teach about people?
4. What does this passage teach about God?

Live It. How will you live more Second today?
Tell It. How will you share what you have learned?

Practice It. Get with a friend or someone in your group. Practice or role-play your "Live and Tell" commitments.

Day 2: **Authority**

Calling the Twelve to him, he began to send them out two by two and gave them authority over impure spirits.

—Mark 6:7

Read the whole passage in Mark 6:6–13.

Nobody is ever ready for that first cruise down the street, for the first drive along the highway. We can read books about driving, learn every model of car, and watch the best drivers, but until we sit in the driver's seat, we are not ready to drive a car. Experience teaches in ways that lecture never can. Practice instructs in ways modeling never will. Even Jesus did not depend on modeling alone to teach his disciples. He gave them responsibilities and authority as they progressed, not fearing their failures or worrying about their inevitable mistakes. He would walk beside them, debrief and question them, pay close attention to their work, and assist them in their endeavors, but he still gave them the authority and opportunity to lead, to fail, and to grow. Making leaders means creating opportunity for others to shine and places for others to lead.

Talk with God

Make me a teacher who helps others succeed, a mentor who gives others the opportunity to shine.

Live It. How can you live more Second today?
Tell It. How will you share what you have learned?

Tweet using #IASauthority to share your thoughts.

Day 3: **Test**

When Jesus looked up and saw a great crowd coming toward him, he said to Philip, "Where shall we buy bread for these people to eat?" He asked this only to test him, for he already had in mind what he was going to do.

—John 6:5–6

Read the whole passage in John 6:1–15.

Tests shock us out of the ordinary and challenge us to grow. They push us to run faster and to think harder. Tests inspire and empower. A test might be an audience if public speaking terrifies us. A test might be watching a child if our patience is short or dieting if food rules our life. A test might be stepping out in faith if worry is our adversary or choosing to listen if blabbering is our habit. We each need different tests and different challenges, but we all need them. We need opportunities to stretch and windows of concentrated effort. A mentor knows the weaknesses of his disciples and challenges accordingly. When was the last time we tailor-made a test for someone in our lives, not something to frustrate or annoy those around us, but something to inspire them, to help them grow? When was the last time we cared enough to name a weakness and provide a challenge?

Talk with God

Help me be a catalyst of growth to those around me.

Live It. How can you live more Second today?
Tell It. How will you share what you have learned?

🐦 Tweet using #IAStest to share your thoughts.

Day 4: Patience

His disciples answered, "But where in this remote place can anyone get enough bread to feed them?"

—Mark 8:4

Read the whole passage in Mark 8:1–13.

Jesus had fed five thousand hungry people, but now he faced another crowd on another day with the same need. Would his disciples remember his previous act? Would they recall the mass feeding and public miracle? Would they pray that heaven would rain down bread or that the sea would pour out its fishy contents? Would they trust Jesus to multiply the loaves or make cakes from the dust? No. They would not. They forgot the lesson. Jesus' previous miracle was lost on their slow minds, his demonstration wasted on their unseeing eyes. He set up the same problem and asked them the same question, gave them opportunity for the same faith, but they failed. Patience was his answer. Repetition and gracious reiteration was his response. What is our response to others when they fail? What is our reaction when lessons are forgotten and faith is lost? Do we lash out or give grace, show annoyance or patience? When we teach and mentor, we must not be surprised at slow growth and failed attempts, of two steps forward and one back.

Talk with God

Give me the patience to teach even when my words are forgotten, as you have so faithfully demonstrated with me.

Live It. How will you live more Second today?
Tell It. How will you share what you have learned?

🐦 Tweet using #IASpatience to share your thoughts.

Day 5: Question

"But what about you?" he asked. "Who do you say I am?"
—Matthew 16:15

Read the whole passage in Matthew 16:13–20.

Humility comes in many shapes. Rarely does it look weak or desperate, mild or indecisive; rather it shows itself in a willingness to learn and a desire to hear others. It asks questions rather than shout answers. It fosters conversation and discussion rather than lecture and lopsided dialogue. It seeks answers through query and discourse and gives others the opportunity to learn alongside. Meekness is not weakness but patience tied with strength and kindness bound with sternness. Jesus had no need for questions, but he often gave more of them than he did answers. He was willing to let others develop their own thoughts and dig around for their own conclusions. What does our teaching look like? How different is ours from his? What is our question-to-answer ratio? Do we pride ourselves in being the Bible-answer person or in being the question-challenge-motivate person? Do we look like Jesus?

Talk with God

Teach me the humility of Jesus, his willingness to ask questions, and his ability to listen.

Live It. How will you live more Second today?
Tell It. How will you share what you have learned?

🐦 Tweet using #IASquestion to share your thoughts.

Day 6: **Correct**

Jesus turned and said to Peter, "Get behind me, Satan! You are a stumbling block to me; you do not have in mind the concerns of God, but merely human concerns."

—Matthew 16:23

Read the whole passage in Matthew 16:21–28.

Our failure to correct and confront often has more to do with self-preservation than love. We tell ourselves that we want to preserve peace or avoid hurting people's feelings. But really we just don't want our own feelings hurt or have our own relational comfort disturbed. We talk about not judging or interfering, but when our wants are delayed or our rights violated, we are all too quick to straighten someone out. Yet Jesus was as quick to give praise as he was correction, honest criticism as kind grace. Fire and brimstone did not always rain from his mouth, but they did fall when appropriate. *Confrontation* is not a dirty word. Awkward conversations and hard talks are not from the devil. They are tools that bring realization and awareness, healing and healthy behavior. We are our brother's keeper and our sister's protector. We are obligated to help each other grow and to challenge each other to stay strong. And that means having the occasional difficult conversation and intervention.

Talk with God

Give me the tact to confront lovingly and the courage to correct faithfully.

Live It. How will you live more Second today?
Tell It. How will you share what you have learned?

🐦 Tweet using #IAScorrect to share your thoughts.

Day 7: Glory

Ascribe to the LORD, you heavenly beings,
ascribe to the LORD glory and strength.
Ascribe to the LORD the glory due his name;
worship the LORD in the splendor of his holiness.
The voice of the LORD is over the waters;
the God of glory thunders,
the LORD thunders over the mighty waters.
The voice of the LORD is powerful;
the voice of the LORD is majestic. . . .
And in his temple all cry, "Glory!"
The LORD sits enthroned over the flood;
the LORD is enthroned as King forever.
The LORD gives strength to his people;
the LORD blesses his people with peace.

—Psalm 29:1–4, 9–11

God is bigger than all our dreams, grander than all our plans. Nothing can defend against his might, nothing can stand in his way. God deserves to be praised simply because he is God. He made everything, rules everything, and is the source of all existence.

Talk with God

Worship.

". . . glory and strength . . ."
God, I worship you because . . .

🐦 Tweet using #IASglory to share your prayers.

Day 1: Entrust

Watch the Jerry Zucha Film

iamsecond.com/jerryzucha

What did you like about, identify with, or learn from Jerry's story?

> *After Paul and Silas came out of the prison, they went to Lydia's house, where they met with the brothers and sisters and encouraged them. Then they left.*
>
> **—Acts 16:40**

Read the whole passage in Acts 16:6–40

What It Says
1. What did you like about this passage?
2. What did you not like or find confusing about this passage?

What It Means
3. What does this passage teach about people?
4. What does this passage teach about God?

Live It. How will you live more Second today?
Tell It. How will you share what you have learned?

Practice It. Get with a friend or someone in your group. Practice or role-play your "Live and Tell" commitments.

Day 2: Comfort

Now I want you to know, brothers and sisters, that what has happened to me has actually served to advance the gospel.

—Philippians 1:12

Read the whole passage in Philippians 1:12–30.

The Philippians saw their mentor and founder wrongly imprisoned and the advance of their cause seemingly threatened. Discouragement set in, and fear raised its voice. Disillusionment occurs when our dreams and expectations meet the difficulty of reality. We know God is all-powerful, that our message is true and our intention sincere, but not everybody listens. Some scoff at our convictions. Others mock our lifestyle and choices. Clouds of doubt and fear can begin to overwhelm. The answer is not to ignore doubt or hide discouragement, but to admit its power and acknowledge its existence. We will find that in naming discouragement we deprive it of its power and strip it of the loneliness it creates. Training leaders and mentoring others will always require a dose of encouragement and a well-timed word of comfort. Whom do we need to encourage today?

Talk with God

Father, give me words of encouragement, the ability to identify doubt and release its grip on others.

Live It. How can you live more Second today?
Tell It. How will you share what you have learned?

🐦 Tweet using #IAScomfort to share your thoughts.

Day 3: Guide

Therefore, my dear friends, as you have always obeyed—not only in my presence, but now much more in my absence . . .

—Philippians 2:12

Read the whole passage in Philippians 2:1–18.

A tour guide does not force people to follow him or demand that people obey his directions. But a guide has walked the route before, and his experience has won him the right to speak. His voice carries wisdom because of his experience, and his gait shows confidence because of his knowledge. Likewise, Paul did not demand people's allegiance, but he still gained their loyalty. He did not demand respect, but he earned it. He did not command obedience, but people gave it. He taught them what he knew and carried people along on his journey. He was not afraid to point out pitfalls or to identify dangerous parts of the path. We are all tour guides in a sense. We may not know everything, but we can walk people through where we have gone before. We may not have all the answers, but we know where the pitfalls lie; we have learned many of life's difficult paths. We are a guide to those who follow behind.

Talk with God

Make me a guide who warns weary travelers and watches over struggling sojourners.

Live It. How can you live more Second today?
Tell It. How will you share what you have learned?

🐦 Tweet using #IASguide to share your thoughts.

Day 4: Visit

I hope in the Lord Jesus to send Timothy to you soon, that I also may be cheered when I receive news about you.

—Philippians 2:19

Read the whole passage in Philippians 2:19–30.

People need people. Books and podcasts can only go so far. Websites and blogs can only teach so much. Information is cheap. Anyone can look up answers online or dig around in books and find pithy statements of cheer and cleverness. But to really develop as people, to grow as individuals, and to learn as disciples of Jesus, we need each other. We need one-on-one interaction, personal involvement. We need time. We can easily smother someone by not letting them alone, by doing it all for them, by constantly assisting and never watching, but we can also fail to properly watch, to personally engage. We often think we can do life alone, but we cannot. None of us can. Life was meant to be lived together. Growth happens best and most quickly with the personal and occasional oversight of mentors.

Talk with God

Teach me to walk the line between always assisting and never watching. Teach me to personally engage without overmanaging.

Live It. How will you live more Second today?
Tell It. How will you share what you have learned?

🐦 Tweet using #IASvisit to share your thoughts.

Day 5: **Safeguard**

Watch out for those dogs, those evildoers, those mutilators of the flesh.

—Philippians 3:2

Read the whole passage in Philippians 3:1–11.

Some insist that they cannot tell others how to live because they have made the same mistakes. But if we stepped on a land mine, would we not tell others to beware? If we stuck our hand on a stove, would we not warn others of the danger? We know these truths in the physical world. Why can't we transfer them to the spiritual and moral as well? After all, moral failure can bring more dangerous consequences than losing a leg or scarring our hands. A person can still be president and require a wheelchair, but he gets impeached if he lies to the grand jury. A person can run companies and build empires and have a physical disfigurement, but pride and vanity and moral indiscretion can topple even the most powerful leaders. How could we better safeguard the spiritual and moral lives of those around us? How could we prevent disaster rather than wait to clean it up?

Talk with God

Give me the strength to have this difficult conversation with a friend or loved one.

Live It. How will you live more Second today?
Tell It. How will you share what you have learned?

🐦 Tweet using #IASsafeguard to share your thoughts.

Day 6: Thank

Yet it was good of you to share in my troubles. Moreover, as you Philippians know, in the early days of your acquaintance with the gospel, when I set out from Macedonia, not one church shared with me in the matter of giving and receiving, except you only.

—Philippians 4:14–15

Read the whole passage in Philippians 4:1–21.

A kind thank-you speaks volumes. It is more than manners or a habit our mothers taught us. It is a heartfelt appreciation for the kindness and love of another human being. When we fail to recognize the efforts of others, we not only display rudeness, but we fail to reinforce the good behavior and moral success of others. Encouragement is more than quoting cute proverbs or popular Bible verses; it is recognizing the specific and tangible strengths of others. It is thanking them for their contributions to our lives and to the kingdom in which we serve. Thanks may come with a firm handshake or teary eyes, a quick note or a public award, but whatever form it takes, thankfulness is important to practice. Whom might we thank today for the impact they have made?

Talk with God

I thank you for your work in my life. I praise you for all you have given me and all you have planned ahead.

Live It. How will you live more Second today?
Tell It. How will you share what you have learned?

🐦 Tweet using #IASthank to share your thoughts.

Day 7: **Pray For**

I thank my God every time I remember you. In all my prayers for all of you, I always pray with joy because of your partnership in the gospel from the first day until now, being confident of this, that he who began a good work in you will carry it on to completion until the day of Christ Jesus.

It is right for me to feel this way about all of you, since I have you in my heart and, whether I am in chains or defending and confirming the gospel, all of you share in God's grace with me. God can testify how I long for all of you with the affection of Christ Jesus.

And this is my prayer: that your love may abound more and more in knowledge and depth of insight, so that you may be able to discern what is best and may be pure and blameless for the day of Christ, filled with the fruit of righteousness that comes through Jesus Christ—to the glory and praise of God.

—Philippians 1:3–11

Let our love for each other prompt our prayers. Let our concern for one another inspire our conversations with God. We are called to love practically, to sacrifice our own comforts and possessions for the sake of others. But we are also called to love prayerfully, to consider others when we talk with God, to pray for others and not just ourselves.

Talk with God

Ask.

"**. . . that** your love may abound . . ."
God, help these people abound more in love . . .

🐦 Tweet using #IASprayfor to share your prayers.

Day 1: Journey

Watch the Kathy Ireland Film

iamsecond.com/kathyireland

What did you like about, identify with, or learn from Kathy's story?

It will be like a man going on a journey, who called his servants and entrusted his wealth to them.

—Matthew 25:14

Read the whole passage in Matthew 25:14–30.

What It Says
1. What did you like about this passage?
2. What did you not like or find confusing about this passage?

What It Means
3. What does this passage teach about people?
4. What does this passage teach about God?

Live It. How will you live more Second today?
Tell It. How will you share what you have learned?

Practice It. Get with a friend or someone in your group. Practice or role-play your "Live and Tell" commitments.

Day 2: **Sheep-Care**

Jesus said, "Feed my lambs."

—**John 21:15**

Read the whole passage in John 21:15–17.

We are all sheep following the same shepherd. We do not always reason to our benefit or behave in our best interest. We need prodding and leadership. We need consequences and tough love. But we are all tasked both to be sheep and to herd sheep. We are instructed to watch out for our fellow brothers and sisters. Though we are lambs, some of us walk a few paces ahead. None of us claims to have all the answers or to carry the shepherd's staff, only that we know some things that others do not and have experienced some things that others still have yet to see. This qualifies us to lead. Peter certainly felt underqualified, even disqualified, to lead and speak for Jesus. But he had walked with Jesus closer and heard him more and loved him longer—and because of that simple truth he was qualified. We all qualify for some kind of leadership. The things we have learned and put to practice entitle us to be teachers of those things. We do not have to wait for someone to receive a diploma or earn a title to exercise leadership.

Talk with God

Help me see the potential for leadership in everyone.

Live It. How can you live more Second today?

Tell It. How will you share what you have learned?

🐦 Tweet using #IASsheepcare to share your thoughts.

Day 3: Sacrifice

Feed my sheep. Very truly I tell you, when you were younger you dressed yourself and went where you wanted; but when you are old you will stretch out your hands, and someone else will dress you and lead you where you do not want to go.

—John 21:17–18

Read the whole passage in John 21:17–22.

We cannot send out disciples who think that the world is full of easy roads and well-marked highways. Those we mentor must know that our road is not easy. It will have its moments of peace and comfort, but we walk the road less traveled. Low-hanging branches, thorny briars, and fallen logs obstruct our path. Storms will wash out the bridges, and fog will cover our eyes. Sacrifice will be the norm, not the exception. If we find the road always easy or the path always well marked, then perhaps we do not journey the road that leads to eternal reward. Before anyone leaves our tutoring, they must know that neither choice should be taken lightly: one road leads comfortably to eternal punishment, but the other offers a lifetime of challenge and sacrifice only later to be rewarded.

Talk with God

Father, teach me to be ready for the tough road that lies ahead and to prepare others for same hardships I may face.

Live It. How can you live more Second today?
Tell It. How will you share what you have learned?

🐦 Tweet using #IASsacrifice to share your thoughts.

Day 4: **Job**

*The reason I left you in Crete was that you might put in order
what was left unfinished and appoint elders in every town,
as I directed you.*

—Titus 1:5

Read the whole passage in Titus 1:1–16.

Most of us who grew up in this faith, who went to church as kids
or went to youth camp as teenagers, know that church is generally
a place to sit. A few may stand on the stage and exercise their gifts,
but most are only allowed to watch. We say we want involvement;
we hope everyone participates and joins in. But there can only be so
many guitar players or speakers or singers or greeters or parking lot
attendants. And when those slots are filled, the rest of us sit idly by
and watch as others "do church." But disciple making must be different. It requires that tasks be assigned, that a job be fulfilled. We
cannot grow in our faith by sitting, and we cannot hope to breach
the gates of hell while twiddling our thumbs. Disciple making is
about much more than lecturing. It is about training people for a
mission and then sending them out to accomplish that mission.

Talk with God

Let me inspire people to join, to equip people to fulfill their call,
and send them out to tear down the kingdom of Satan.

Live It. How will you live more Second today?
Tell It. How will you share what you have learned?

🐦 Tweet using #IASjob to share your thoughts.

Day 5: **Sound Doctrine**

You, however, must teach what is appropriate to sound doctrine.

—Titus 2:1

Read the whole passage in Titus 2:1–15.

Milk is appropriate for a time. Applesauce and pureed squash are suitable for a certain period of childhood development. But we must not be content to let mature people survive on such meager diets. Roasted meats and skewered shrimp and chicken pot pie should be the mainstay of our meals. Our spiritual diet is no different. It is important for people to drink the milk of the gospel, the foundation of our faith, the story of Jesus and his sacrifice. But we also must push people to address the issues of gluttony and materialism, to face sexual temptation and pride, not to run from confrontation or be ruled by anger. We must teach the doctrines and practices of our faith, not just the building blocks. We must require maturity and sound teaching, not just a ticket out of hell. We must prepare people for our departure and their own day of judgment. We must remember that we will not be coddling them when God requires their accounts.

Talk with God

Give me the foresight to push people to maturity and to prepare them for their day of reckoning.

Live It. How will you live more Second today?
Tell It. How will you share what you have learned?

🐦 Tweet using #IASsounddoctrine to share your thoughts.

Day 6: Mature

At one time we too were foolish, disobedient, deceived and enslaved by all kinds of passions and pleasures. We lived in malice and envy, being hated and hating one another.

—Titus 3:3

Read the whole passage in Titus 3:1–15.

A disciple maker must be organized with his relational investments and careful with his mentoring energy. We model to all; our families, our friends, our coworkers, and our classmates—the whole world sees the manner of our lives. But we personally engage with only a few. We assist and watch over only a handful. Even the master trainer, Jesus himself, regularly engaged with only twelve. But eleven of those twelve went on change the world. Jesus poured himself into learners, into those who progressed, whose lives reformed and changed. They were once foolish and disobedient and enslaved to pleasure, like the rest of us, but the difference with Jesus and the difference with Paul is that they invested most in those who obeyed most, who changed the most, and who pushed to grow and evolve.

Talk with God

Make me a disciple worthy of your investment and a disciple-maker following in your steps.

Live It. How will you live more Second today?
Tell It. How will you share what you have learned?

🐦 Tweet using #IASmature to share your thoughts.

Day 7: **Kept**

To him who is able to keep you from stumbling and to present you before his glorious presence without fault and with great joy—to the only God our Savior be glory, majesty, power and authority, through Jesus Christ our Lord, before all ages, now and forevermore! Amen.

—**Jude 24–25**

Prayer offers an avenue of protection unavailable by other means. Our conversations with God can bring strength and wisdom not found anywhere else. If we forget to prayer for our brothers and sisters, if we fail to come to God with their struggles and difficulties then we leave them without an essential blanket of protection.

Talk with God

Protect.

"**. . . keep** you from stumbling . . ."
God, protect these people from stumbling . . .

Tweet using #IASkept to share your prayers.

Go Local

Weeks 40–43
Week 40: Jerusalem
Week 41: Word and Deed
Week 42: Where God Sends
Week 43: Paul's Plan

It is in our local communities where our light will shine the brightest, our families and friends who are most likely to hear our message. Going local means strategically and thoughtfully approaching our own network of relationships in the hopes of reaching them with the message of Jesus. While all of us must participate in reaching the ends of the earth, in bringing the message of Jesus to every people on the planet, our efforts will most naturally concentrate with those people we already know. We do not need to travel the globe to find a lost soul or leave our city to find a person searching for God. Our local communities and our own networks of friends and family are ripe areas for harvest.

Day 1: Local

Watch the Brant Hansen Film

  iamsecond.com/branthansen

What did you like about, identify with, or learn from Brant's story?

But you will receive power when the Holy Spirit comes on you; and you will be my witnesses in Jerusalem, and in all Judea and Samaria, and to the ends of the earth.

—Acts 1:8

Read the whole passage in Acts 1:1–11.

What It Says
1. What did you like about this passage?
2. What did you not like or find confusing about this passage?

What It Means
3. What does this passage teach about people?
4. What does this passage teach about God?

Live It. What is your local mission? Who will you reach out to in your community? Your friends, workplace, school, neighborhood, a certain demographic, or a group with specific needs (alcoholics, homeless, etc.)?

Tell It. Who else needs to hear about your desire to reach this group?

Practice It. Gather your friends and make a plan as a group. Go through this week's challenges together to develop a plan and make an impact in your community.

Day 2: **Dream**

If it pleases the king and if your servant has found favor in his sight, let him send me to the city in Judah where my fathers are buried so that I can rebuild it.

—Nehemiah 2:5

Read the whole passage in Nehemiah 1:1–2:5.

Nehemiah understood his community needed rebuilding, that its broken walls were a symbol of broken people. He dared to dream of rebuilding those walls, despite the impossible hurdles and the sure headaches that lay ahead. What does your community need? What wall needs rebuilding in your city or neighborhood? How big can you dream?

Talk with God

God, give me your dream for my community. What would you like to see happen in my local area?

Live It. Have a "Dream Session." Get two large pieces of paper and markers. Draw two different pictures on each piece of paper. On the first piece of paper draw a picture that represents the challenges the community faces. On another sheet draw a picture that represents your dreams and hopes for the community.

Tell It. Discuss these pictures and their meaning for you with your group. What elements or images are in these pictures? Why have you included each of these images? What do you want your community to look like?

For more ideas, talk with other I am Second groups in your area or go to www.iamsecond.com/volunteer.

Tweet using #IASdream to share your dreams.

Day 3: Plan

By night I went out through the Valley Gate toward the Jackal Well and the Dung Gate, examining the wall of Jerusalem.

—Nehemiah 2:13

Read the whole passage in Nehemiah 2:6–16.

Nehemiah knew what he needed before he asked. He knew he needed the king's permission, time off from work, safe-conduct to the land, and timber to rebuild the wall. He examined everything carefully and planned what he could before beginning his task. What plans might you need to make before pursuing a dream for you community?

Talk with God

Father, you have blessed our community with a host of resources. Give us the wisdom to know the best way to use what you have given us.

Live It. Have a "Planning Session." Get a large piece of paper and brainstorm what resources your community has that could help make your dream come true.

Tell It. Discuss these resources and their potential with your group. What resources are the most obvious fit for your goals? How might you gain access to these resources? Who else needs to be included in your group to help make your dream come true?

For more ideas, talk with other I am Second groups in your area or go to www.iamsecond.com/volunteer.

🐦 Tweet using #IASplan to share your plans.

Day 4: **Organize**

*Then I said to them, "You see the trouble we are in:
Jerusalem lies in ruins, and its gates have been burned with
fire. Come, let us rebuild the wall of Jerusalem."*

—Nehemiah 2:17

Read the whole passage in Nehemiah 2:17–20.

Time to recruit. Getting the right people on the team for any project no matter how big or small is absolutely essential. If you have a dream for your community, a picture of what you hope it can become, then find people who share your passion and who can partner with you in making that dream come true.

Talk with God

Bring the right people at the right time to do the right tasks so that your dream for our community will come true.

Live It. Have a "Team Session." Identify who in your community is the eyes, ears, heart, hands, etc.
Tell It. What experiences or stories have you heard that made you choose these people? How can you include these people in your dream?

For more ideas, talk with other I am Second groups in your area or go to www.iamsecond.com/volunteer.

🐦 Tweet using #IASorganize to tell us about your team.

Day 5: Interest

They all plotted together to come and fight against Jerusalem and stir up trouble against it. But we prayed to our God and posted a guard day and night to meet this threat.

—Nehemiah 4:8–9

Read the whole passage in Nehemiah 4:1–23.

Not everyone will see your dream the same. Some will have an interest in seeing it success, others in seeing it fail. Think through the kind of people that may have an interest (good or ill) in your dream for your community.

Talk with God

Hardship and opposition will surely come. Father, prepare us to face whatever lies ahead.

Live It. Have an "Interest Session." Get a large piece of paper. List out all of the people or kinds of people who will have an interest in your dream. Who might be the beneficiaries, opponents, or decision makers?

Tell It. Discuss these people with your group. Which groups will you inform, consult, partner with, or monitor? How can you prepare for opposition?

For more ideas, talk with other I am Second groups in your area or go to www.iamsecond.com/volunteer.

🐦 Tweet using #IASinterest to share your thoughts.

Day 6: Celebrate

At the dedication of the wall of Jerusalem, the Levites were sought out from where they lived and were brought to Jerusalem to celebrate joyfully the dedication with songs of thanksgiving and with the music of cymbals, harps and lyres.

—Nehemiah 12:27

Read the whole passage in Nehemiah 12:27–43.

What will you celebrate? What goals will you aim at? If you really want to see God do big things in your community, you must know what it is you are asking God to do. Take some time and think through what specific goals or successes are required for your dream to come true for your community.

Talk with God

We praise you for what you have planned ahead of us and celebrate what lies in the future.

Live It. Have a "Goals Session." Get a piece of paper. Draw a series of pictures that represent the different steps or stages of your plan.

Tell It. Discuss what tasks, meetings, work dates, projects, measurable goals, or victories you foresee in the future. What might the timeline for each of these steps be? How can you celebrate the completion of each of these steps?

🐦 Tweet using #IAScelebrate to share your victories.

Day 7: **Walls**

I rejoiced with those who said to me,
*"Let us go to the house of the L*ORD*."*
Our feet are standing
in your gates, Jerusalem.
Jerusalem is built like a city
that is closely compacted together.
That is where the tribes go up—
*the tribes of the L*ORD*—*
*to praise the name of the L*ORD
according to the statute given to Israel.
There stand the thrones for judgment,
the thrones of the house of David.
Pray for the peace of Jerusalem:
"May those who love you be secure.
May there be peace within your walls
and security within your citadels."
For the sake of my family and friends,
I will say, "Peace be within you."
*For the sake of the house of the L*ORD *our God,*
I will seek your prosperity.

—Psalm 122

God is concerned about your community. He cares what goes on in your neighborhood and city. Ask him about his hopes for your community. Talk with God about the real issues affecting your community.

Talk with God

Ask.

"For the sake of my family and friends . . ."
God, I pray for my local community . . .

Tweet using #IASwalls to share your prayers.

Day 1: Good and Gospel

Watch the Tyrone Flowers Film

iamsecond.com/tyroneflowers

What did you like about, identify with, or learn from Tyrone's story?

> *The blind receive sight, the lame walk, those who have leprosy are cleansed, the deaf hear, the dead are raised, and the good news is proclaimed to the poor.*
>
> **—Luke 7:22**

Read the whole passage in Luke 7:11–23.

What It Says
1. What did you like about this passage?
2. What did you not like or find confusing about this passage?

What It Means
3. What does this passage teach about people?
4. What does this passage teach about God?

Live It. How will you live more Second today?
Tell It. How will you share what you have learned?

Practice It. Get with a friend or someone in your group. Practice or role-play your "Live and Tell" commitments.

Day 2: In Chains

I appeal to you for my son Onesimus, who became my son while I was in chains.

—Philemon 10

Read the whole passage in Philemon 1–25.

Jesus changes things. Onesimus was Philemon's slave. But Paul made a challenge—not a command, not a requirement, but a bold ask that a legal right be ignored and a culturally accepted practice be stopped. That is the effect of the gospel, the message of Jesus. The poor find empowerment, the oppressed find a voice, and slaves find freedom. All the evils of our world began with sin, our attempt at deity and self-rule. But when God becomes First, when we put him where he belongs, his interests and his plans ahead of our own, then everything begins to change. The things we once saw as normal now seem terrible. What we once participated in or were applauded for now we hate. But our cultural baggage is heavy and its blinders strong. What injustice still finds a home in our communities? What inequality still evades our capture? What lie do we continue to believe?

Talk with God

Help me look through the fog of my culture to see the evils that I harbor and the injustices that I ignore.

Live It. How can you live more Second today?
Tell It. How will you share what you have learned?

🐦 Tweet using #IASinchains to share your thoughts.

Day 3: Real Fix

Were not all ten cleansed? Where are the other nine?

—Luke 17:17

Read the whole passage in Luke 17:11–21.

Warm bread does not end poverty, and new laws do not end hatred. The evil and injustices of our world continue despite our best efforts because a deeper problem exists. Our world is haunted by poverty and prejudice, by corruption and destruction, because the world has not yet given up its rebellion. We can heal lepers or feed hungry mouths, but unless hearts are changed, unless the issues are addressed, then the broken systems that produce these tragedies will continue to flourish. Jesus offered healing and gave humanitarian aid, but he also never neglected to offer the true fix for our problems, the true answer to our ailments. Let us never forget his example, his lead in offering tangible and intangible cures, physical and spiritual solutions.

Talk with God

God, I commit to love this world with both word and deed, with both physical aid and spiritual medicine.

Live It. How can you live more Second today?
Tell It. How will you share what you have learned?

Tweet using #IASrealfix to share your thoughts.

Day 4: Poor

Truly I tell you, it is hard for someone who is rich to enter the kingdom of heaven.

—Matthew 19:23

Read the whole passage in Matthew 19:16–26.

Each of us reading this page has the wealth of an education. Each of us with access to clean water is among the world's richest. We often look on the poor as less fortunate, and in many ways they are. The poor have limited access to health care, education, and more. But they also possess something most of us never will: a sense of need and an understanding that our world is broken. The rich do not need God to feed their families or heal their children. They do not need God to fix their world or save their countries. They can do it themselves. God has no place in most of their daily tasks or weekly goals. But the poor know this world offers no lasting hope. While many of us delude ourselves into trusting money, the poor have never tasted such temptation. So before we dump our false faith in money into the homes of poor villagers or the streets of poor neighborhoods, let us ask what we can give beyond just our money.

Talk with God

Whether I am rich or poor, teach me to always depend on you and teach others to do the same.

Live It. How will you live more Second today?
Tell It. How will you share what you have learned?

Tweet using #IASpoor to share your thoughts.

Day 5: Money

No one can serve two masters. Either you will hate the one and love the other, or you will be devoted to the one and despise the other. You cannot serve both God and money.

—Luke 16:13

Read the whole passage in Luke 16:1–13.

Our money is tied to our hearts. It reveals our true loyalty and first love. If we hoard it, we tell of our distrust of God's promise. If we waste it, we shout of our disregard of his kingdom. If we spend it on houses, cars, or fancy clothes, we speak of our attachment to this world. But our money can also tell a different story. We can enrich ourselves to enrich our world and advance his kingdom. We can invest in serving the poor and helping the widows, in caring for orphans and empowering the oppressed. We can finance the telling of Jesus' story and the spread of his message. We can spend to love our neighbors, or we can spend to love ourselves. We can build our own kingdom, or we can invest in his. The choice is ours. We can serve one or the other. What is our money saying about our lives?

Talk with God

Make me a wise investor. Teach me to view my money as a trust dedicated to your ends, not a slush fund for my own whims and fancies.

Live It. How will you live more Second today?
Tell It. How will you share what you have learned?

Tweet using #IASmoney to share your thoughts.

Day 6: Lazarus

Son, remember that in your lifetime you received your good things, while Lazarus received bad things, but now he is comforted here and you are in agony.

—Luke 16:25

Read the whole passage in Luke 16:19–31.

Wealth provides great opportunity and great danger. With it we can move mountains and reform cities; we can bring change and promote love, spread the message of Jesus or demonstrate his goodness. But wealth can also blind, give confidence when none is warranted, and teach pride when none is appropriate. It can make us feel self-sufficient though God sustains us all, invulnerable though death will strip us all bare. We are each given one life to show our mettle and determine our destiny, one chance to choose our side. We can sit back and enjoy the pleasures of this world, or we can push for eternal rewards. God wants our words to speak of his greatness and our money to reveal his love. He does not want one without the other. He desires both word and deed.

Talk with God

I ask for riches but only to advance your kingdom, for wealth but only to steward your investment.

Live It. How will you live more Second today?
Tell It. How will you share what you have learned?

🐦 Tweet using #IASlazarus to share your thoughts.

Day 7: Reward

Yes, my soul, find rest in God;
my hope comes from him.
Truly he is my rock and my salvation;
he is my fortress, I will not be shaken.
My salvation and my honor depend on God;
he is my mighty rock, my refuge.
Trust in him at all times, you people;
pour out your hearts to him,
for God is our refuge.
One thing God has spoken . . .
two things I have heard:
"Power belongs to you, God,
and with you, Lord, is unfailing love";
and, "You reward everyone
according to what they have done."

—Psalm 62:5–8, 11–12

God rewards everyone for what they have done. Some of those rewards will come in this life. But the ultimate judgment and the final rewards will be when we enter the next life. We will give an account for what we have done with our lives and the resources we have been given. What would we surrender to God now, if we knew we would stand before him tomorrow?

Talk with God

Surrender.

"You reward everyone according to what they have done," **God, I** commit my money, my resources, my time, my wealth to you . . .

Tweet using #IASreward to share your prayers.

Day 1: Tomorrow

Watch the Tony Dungy Film

  iamsecond.com/tonydungy

What did you like about, identify with, or learn from Tony's story?

> *Instead, you ought to say, "If it is the Lord's will, we will live and do this or that."*
>
> **—James 4:15**

Read the whole passage in James 4:13–16.

What It Says
1. What did you like about this passage?
2. What did you not like or find confusing about this passage?

What It Means
3. What does this passage teach about people?
4. What does this passage teach about God?

Live It. How will you live more Second today?
Tell It. How will you share what you have learned?

Practice It. Get with a friend or someone in your group. Practice or role-play your "Live and Tell" commitments.

Day 2: **Heaven-Sent**

For I have come down from heaven not to do my will but to do the will of him who sent me.

—John 6:38

Read the whole passage in John 6:30–59.

Jesus' mission was not his own but that of his Father's. He did not invent his life's path or negotiate his life's goal. He knew his role and pursued that end. Sometimes we forget that God has a plan for each us, a heavenly mission for all of us to complete. To some he speaks directly, appearing in dreams or while in prayer, but to many his plans are revealed through long hours in the Bible or deep discussions with friends and family, through opportunity or natural ability. To all he says, "Go and make disciples"; to some he tells where or to whom. To all he says, "Love your neighbor"; to some he provides blueprints and strategy. But whether God gives us the specifics or only the principles, our mission still stands and our goal still exists. Will we obey our heavenly call?

Talk with God

Guide my life toward the goals you have planned and my years toward the mission you have commanded.

Live It. How can you live more Second today?
Tell It. How will you share what you have learned?

🐦 Tweet using #IASheavensent to share your thoughts.

Day 3: **Enabled**

This is why I told you that no one can come to me unless the Father has enabled them.

—John 6:65

Read the whole passage in John 6:60–65.

Jeremiah toiled in vain. Isaiah shouted at deaf ears. Ezekiel displayed his message to a blind audience. Micah, Zephaniah, Malachi, and the rest of the prophets of the Bible spoke to crowds who did not care and people who would not listen. They died in exile, in torture chambers, and in prisons. They pursued their missions never seeing their completion. But success is measured in obedience, not in conversions. This does not excuse ignorance or ineptitude, foolishness or wastefulness, but when we give our finest, plan our hardest, and work our best, God is content. The results are his to manage and his to judge. Hearts turn only at his voice and only with his aid. So while we are called to share his message and make disciples, only he empowers the success of our work.

Talk with God

I ask that you give me success as I share your story, not for my own pride, but so you will be praised even more loudly.

Live It. How can you live more Second today?
Tell It. How will you share what you have learned?

🐦 Tweet using #IASenabled to share your thoughts.

Day 4: **Message**

At once he began to preach in the synagogues that Jesus is the Son of God.

—Acts 9:20

Read the whole passage in Acts 9:19–31.

We are sent with a very specific message. Jesus, the Son of God, came down from heaven and was born a baby. He lived among us but escaped the stain of sin and the mark of any error. He preached the way to God but was rejected and hated, despised and crucified on a cross. He died to offer forgiveness, suffered to take our place. He conquered death so we could have life. He died, but three days later he rose again. And for all who believe in this story and trust in this Jesus, God offers forgiveness and life, a relationship with him and a place in his kingdom. This is the good news we carry and the message we herald. We may talk about self-esteem and business management. We may discuss solutions to poverty and answers to the world's ailments or a host of other topics, but this core message must never cease to leave our lips. It should constantly drip through our conversations and bleed out of our lives.

Talk with God

God, make me ever more persistent in telling your story and sharing your message.

Live It. How will you live more Second today?
Tell It. How will you share what you have learned?

🐦 Tweet using #IASmessage to share your thoughts.

Day 5: Boatless

"Come, follow me," Jesus said, *"and I will send you out to fish for people."*

—**Matthew 4:19**

Read the whole passage in Matthew 4:18–22.

We are fishers of people and seekers of lost souls. We do not let worry trample our spirits or fatigue dampen our efforts. We are not slowed by the storms of life or confused by the winds of our culture. We run forward knowing our goal and believing in our mission. We push through disappointment and discouragement. We ignore rejection and judgment. Laziness and distraction are foreigners. Focus and determination is our motto. We are trumpets in the hands of God and music to the brokenhearted. We are filled by his Spirit and moved by the story of his Son. We are his agents of change, his revolutionaries, and his special forces. We are fishers of people.

Talk with God

Give me the strength to live up to your call.

Live It. How will you live more Second today?
Tell It. How will you share what you have learned?

Tweet using #IASboatless to share your thoughts.

Day 6: Leaving

*"Truly I tell you," Jesus replied, "no one who has left home
or brothers or sisters or mother or father or children or fields
for me and the gospel will fail to receive a hundred times as
much in this present age: homes, brothers, sisters, mothers,
children and fields—along with persecutions—and in the
age to come eternal life."*

—Mark 10:29–30

Read the whole passage in Mark 10:28–31.

Jesus will call us to suffer and sacrifice if we follow him. We
will be called to bet our homes, to risk our families, to endanger
our careers and honor, our wealth and relationships, all for his sake.
Living Second means everything is on the line, the bet is all in, and
nothing kept in our back pockets. We put everything on the table,
and we gamble our lives, liberties, and happiness. But every penny
we bet, every friend we lose or hardship we face, he will repay us in
full with 10,000 percent interest. The world may call us fools for
betting so high, for risking so much, but the house always wins,
and we are heirs to the Owner's fortunes and participants in all his
wealth. We may not see it today or tomorrow or next year, but we
will see our risk pay off.

Talk with God

Despite all the struggles I face, I trust that in the end you will be
worth far more than anything I have to risk.

Live It. How will you live more Second today?
Tell It. How will you share what you have learned?

Tweet using #IASleaving to share your thoughts.

Day 7: Shadows

*The L*ORD *is my shepherd, I lack nothing.*
    He makes me lie down in green pastures,
He leads me beside quiet waters,
    he refreshes my soul.
He guides me along the right paths
    for his name's sake.
Even though I walk
    through the darkest valley,
I will fear no evil,
    for you are with me;
Your rod and your staff,
    they comfort me.
You prepare a table before me
    in the presence of my enemies.
You anoint my head with oil;
    my cup overflows.
Surely your goodness and love will follow me
    all the days of my life,
*And I will dwell in the house of the L*ORD
    forever.

—Psalm 23

Though life may still have its dark valleys, God will walk beside us. Though our enemies may still surround and threaten us, God will remain loyal. He does not promise to make life easy or erase its difficulties, but he does promise to remain with us.

Talk with God

Protect.

"I will fear no evil . . ."
God, protect me from dangers unknown and foes unseen . . .

🐦 Tweet using #IASshadows to share your prayers.

Day 1: Multiply

Watch the Alex Kendrick Film

iamsecond.com/alexkendrick

What did you like about, identify with, or learn from Alex's story?

> *While they were worshiping the Lord and fasting, the Holy Spirit said, "Set apart for me Barnabas and Saul for the work to which I have called them."*
>
> **—Acts 13:2**

Read the whole passage in Acts 13–14.

What It Says

1. What did you like about this passage?
2. What did you not like or find confusing about this passage?

What It Means

3. What does this passage teach about people? What is Paul's process, strategy, or plan as he multiplies new churches?
4. What does this passage teach about God?

Live It. How will you live more Second today?

Tell It. How will you share what you have learned?

Practice It. Get with a friend or someone in your group. Practice or role-play your "Live and Tell" commitments.

Day 2: Talk with God

So after they had fasted and prayed, they placed their hands on them and sent them off.

—Acts 13:3

Read the whole passage in Acts 13:1–3.

We lack for one of two reasons: either we ask out of selfish ambition, or we forget to ask at all. Whatever we hope to see accomplished in our lives and for his kingdom, we must ask God for his help. No plan worth planning will ever succeed without him, and no task worth doing will ever find completion apart from his empowerment. Our prayers do not need to be long-winded or full of fancy words, but they do need to be sincere and persistent and unrelenting. We must pray for ourselves and pray for others and ask for prayers from others. We must never forget that we speak to a living God and a loving Father. He stands ready to hear us and hungry to talk with us.

Talk with God

God, I ask that your will be done here on earth as it is in heaven. Use me to advance your kingdom and to remember the needs of your servant.

Live It. How can you live more Second today?
Tell It. How will you share what you have learned?

🐦 Tweet using #IAStalkwithgod to share your thoughts.

Day 3: **Share**

We tell you the good news: What God promised our ancestors he has fulfilled for us, their children, by raising up Jesus.

—Acts 13:32–33

Read the whole passage in Acts 13:13–41.

We are not mere do-gooders or plain humanitarians. We are bearers of a life-and-death message, agents of an eternal kingdom with gates held wide for all who wish to enter. Jesus is not exclusive to certain demographics or certain cultures or particular types of people. His message applies to all, his appeal to everyone. And we carry this message every time we tell the story of Jesus' death and resurrection, the forgiveness he grants, and the free gift he offers. We do not pander religion or propagate philosophy, but we tell the story of a real God with a real offer of grace. How faithful are we at telling this story? How ready are we to share it with our friends and family? How proud are we to exercise our rights as ambassadors of his kingdom?

Talk with God

God, I want my life to be about sharing you with the world, of telling your story to the masses.

Live It. How can you live more Second today?
Tell It. How will you share what you have learned?

🐦 Tweet using #IASshare to share your thoughts.

Day 4: Make Disciples

Then they returned to Lystra, Iconium and Antioch,
strengthening the disciples and encouraging them to remain
true to the faith.

—Acts 14:21–22

Read the whole passage in Acts 14:1–22.

Paul never dropped evangelism tracts from helicopters or tossed "Jesus Saves" stickers into the street. He preached the message of Jesus, told his story, and then immediately began discipleship. There was no delay between acceptance of Jesus and activation of faith, between hearing about his story and living out its truth. There was no separation between telling about Jesus and instructing in the ways of Jesus. We have often lost this truth in our efforts to share Jesus with others. We stop at resurrection but forget that the New Testament goes on for many chapters more. We talk about healing but only give the prescription, never helping to administer the daily treatment. We are called to make disciples, not merely converts—but how often do we live out this truth?

Talk with God

Teach me to work toward long-term discipleship and mentoring with those you have entrusted to me.

Live It. How will you live more Second today?
Tell It. How will you share what you have learned?

Tweet using #IASmakedisciples to share your thoughts.

Day 5: Gather Together

Paul and Barnabas appointed elders for them in each church and, with prayer and fasting, committed them to the Lord, in whom they had put their trust.

—Acts 14:23

Read the whole passage in Acts 14.

Paul made more than individual converts or isolated disciples. He established new spiritual communities to nurture new believers, new churches to care for these young followers of God. They met in homes or synagogues or anywhere else they could find. Their gatherings lacked our modern frills, professional preachers and sound systems and tall buildings, but they lacked none of the essentials. They studied the Bible, talked with God, commemorated Jesus' death, and encouraged each other to love God more dearly. These were the simple goals of their gatherings. Let their simplicity be a reminder of the essentials of our gatherings and a filter to see what is really important about what we call *church*.

Talk with God

Give me the wisdom to know how to follow in Paul's example to start new spiritual communities of disciples.

Live It. How will you live more Second today?
Tell It. How will you share what you have learned?

🐦 Tweet using #IASgathertogether to share your thoughts.

Day 6: Develop Leaders

Paul and Barnabas appointed elders for them in each church and, with prayer and fasting, committed them to the Lord, in whom they had put their trust.

—Acts 14:23

Read the whole passage in Acts 14:23–28.

Leadership is essential. It can take many forms and wear many colors, but it must always be present. Paul appointed elders for every church and watchmen over every gathering. They had little training and even less experience. Paul modeled the pattern of doctrine and passed on the truth of God. He assisted them when trouble rose and guided them when difficulties raged. He watched over them as he traveled to the next city, wrote to them to remind them, and revisited to strengthen them further. But no matter how limited his time with them, in each city he trusted God to lead his people and the Spirit to protect his church. How often do we feel the need to micromanage God's kingdom? How often does our inability to trust God's Spirit squash the leadership potential of others?

Talk with God

God, make me a leader factory, a person addicted to developing potential and passionate about seeing others succeed.

Live It. How will you live more Second today?
Tell It. How will you share what you have learned?

Tweet using #IASdevelopleaders to share your thoughts.

Day 7: Fragrance

But thanks be to God, who always leads us as captives in Christ's triumphal procession and uses us to spread the aroma of the knowledge of him everywhere. For we are to God the pleasing aroma of Christ among those who are being saved and those who are perishing. To the one we are an aroma that brings death; to the other, an aroma that brings life. And who is equal to such a task? Unlike so many, we do not peddle the word of God for profit. On the contrary, in Christ we speak before God with sincerity, as those sent from God.

—2 Corinthians 2:14–17

Our lives should smell like Jesus. The way we live and speak should so reflect Jesus' heart that the world is compelled to either love us or hate us, to accept God's message or reject his salvation. Praise God that we get to participate in such important work. Thank him for the honor of carrying his scent to the world.

Talk with God

Worship.

"Thanks be to God . . ."
God, thank you for using me to spread your message . . .

Tweet using #IASfragrance to share your prayers.

Session Eleven

Go Global

Weeks 44–48
Week 44: Samaria
Week 45: Ends of the Earth
Week 46: Why Go?
Week 47: Commissioned
Week 48: Paul's Plan

We have been made witnesses to God's truth and heralds of his message. No corner of this planet is to go without knowing this hope. No nation or people group is to exist without hearing it. We are sent to the ends of the earth, anywhere his name is not known, to shout his message. This includes the forgotten widows and the neglected poor. This includes the outcasts and the ostracized. This includes distant tribes and foreign neighbors. We are commissioned to go and spread the love and message of God everywhere and to everyone. Dare to join the global effort of God's kingdom and participate in the spreading of his fame.

Day 1: Nearby

Watch the Rudy Kalis Film

iamsecond.com/rudykalis

What did you like about, identify with, or learn from Rudy's film?

> *But you will receive power when the Holy Spirit comes on you; and you will be my witnesses in Jerusalem, and in all Judea and Samaria, and to the ends of the earth.*
>
> **—Acts 1:8**

Read the whole passage in Acts 1:1–11.

What It Says

1. What did you like about this passage?
2. What did you not like or find confusing about this passage?

What It Means

3. What does this passage teach about people?
4. What does this passage teach about God?

Live It. What is your nearby mission? What can you and your group do to reach those who are near you but outside your normal circle of acquaintances?

Tell It. Who else needs to hear about your desire to reach this group?

Practice It. Gather your friends and make a plan as a group. Review your "Go Local" plan and find a way to address this group's needs in that plan.

Day 2: Leper

Jesus reached out his hand and touched the man. "I am
willing," he said.
"Be clean!" And immediately the leprosy left him.

—Luke 5:13

Read the whole passage in Luke 5:12–16.

Every society has a group of people whom nobody will touch. Maybe its drug dealers or sex offenders, HIV/AIDS victims or homosexuals. Whatever their label, they exist apart from the rest of us. They cannot join our crowds or hang with our friends. But Jesus did not agree with his culture's prejudice or go along with its segregation. If we follow him, then we must copy his example. We must learn to overcome our own intolerance, swallow our pride, and love the unloved. Who makes us cringe? Who makes us uncomfortable? What group of people do we avoid like the lepers and secretly hate like the tax collectors? And what would it look like to love them as Jesus loves us?

Talk with God

God, ruin my prejudice and change my heart. Teach me to love others the way you have loved me.

Live It. How can you live more Second today?
Tell It. How will you share what you have learned?

Tweet using #IASleper to share your thoughts.

Day 3: **Tax Collectors**

But the Pharisees and the teachers of the law who belonged to their sect complained to his disciples, "Why do you eat and drink with tax collectors and sinners?"

—Luke 5:30

Read the whole passage in Luke 5:27–35.

Believers tend to create a unique subculture, our own list of likes and dislikes, our favorite enemies and sacred punching bags. And while God never asked us to be soft on sin, he did teach us to love our enemies, to treat others as we would want to be treated. While tax collectors no longer top our hate list, we have found others to fill their place. Maybe they tattoo their skin or experiment with their sexuality or beg on street corners or vote for the other party—but God calls us to love them and to befriend them. He requires that we demonstrate our love and share his story with each of them. To call them friends may lose us our Christian friends or our reputation in polite society, but God calls for nothing less than unqualified love for the tax collectors of our day.

Talk with God

God, teach me to love the least of these and the worst of these.

Live It. How can you live more Second today?
Tell It. How will you share what you have learned?

🐦 Tweet using #IAStaxcollectors to share your thoughts.

Day 4: **Needy**

*When the Lord saw her, his heart went out to her and he
said, "Don't cry."*

—Luke 7:13

Read the whole passage in Luke 7:11–17.

Maybe their family life is more broken, their finances more
dire, or their history more checkered. Regardless of political persuasion or cultural background, we are called to care for these
needy people. Our faith demands that the helpless are helped. We
may disagree with how best to help needy people, but we must
never argue against helping. Jesus' call to reach Samaria should
inspire us to help the helpless and love the unloved. When was the
last time we volunteered at a battered women's shelter or mentored
a troubled kid? When was the last time our love reached beyond
those who knew how to love us back?

Talk with God

Give me a heart that breaks for the brokenhearted and loves the
unloved.

Live It. How will you live more Second today?
Tell It. How will you share what you have learned?

Tweet using #IASneedy to share your thoughts.

Day 5: Unclean

And a woman was there who had been subject to bleeding for twelve years, but no one could heal her.

—**Luke 8:43**

Read the whole passage in Luke 8:40–56.

The "unclean" of our society are perhaps recovering alcoholics or divorcées or adulterers or single parents. These are people we accept but only as second-class citizens. We deny them serious responsibility and restrict them from active ministry. Though they have the most potent stories to tell and the most important lessons to teach, we silence their voices. They have made mistakes or been victims of circumstance, but we label them as disabled. Though it is the weak God most enjoys to use and the poor in spirit he most delights in utilizing, we have neglected their talent. What would it take for us to release the bonds of judgment and to activate the ministries of the "unclean"? What would it look like to stop feeling sorry for ourselves and realize that no matter our background, God has a plan for our lives?

Talk with God

You are bigger than my past and greater than my failures. I know you can still use me and those like me. Give me a place to serve.

Live It. How will you live more Second today?
Tell It. How will you share what you have learned?

Tweet using #IASunclean to share your thoughts.

Day 6: Inconvenient

Jesus asked the Pharisees and experts in the law, "Is it lawful to heal on the Sabbath or not?"

—Luke 14:3

Read the whole passage in Luke 14:1–6.

Too long have we allowed tradition rather than the Bible to make our decisions. Too long we have obsessed over the size of our buildings and the height of our steeples when God only cares about the people. We argue over the shape of our musical instruments and the location of our next cookout, all the while only a fraction of our offerings ever leaves the church parking lot, only a poor pittance serves anyone but ourselves. We bicker over titles and who leads what committee; meanwhile those we work with have never heard the message of Jesus, and those we live next to have never heard our story or witnessed God's love. Reaching Samaria may involve unorthodox methods and unusual thinking. It may require that we reexamine our traditions or set aside our internal disputes. But it is a goal well worth the effort.

Talk with God

God, take the blinders off my eyes. Let me discern between the traditions of men and the commands of your Bible.

Live It. How will you live more Second today?
Tell It. How will you share what you have learned?

🐦 Tweet using #IASinconvenient to share your thoughts.

Day 7: Clap

Clap your hands, all you nations;
shout to God with cries of joy.
*For the L*ᴏʀᴅ *Most High is awesome,*
the great King over all the earth.
He subdued nations under us,
peoples under our feet.
He chose our inheritance for us,
the pride of Jacob, whom he loved.
God has ascended amid shouts of joy,
*the L*ᴏʀᴅ *amid the sounding of trumpets.*
Sing praises to God, sing praises;
sing praises to our King, sing praises.
For God is the King of all the earth;
sing to him a psalm of praise.
God reigns over the nations;
God is seated on his holy throne.
The nobles of the nations assemble
as the people of the God of Abraham,
For the kings of the earth belong to God;
he is greatly exalted.

—Psalm 47

Talk with God

Ask.

". . . kings of the earth . . ."
God, I want my neighbors, my city, the rulers and kings of the
world to know you . . .

Tweet using #IASclap to share your prayers.

Day 1: Far Away

Watch the Christine Petric Film

iamsecond.com/christinepetric

What did you like about, identify with, or learn from Christine's story?

But you will receive power when the Holy Spirit comes on you; and you will be my witnesses in Jerusalem, and in all Judea and Samaria, and to the ends of the earth.

—Acts 1:8

Read the whole passage in Acts 1:1–11.

What It Says
1. What did you like about this passage?
2. What did you not like or find confusing about this passage?

What It Means
3. What does this passage teach about people?
4. What does this passage teach about God?

Live It. What is your global mission? How will you or your group get involved in God's global mission?

Tell It. Who else needs to hear about your desire to go global?

For information about how to go global with I am Second, go to www.iamsecond.com/expeditions.

Day 2: Earth

I will bless those who bless you,
and whoever curses you I will curse;
and all peoples on earth
will be blessed through you.

—**Genesis 12:3**

Read the whole passage in Genesis 12:1–9.

God gave us free will. The ability to say no. And in the very beginning, we exercised that ability and tore ourselves from God's presence. We bowed our knees to the prince of darkness rather than to the Prince of Peace and to the king of lies rather than to the King of kings. But despite our rebellion, God has not forgotten his people. He has not let go of his special creation. He has set a plan in motion that will bring praise from every people and every nation. Not a spot on this earth will be untouched by his love or unaltered by his forgiveness. Individuals will still reject him, nations still run their own way. But his message still rings through the villages and down the small alleyways. His blessings still reach people in every demographic and every language. And he will use us in our own small ways to participate in his grand plan to reach the ends of the earth.

Talk with God

God, show me my part in your global strategy.

Live It. How can you live more Second today?
Tell It. How will you share what you have learned?

🐦 Tweet using #IASearth to share your thoughts.

Day 3: **All People**

*And I, when I am lifted up from the earth, will draw all
people to myself.*

—John 12:32

Read the whole passage in John 12:23–33.

God insists on his blessings being shared and his forgiveness
being given. He goes out ahead of us and speaks in dreams and
visions, through books and television, through missionaries and
faithful messengers. But he calls each of us to join him, to lift up
Christ, and to shout his story. He tells us to be messengers to all
the earth and bringers of good news to all peoples. Modern transportation and communication now make it possible to journey to
the ends of the earth and back without even missing an e-mail. But
will we take advantage of this gift and the immense opportunity to
bring God to people who have never heard his name?

Talk with God

God, show me where to go to share your name and where to give to
allow others to do the same.

Live It. How can you live more Second today?
Tell It. How will you share what you have learned?

🐦 Tweet using #IASallpeople to share your thoughts.

Day 4: **Salty**

You are the salt of the earth. But if the salt loses its saltiness, how can it be made salty again? It is no longer good for anything, except to be thrown out and trampled underfoot.

—Matthew 5:13

Read the whole passage in Matthew 5:13–16.

We are not mere residents in a strange world but revolutionaries ready to turn it upside down. We are more than aliens and foreigners in a land that does not know us; we are agents of change and persons of influence. We salt the earth with our message and whet the spiritual appetite of our communities. We have no other purpose on this earth and no other reason for our stay here. We bear his image and share his story. We work for his kingdom and serve his purpose. That is our calling. If we refuse this mission or reject his mandate, then we forfeit the very goal of our lives. When we look at our lives, do his goals weave through our daily tasks? Does his story shout through the patterns of our daily worries?

Talk with God

Help me flavor this world and salt this planet with your truth. Make me different than those around me and an agent of change to those I talk with.

Live It. How will you live more Second today?
Tell It. How will you share what you have learned?

🐦 Tweet using #IASsalty to share your thoughts.

Day 5: Celebration

"For this son of mine was dead and is alive again; he was lost and is found." So they began to celebrate.

—Luke 15:24

Read the whole passage in Luke 15:11–32.

God is not dead. His plan is not stalled, and his work is not slowed. He moves forward in our midst and stirs through our world. People from every country and every culture are learning his story and discovering his forgiveness. Missionaries still carry his message, and his people still wave his flag. The lame are still finding new legs through his healing and the blind finding new eyes through his touch. We can hear of his greatness along the edges of our world, in the depths of the jungles, in the heat of the deserts, and on the breeze of the islands. People still rise from the dead and are found in their lostness. And we, his people, can rejoice and sing of the amazing work that God is still doing around the world.

Talk with God

God, I praise you that you are still active and involved in our world, still saving the lost and giving life to the dead.

Live It. How will you live more Second today?
Tell It. How will you share what you have learned?

🐦 Tweet using #IAScelebration to share your thoughts.

Day 6: **Thirsty**

Let anyone who is thirsty come to me and drink. Whoever believes in me, as Scripture has said, rivers of living water will flow from within them.

—John 7:37–38

Some think they cannot be forgiven, that their sin is too great or their past too terrible. But God's promise is bigger, and his forgiveness wider than any wrong we could commit or evil we could think. There are no exclusions to his offer or exceptions to his gift. He offers freely and openly to all with ears to hear and eyes to see, to whoever hungers and whoever thirsts. He holds his gift out to everyone without prejudice and without hesitation. God's message is not for a select few, but for everyone. We are his messengers to the world, not just to our neighborhood. What have we done to participate in this global endeavor?

Talk with God

Show me how to get involved in what you are doing around the world, not just here at home.

Live It. How will you live more Second today?
Tell It. How will you share what you have learned?

🐦 Tweet using #IASthirsty to share your thoughts.

Day 7: **Forever Power**

Shout for joy to God, all the earth!
Sing the glory of his name;
make his praise glorious.
Say to God, "How awesome are your deeds!
So great is your power
that your enemies cringe before you.
All the earth bows down to you;
they sing praise to you,
they sing the praises of your name."
Come and see what God has done,
his awesome deeds for mankind!
He turned the sea into dry land,
they passed through the waters on foot—
come, let us rejoice in him.
He rules forever by his power,
his eyes watch the nations—
let not the rebellious rise up against him.

—Psalm 66:1–7

How often do we spend our time with God asking him for our laundry list of wants? How often do we forget that God is not Santa Claus but our Father, Friend, and Counselor? Take some time today to just worship God for who he is and what he has done. Thank him for his intervention in your life and his work in this world.

Talk with God

Worship.

"Shout for joy . . ."
God, thank you for all you have done in my life and in the lives around me . . .

🐦 Tweet using #IASforeverpower to share your prayers.

Day 1: Every Tribe

Watch the Ken Hutcherson Film

iamsecond.com/kenhutcherson

What did you like about, identify with, or learn from Ken's story?

> *With your blood you purchased for God*
> *persons from every tribe and language and people and nation.*
> **—Revelation 5:9**

Read the whole passage in Revelation 5:9–12.

What It Says
1. What did you like about this passage?
2. What did you not like or find confusing about this passage?

What It Means
3. What does this passage teach about people?
4. What does this passage teach about God?

Live It. How will you live more Second today?
Tell It. How will you share what you have learned?

Practice It. Get with a friend or someone in your group. Practice or role-play your "Live and Tell" commitments.

Day 2: **Eternity**

*Very truly I tell you, whoever hears my word and believes
him who sent me has eternal life and will not be judged but
has crossed over from death to life.*

—**John 5:24**

Read the whole passage in John 5:19–24.

Eternity should be our motivation. Life and death our inspiration. Our message is not about "real" housewives or car engines or political elections but about the Son of God invading our world and dying on a cross to rescue us from darkness. We share a message of substance and importance. It trumps cable news and makes child's play out of national newspapers. We bring the story that shaped history and the God who created space and time. Nothing is more important and no one claims higher rank. Will we believe our message enough to share it, to make it a centerpiece of every conversation and a goal of every interaction? Will we adhere to its priority and listen to its urgency?

Talk with God

Make your word fire in my bones and your story breath in my lungs.

Live It. How can you live more Second today?
Tell It. How will you share what you have learned?

🐦 Tweet using #IASeternity to share your thoughts.

Day 3: **Judgment**

*I told you that you would die in your sins; if you do not
believe that I am he, you will indeed die in your sins.*

—**John 8:24**

Read the whole passage in John 8:12–26.

We sit on a perilous branch and on a dangerous cliff. We have an
unknown number of years on this earth and an undisclosed number of opportunities to hear his message. Death stands at our door
and judgment awaits our answer. We are promised no tomorrow
and guaranteed no second chance. Our friends may never again see
the light of day or our family the glow of night. This world may not
survive the year or our universe the blink of an eye. We must let the
urgency of the coming judgment persuade us to share Jesus and the
certainty of death to encourage our faithful witnessing. Though we
carry a message of great hope, a promise of terrible consequence
will answer its rejection.

Talk with God

Help me spend my short time here on earth well.

Live It. How can you live more Second today?
Tell It. How will you share what you have learned?

🐦 Tweet using #IASjudgment to share your thoughts.

Day 4: Freedom

If you hold to my teaching, you are really my disciples. Then you will know the truth, and the truth will set you free.

—John 8:31–32

Read the whole passage in John 8:27–47.

Our message is more than a self-help pep talk. We carry the key to unlock every bondage and the cure to every ailment. Death will fail at the sound of God's truth. The grave will give up its dead at the sound of Jesus' trumpet. Even in this life, freedom begins its reign in believer's lives. While trouble may still come, we are free to smile, knowing that the end is already won. While pain and death will visit, we can laugh, knowing that it will never last. That is the strength of our message and the motivation for us to shout it with our lives.

Talk with God

Make me a voice of freedom in this world and a messenger of your grace.

Live It. How will you live more Second today?
Tell It. How will you share what you have learned?

🐦 Tweet using #IASfreedom to share your thoughts.

Day 5: Life

I am the resurrection and the life. The one who believes in me will live, even though they die; and whoever lives by believing in me will never die.

— John 11:25–26

Read the whole passage in John 11:1–44.

Our bodies were never meant to decay, to succumb to cancer or illness or even death. Our original DNA spelled eternity, and our first design promised only life. Sin brought death and, with it, frailty and weakness. But Jesus offers new life. He promises escape from death's grip. If we believe in his words, accept his sacrifice, trust his death and resurrection and promise of new life, then we can return to our original destiny and never taste the bitterness of the grave. Though we will exit this world, our lives will continue and our bodies will resurrect. We hold on to hope when the world can only delay the inevitable. We speak of eternity when others can only offer temporal pleasure.

Talk with God

Fill my words with your hope and my speech with your promises.

Live It. How will you live more Second today?
Tell It. How will you share what you have learned?

🐦 Tweet using #IASlife to share your thoughts.

Day 6: Rooms

*My Father's house has many rooms; if that were not so,
would I have told you that I am going there to prepare a
place for you?*

—John 14:2

Read the whole passage in John 14:1–12.

We may face trouble here on earth, but peace awaits our eternity. We may know poverty or need in this life, but a mansion awaits us in heaven and glorious wealth in our future. We do not preach a message of judgment or condemnation but one of peace, love, and forgiveness. We are promised great reward and forever rest, perfect paradise and unbroken happiness. These are the promises that we announce to the world and the gifts that God holds out in grace. We do not earn it, for nothing ever could. We do not deserve it, for no one ever would. But we are promised it anyway. For everyone who believes and anyone who accepts the message of Jesus, heaven—and all its perfection—is our destiny.

Talk with God

I praise you for your gifts and thank you endlessly for your grace.

Live It. How will you live more Second today?
Tell It. How will you share what you have learned?

🐦 Tweet using #IASrooms to share your thoughts.

Day 7: **Peoples**

Praise our God, all peoples,
let the sound of his praise be heard;
He has preserved our lives
and kept our feet from slipping.
For you, God, tested us;
you refined us like silver.
You brought us into prison
and laid burdens on our backs. . . .
Come and hear, all you who fear God;
let me tell you what he has done for me.
I cried out to him with my mouth;
his praise was on my tongue.
If I had cherished sin in my heart,
the Lord would not have listened;
But God has surely listened
and has heard my prayer.
Praise be to God,
who has not rejected my prayer
or withheld his love from me!

—Psalm 66:8–11, 16–20

God deserves the praise of every people and every person needs the knowledge of his existence and the kindness of his love. We are his ambassadors. It is our responsibility to get the word out. But the all-important first step to any endeavor is to talk with God. Praise God for what he has done and ask him to bring his praise to all peoples.

Talk with God

Worship.

"Praise our God, all peoples . . ."
God, I want everyone to praise you . . .

🐦 Tweet using #IASpeoples to share your prayers.

Day 1: Volunteer

Watch the Sujo Johns Film

iamsecond.com/sujojohns

What did you like about, identify with, or learn from Sujo's story?

> *Then I heard the voice of the Lord saying, "Whom shall I send? And who will go for us?"*
> *And I said, "Here am I. Send me!"*
>
> **—Isaiah 6:8**

Read the whole passage in Isaiah 6:1–13.

What It Says
    1. What did you like about this passage?
    2. What did you not like or find confusing about this passage?

What It Means
    3. What does this passage teach about people?
    4. What does this passage teach about God?

Live It. How will you live more Second today?
Tell It. How will you share what you have learned?

Practice It. Get with a friend or someone in your group. Practice or role-play your "Live and Tell" commitments.

Day 2: **Loyalty**

*Then the fire of the L*ord *fell and burned up the sacrifice,
the wood, the stones and the soil, and also licked up the
water in the trench. When all the people saw this, they fell
prostrate and cried, "The L*ord*—he is God! The L*ord*—he is
God!"*

—1 Kings 18:38–39

Read the whole passage in 1 Kings 18:1–46.

Elijah lived in a time when Abraham's descendants had forgotten their God. They ran after the gods of their neighbors and
the idols of foreign peoples. They walked away from the God who
brought them out of Egypt and the God who had made them into
his special people. Elijah called them back. He challenged them to
abandon their fake gods and return to their first love. But it took
the defeat of a host of false priests and fire falling from heaven to
convince them of this. May our love come much quicker and our
loyalty stand firmer. How quickly we all forget what God has done
in our lives. We are sent as his messengers and commissioned as his
representatives; let us remember what he has done in our lives as we
represent him to the world.

Talk with God

God, give me the strength to stay loyal to you even through the
darkest times of doubt.

Live It. How can you live more Second today?
Tell It. How will you share what you have learned?

🐦 Tweet using #IASloyalty to share your thoughts.

Day 3: **Burning Plows**

He took his yoke of oxen and slaughtered them. He burned the plowing equipment to cook the meat and gave it to the people, and they ate. Then he set out to follow Elijah and became his servant.

—1 Kings 19:21

Read the whole passage in 1 Kings 19:8–21.

"When I am older," some say. "When I have saved enough money," others insist. "If I get this job or make this income bracket," still more promise. How dare we tell God to wait? God has no interest in our delayed obedience. Elisha heard God's call, barbequed his farm equipment, ate his retirement, and stepped out in immediate, radical, costly obedience. Some of us may need to continue working our jobs and being salt and light in those areas of the world. Some of us may need to continue building our retirements and saving for our children that they may enter life unencumbered by debt or worry. But others of us may need to sell everything, to burn our bridges and leave our homes, to accept his call and step out in faith. How many of us are willing to kindle that fire, if he asks?

Talk with God

God, I will light on fire everything I own, if you ask. I am all yours, me and everything I possess. Just say the word, and in flames it all will go.

Live It. How can you live more Second today?
Tell It. How will you share what you have learned?

🐦 Tweet using #IASburningplows to share your thoughts.

Day 4: **Appointed**

Do not say, "I am too young." You must go to everyone I
send you to and say whatever I command you. Do not be
afraid of them, for I am with you and will rescue you.

—**Jeremiah 1:7–8**

Read the whole passage in Jeremiah 1:1–10.

The job he offers has no prerequisites, no work experience needed, no résumé necessary. We do not need to be a certain age or possess certain talents. Skill is unnecessary, and ability is non-essential. God equips us for the work to which he calls us. He gives us his words and fills us with his power. He will train as we go and provide for us as we work. The interview for this position has only one question: "Will you go?" The answer is ours to give. Accept it and hardship will come, difficulty will be our wage, and sacrifice will be our lot. But a reward awaits us in heaven, one that outstrips our imagination and outweighs all the gold on earth. If we decline the offer, normalcy will be our destiny, and mediocrity will mark our lives; we will toil at work and trudge through our lives without purpose, without aim, and without reward. Which will you choose?

Talk with God

God, I choose you. I do not know what awaits me or what you have in store for my life. But I trust you enough to say that I am all in.

Live It. How will you live more Second today?
Tell It. How will you share what you have learned?

🐦 Tweet using #IASappointed to share your thoughts.

Day 5: Hardened

You are not being sent to a people of obscure speech and strange language, but to the people of Israel—not to many peoples of obscure speech and strange language, whose words you cannot understand. Surely if I had sent you to them, they would have listened to you.

—Ezekiel 3:5–6

Read the whole passage in Ezekiel 2–3.

Our obedience should not be determined by the likelihood of our success. Family members can be our toughest critics and our hardest audience. But we are still called to show them God's love and tell them about his message. Our own culture can be our biggest challenge and the slowest to respond. But the response of those around us will not be the criteria of our judgment. We are called to be active in sharing Jesus wherever we find ourselves, regardless of the fruit of our work. We do not need to pester people with the gospel, but we do need to inform them. We do not need to annoy people with constant Jesus-talk, but we do need to make them aware. How aware are the people in our lives?

Talk with God

God, give me the courage to share Jesus with those who reject your message and who harden their hearts.

Live It. How will you live more Second today?
Tell It. How will you share what you have learned?

🐦 Tweet using #IAShardened to share your thoughts.

Day 6: Watchman

When I say to the wicked, "You wicked person, you will surely die," and you do not speak out to dissuade them from their ways, that wicked person will die for their sin, and I will hold you accountable for their blood.

—Ezekiel 33:8

Read the whole passage in Ezekiel 33:1–33.

We have a message that holds the power of life and death. We believe in a Savior who can rescue us from the grave and cure us of our sickness. We follow a God who demands confession or death, who offers eternal forgiveness or forever damnation. And it is we who are charged to let this world know of his ultimatum. If we muzzle the alarm, he will charge us with their deaths. If we hide the light or keep secret his offer, then we hold their blood on our hands. We are not obligated to wake everyone from their sleep, but we are under orders to shake their beds and turn on the lights. We are not forced to fight off death, but we are to warn of its coming and to shout of its remedy. How much shouting have we done with our lives? How many lights have we tried to turn on or beds to shake? Have we been a watchman asleep at our post or a dutiful herald of the coming judgment?

Talk with God

Forgive me for my failures as a watchman.

Live It. How will you live more Second today?
Tell It. How will you share what you have learned?

🐦 Tweet using #IASwatchman to share your thoughts.

Day 7: Worthy

You are worthy, our Lord and God,
to receive glory and honor and power,
For you created all things,
and by your will they were created
and have their being. . . .
You are worthy to take the scroll
and to open its seals,
Because you were slain,
and with your blood you purchased for God
persons from every tribe and language and people and nation.
You have made them to be a kingdom and priests to serve our God,
and they will reign on the earth. . . .
Worthy is the Lamb, who was slain,
to receive power and wealth and wisdom and strength
and honor and glory and praise! . . .
To him who sits on the throne and to the Lamb
be praise and honor and glory and power,
for ever and ever!

—Revelation 4:11; 5:9–10, 12–13

We serve a worthy God. Any comfort given up for him is worthwhile. All rights laid down for his name are given for a deserving God. Any life lost for his sake is worth the price. He rewards all who serve and remembers all who sacrifice in his name.

Talk with God

Worship.

"You are worthy . . ."
God, I want the nations to follow you because you alone are worthy . . .

🐦 Tweet using #IASworthy to share your prayers.

Day 1: Multiply

Watch the Josh Turner Film

iamsecond.com/joshturner

What did you like about, identify with, or learn from Josh's story?

Every Sabbath he reasoned in the synagogue, trying to persuade Jews and Greeks.

—Acts 18:4

Read the whole passage in Acts 18:1–22.

What It Says
1. What did you like about this passage?
2. What did you not like or find confusing about this passage?

What It Means
3. What does this passage teach about people?
4. What does this passage teach about God?

Live It. How will you live more Second today?
Tell It. How will you share what you have learned?

Practice It. Get with a friend or someone in your group. Practice or role-play your "Live and Tell" commitments.

Day 2: **Talk with God**

*One night the Lord spoke to Paul in a vision: "Do not be
afraid; keep on speaking, do not be silent. For I am with you,
and no one is going to attack and harm you, because I have
many people in this city."*

—**Acts 18:9–10**

Read the whole passage in Acts 18:6–10.

We usually think of prayer as a time when we talk with God,
when we present our requests, confess our sins, and express our
love. But sometimes we forget that God also speaks back. While
his voice is infrequent and his direct messages few and far between,
he is neither shy nor mute. He is able to intervene in our world and
break the silence in our heads. He may speak in dreams or visions,
through conviction or a still, small voice, but when he does it will
be unmistakable. We must ready our ears and train our minds to
think that our time in prayer is a meeting with God and a conversation with the Almighty and not just our oral journaling.

Talk with God

God, my ears are open. Speak to me when you want.

Live It. How can you live more Second today?
Tell It. How will you share what you have learned?

🐦 Tweet using #IAStalkwithgod to share your thoughts.

Day 3: Share

Paul devoted himself exclusively to preaching, testifying to the Jews that Jesus was the Messiah.

—Acts 18:5

Read the whole passage in Acts 18:1–5.

We are messengers. We bring a simple and unchanging message. It is the same message that Paul spoke to the Greeks and the same message that Jesus preached to the Jews. It is the same message in Africa, Asia, and the Americas. Jesus died for our sins and rose again three days later. That is our mantra, our elevator speech, our Facebook status, and our daily tweet. Nothing can improve it, and nothing can alter its truthfulness or raise its eloquence. We only need to share it, to tell it in every way possible, to live it with our lives and speak it with our lips. We may change the words but never the meaning. We may alternate its presentation but never its essence. We did not create the message, but we are commissioned to pass it on.

Talk with God

Shout your story through my lips and your message through my life.

Live It. How can you live more Second today?
Tell It. How will you share what you have learned?

🐦 Tweet using #IASshare to share your thoughts.

Day 4: Make Disciples

So Paul stayed for a year and a half, teaching them the word of God.

—Acts 18:11

Read the whole passage in Acts 18:1–11.

The church at Corinth sat under Paul's teaching for a year and a half, received at least two of Paul's letters, and was the destination of several visits. They felt Paul's wrath when they erred and his care when they struggled. They learned about his love of Jesus, his hate of sin, and his pattern of godliness. Discipleship is not a quick-fix package. It is more than a book or a class or a series of lectures. It is the sharing of life and the passing on of a pattern of living. It requires hard work, a willingness to confront and correct, and the patience to see people through their failures. But despite the hardships and the pitfalls, making disciples is the call of our lives and the purpose of our stay here on earth.

Talk with God

I want to see more than momentary decisions or fleeting commitments; I want to see disciples made for your kingdom.

Live It. How will you live more Second today?
Tell It. How will you share what you have learned?

🐦 Tweet using #IASmakedisciples to share your thoughts.

Day 5: Gather Together

Then Paul left the synagogue and went next door to the
house of Titius Justus, a worshiper of God.

—**Acts 18:7**

Read the whole passage in Acts 18:1–11.

Most discipleship will not take place within church walls. Just as schools have no monopoly on learning and classrooms serve only as launching pads to the real stuff of life, so church buildings witness only a portion of our teaching and only a fraction of the discipleship process. Our gatherings occur whenever we share a meal and remember Jesus' sacrifice, whenever we open our Bibles and learn from its contents, whenever we bow our heads and speak with our Father. We are not restricted to steepled buildings or to sacred spaces. We are called to bring the church to the world and not the world to church.

Talk with God

God, I ask that you bless your church wherever she meets and your community where she gathers.

Live It. How will you live more Second today?
Tell It. How will you share what you have learned?

🐦 Tweet using #IASgathertogether to share your thoughts.

Day 6: **Develop Leaders**

Paul stayed on in Corinth for some time. Then he left the brothers and sisters and sailed for Syria, accompanied by Priscilla and Aquila.

—Acts 18:18

Read the whole passage in Acts 18:12–21.

Paul never intended to stay in any one place forever. He saw his role as a mobilizer, a catalyst for leadership development. He stayed only to multiply and spoke only to train up others. He searched for ready learners like Priscilla and Aquila, men and women who would take up the challenge of making disciples, who would pass on what they learned and multiply others who would do the same. How much of our lives are spent trying to climb ladders and rise to the top, when true discipleship aims to push others up the ladder and see others succeed beyond their natural capabilities? How much of our lives are wasted worrying about whether people respect our positions, when all the while God desires that we give up our positions and train others to take our places?

Talk with God

Teach me to train up those around me, to develop and reproduce spiritual leaders.

Live It. How will you live more Second today?
Tell It. How will you share what you have learned?

🐦 Tweet using #IASdevelopleaders to share your thoughts.

Day 7: Kings of Earth

*May all the kings of the earth praise you, L*ORD*,*
  when they hear what you have decreed.
*May they sing of the ways of the L*ORD*,*
  *for the glory of the L*ORD *is great.*
*Though the L*ORD *is exalted, he looks kindly on the lowly;*
  though lofty, he sees them from afar.
Though I walk in the midst of trouble,
  you preserve my life.
You stretch out your hand against the anger of my foes;
  with your right hand you save me.
*The L*ORD *will vindicate me;*
  *your love, L*ORD*, endures forever—*
  do not abandon the works of your hands.

—Psalm 138:4–8

We think too small. We think about our community or our group of friends or our workplace. But God wants the whole world to hear about him. God wants kings and queens, presidents and cultural icons, scientists and leaders. God wants everyone. Are we bold enough to ask him for something so big?

Talk with God

Worship.

"May the kings of the earth praise you . . ."
God, I want the whole world to worship you because you are . . .

Tweet using #IASkingsofearth to share your prayers.

Session Twelve

Commit

Living Second means obeying he who is First. We bear the image of our Creator. We wear the jersey of his team and the banner of his kingdom. The practice of our lives shine on God, and the witness of our actions reflect on his name. Our effectiveness as his servants depends on our obedience to his will. While forgiveness is always at a ready supply, God insists we strive for perfection, that obedience always be our goal. We shame him when we fail, but we reflect his greatness when we love. Obedience is recognizing we can do great things with him and nothing without him. Let this just be the beginning of a long journey of following God and a lifelong commitment to keep God First.

Day 1: Tarshish

Watch the Parks Film

www.iamsecond.com/theparks

What did you like about, identify with, or learn from the Parkses' story?

> But Jonah ran away from the LORD and headed for Tarshish. He went down to Joppa, where he found a ship bound for that port. After paying the fare, he went aboard and sailed for Tarshish to flee from the LORD.
>
> **—Jonah 1:3**

Read the whole passage in Jonah 1.

What It Says
   1. What did you like about this passage?
   2. What did you not like or find confusing about this passage?

What It Means
   3. What does this passage teach about people?
   4. What does this passage teach about God?

Live It. How will you live more Second today?
Tell It. How will you share what you have learned?

Practice It. Get with a friend or someone in your group. Practice or role-play your "Live and Tell" commitments.

Day 2: **Drafted**

But Moses said, "Pardon your servant, Lord. Please send someone else." Then the LORD's anger burned against Moses.

—**Exodus 4:13–14**

Read the whole passage in Exodus 4:1–17.

God hates our reluctance. He did not ask us to volunteer for his service. We were drafted. He chose us before the universe existed and selected us before our mothers ever took their first breaths. He formed our lips to speak his words. He shaped our legs to run his errands, our hands to work his assignments. We may think that our lives are ours for the taking, our plans for the making, but he alone rules the universe. He did not ask us our opinions when he shaped the stars or for our thoughts when he set the world on its axis. He made the rules all by himself, and he set his plans without our input. So while we may ask for his assistance in carrying out his orders or for his grace in forgiving our mistakes, we may not ask to be discharged from his service or released from his command.

Talk with God

God, forgive me for my reluctance, for being so slow to heed your instruction and to hear your commands.

Live It. How can you live more Second today?
Tell It. How will you share what you have learned?

🐦 Tweet using #IASdrafted to share your thoughts.

Day 3: Let Go

Pharaoh said, "Who is the L<small>ORD</small>, that I should obey him and let Israel go? I do not know the L<small>ORD</small> and I will not let Israel go."

—Exodus 5:2

Read the whole passage in Exodus 5:1–3.

We all have holdouts in our lives, little areas that we refuse to let go. We think God is content to walk through our kitchen and roam around our bedroom or sit in our living room. But he is not. He wants the deed to the house. He knocks on the door not to be a guest but the owner. He wants every room, every closet, every pantry, and every cupboard of our lives. He will accept nothing less than everything. We think that our romantic escapades are on our own time, that our careers are for our own advancement, or our homes and bank accounts at our own discretion. But if we claim to follow Jesus, then his name is on the deed to our lives, his purpose sits at the top of our priorities, and his kingdom the point of all our wealth and all our time. What are you still trying to hold on to?

Talk with God

God, you own me. I let go of everything and hold nothing back.

Live It. How can you live more Second today?
Tell It. How will you share what you have learned?

🐦 Tweet using #IASletgo to share your thoughts.

Day 4: **Victory**

The Egyptians will know that I am the Lord when I stretch out my hand against Egypt and bring the Israelites out of it.

—Exodus 7:5

Read the whole passage in Exodus 7:1–24.

God always wins. We may try to hold out against him and suffer the fate of his enemies, or we can join him. We can fight a battle we will never win, or we can side with the one who will never lose. We can enter a war we have no hope to win, or we can march with the victor who has all the troops and all the weapons. The battle is not between flesh and blood, nations or empires, but between God and his enemies. But unlike any other war, the end has already been sealed. Jesus won when he rose from the grave. God was victorious when he hatched the plan of our redemption. The war is nothing more than a mop-up job. The enemy runs defeated and panicked. We have a choice. We can accept his offer of grace, the sacrifice of his Son, and the resurrection of the same; we can trust him in faith and accept Jesus alone for our salvation, or we can remain his enemy. The choice is ours.

Talk with God

God, I'm weary of fighting you. I ask for mercy for my rebellion and forgiveness for my sins. I trust only in your offer for forgiveness through Jesus, in his death and resurrection, and I beg for your grace.

Live It. How will you live more Second today?
Tell It. How will you share what you have learned?

🐦 Tweet using #IASvictory to share your thoughts.

Day 5: Plagued

For by now I could have stretched out my hand and struck you and your people with a plague that would have wiped you off the earth. But I have raised you up for this very purpose, that I might show you my power and that my name might be proclaimed in all the earth.

—Exodus 9:15–16

Read the whole passage in Exodus 8:1–9:34.

Pharaoh was given his armies to prove a point and his power to make a statement. He was made king of Egypt and crowned chief among nations so that God could teach a lesson. Pharaoh could stiffen his neck and bulge his muscles, but God held all the power. Pharaoh could throw his armies with all his fury and all his arrogance, but he would never prevail. We can try to assert our independence from God. We can pretend that we rule our own fiefdoms, but we only deceive ourselves. God will humble us and, if necessary, humiliate and destroy us. But in the end every knee will bow and every mouth confess that he is God. While he may not give us easy assignments, obedience is the only wise choice. All other options lead to ruin.

Talk with God

I submit to your rule and your authority. I commit to obey your commands and listen to your voice.

Live It. How will you live more Second today?
Tell It. How will you share what you have learned?

🐦 Tweet using #IASplagued to share your thoughts.

Day 6: **Rebellion**

*At midnight the L*ORD *struck down all the firstborn in Egypt, from the firstborn of Pharaoh, who sat on the throne, to the firstborn of the prisoner, who was in the dungeon, and the firstborn of all the livestock as well.*

—**Exodus 12:29**

Read the whole passage in Exodus 12:29–51.

God plays no games. Our rebellion will be struck down and our insurrection ended. He gives us grace but only so we have the opportunity to repent. He grants us a stay on punishment but only so we might change our ways and mend our wrongs. If we fail to change, if we close our ears and continue our struggle against him and our rejection of his rule, then be warned, his wrath is heavy and his anger devastating. Life is but a testing ground, and he has no problem ending the test and giving us a failing grade. He may call his children home early and his enemies to eternal punishment. We all are accountable for the lives we lead. Let this be a challenge for us to examine our lives and check our behaviors and intentions. Do we harbor rebellion? Do we grant mutiny a home? What needs to be changed for our lives to satisfy his requirements?

Talk with God

God, I confess my failures and beg for your forgiveness. I commit to change my ways and to struggle forward. Overlook my sins and give me strength to live rightly.

Live It. How will you live more Second today?
Tell It. How will you share what you have learned?

🐦 Tweet using #IASrebellion to share your thoughts.

Day 7: Mercy

LORD, do not rebuke me in your anger
or discipline me in your wrath.
Have mercy on me, LORD, for I am faint;
heal me, LORD, for my bones are in agony.
My soul is in deep anguish.
How long, LORD, how long?
Turn, LORD, and deliver me;
save me because of your unfailing love.
Among the dead no one proclaims your name.
Who praises you from the grave?
I am worn out from my groaning.
All night long I flood my bed with weeping
and drench my couch with tears.
My eyes grow weak with sorrow;
they fail because of all my foes.

—Psalm 6:1–7

Humanity was not created with error or sin in mind. We were not designed to rebel against God. We were formed to serve God, but we were also given free choice. And though we have all freely chosen to reject God's way, to choose error rather than righteousness, we can also choose to confess those sins and return each and every day to the one who always forgives.

Talk with God

Forgive.

"Have mercy on me . . ."
God, make me a better follower of you and have patience with me when I fail . . .

🐦 Tweet using #IASmercy to share your prayers.

Day 1: The Sea

Watch the Nate Larkin Film

www.iamsecond.com/natelarkin

What did you like about, identify with, or learn from Nate's story?

"In my distress I called to the LORD, and he answered me."
—**Jonah 2:7**

Read the whole passage in Jonah 2:1–10.

What It Says
1. What did you like about this passage? What are the kinds of things that Jonah talked with God about?
2. What did you not like or find confusing about this passage?

What It Means
3. What does this passage teach about people?
4. What does this passage teach about God?

Live It. Take some time and talk with God as a group. Use Jonah's prayer as a model for your own.
Tell It. How will you share what you have learned?

Day 2: Confession

Therefore let all the faithful pray to you
*   while you may be found;*
Surely the rising of the mighty waters
*   will not reach them.*
You are my hiding place;
*   you will protect me from trouble*
*   and surround me with songs of deliverance.*
I will instruct you and teach you in the way you should go;
*   I will counsel you with my loving eye on you.*
Do not be like the horse or the mule,
*   which have no understanding*
but must be controlled by bit and bridle
*   or they will not come to you.*
Many are the woes of the wicked,
*   but the LORD's unfailing love*
*   surrounds the one who trusts in him.*
Rejoice in the LORD and be glad, you righteous;
Sing, all you who are upright in heart!

—Psalm 32:6–11

Confession brings healing. God already knows our mistakes, even better than we do ourselves. Nothing shocks him, and no wrong can surprise him. We can continue in our stubbornness, persist in denying our weaknesses, or we can begin the process of healing and ask for forgiveness.

Talk with God

Forgive.

"Do not be like the horse or the mule . . ."
God, forgive me for my failures, have mercy in my mistakes . . .

Tweet using #IASconfession to share your prayers.

Day 3: **Discipline**

LORD, do not rebuke me in your anger
or discipline me in your wrath.
Your arrows have pierced me,
and your hand has come down on me.
Because of your wrath there is no health in my body;
there is no soundness in my bones because of my sin.
My guilt has overwhelmed me
like a burden too heavy to bear. . . .
For I am about to fall,
and my pain is ever with me.
I confess my iniquity;
I am troubled by my sin.

—Psalm 38:1–4, 17–18

Trouble in this life has many causes. Some is due to the evil and wrongdoing of others. Some to the broken system of our world and its governments. Some comes due merely to the fallen nature of our world, a testament to humanities separation from God. But some of our trouble is self-made, brought on by our own poor decisions and moral failings.

Talk with God

Forgive.

"I confess my inequity . . ."
God, forgive me for my failures, have mercy in my mistakes . . .

🐦 Tweet using #IASdiscipline to share your prayers.

Day 4: **Pure Heart**

Cleanse me with hyssop, and I will be clean;
*   wash me, and I will be whiter than snow.*
Let me hear joy and gladness;
*   let the bones you have crushed rejoice.*
Hide your face from my sins
*   and blot out all my iniquity.*
Create in me a pure heart, O God,
*   and renew a steadfast spirit within me.*
Do not cast me from your presence
*   or take your Holy Spirit from me.*
Restore to me the joy of your salvation
*   and grant me a willing spirit, to sustain me.*

—Psalm 51:7–12

Come clean with God. He knows all and offers to forgive all. He wants to remake us to be more like him, to reshape our hearts to reflect his love more clearly. But he wants us to admit our wrongs and humbly accept his aid.

Talk with God

Forgive.

"Create in me a pure heart . . ."
God, forgive me for . . .

 Tweet using #IASpureheart to share your prayers.

Day 5: Wrath

*Hear my prayer, L*ORD*;*
let my cry for help come to you.
Do not hide your face from me
when I am in distress.
Turn your ear to me;
when I call, answer me quickly.
For my days vanish like smoke;
my bones burn like glowing embers.
My heart is blighted and withered like grass;
I forget to eat my food.
In my distress I groan aloud
and am reduced to skin and bones.
I am like a desert owl,
like an owl among the ruins.
I lie awake; I have become
like a bird alone on a roof.

—Psalm 102:1–7

Like any good parent, God is not afraid to punish, to use discomfort to reform our hearts or pain to shake us from our slumber. Not every hard time is due directly to our personal sin, but we must be aware that God can and does punish his children. Make confession a daily habit and do not tempt his anger.

Talk with God

Forgive.

". . . when I call, answer me quickly."
God, forgive my wrongs and save me from my struggles.

🐦 Tweet using #IASwrath to share your prayers.

Day 6: Cry

Out of the depths I cry to you, Lord;
Lord, hear my voice.
Let your ears be attentive
to my cry for mercy.
If you, Lord, kept a record of sins,
Lord, who could stand?
But with you there is forgiveness,
so that we can, with reverence, serve you.
I wait for the Lord, my whole being waits,
and in his word I put my hope.
I wait for the Lord
more than watchmen wait for the morning,
more than watchmen wait for the morning.
Israel, put your hope in the Lord,
for with the Lord is unfailing love
and with him is full redemption.
He himself will redeem Israel
from all their sins.

—Psalm 130

Failure is a guarantee of our existence; weakness is a fact of life. God is no more surprised by our mistakes and lapses in judgment than we are. He hates our sin, but he also loves our repentance. So when we find ourselves mired in failure or scarred by our wrongs, let us run to God for forgiveness.

Talk with God

Forgive.

"**. . . with** you there is forgiveness . . ."
God, forgive me for my failures, have mercy in my mistakes . . .

🐦 Tweet using #IAScry to share your prayers.

Day 7: **Relief**

Lord, hear my prayer,
listen to my cry for mercy;
In your faithfulness and righteousness
come to my relief.
Do not bring your servant into judgment,
for no one living is righteous before you.
The enemy pursues me,
he crushes me to the ground;
He makes me dwell in the darkness
like those long dead.
So my spirit grows faint within me;
my heart within me is dismayed.
I remember the days of long ago;
I meditate on all your works
and consider what your hands have done.
I spread out my hands to you;
I thirst for you like a parched land.

—Psalm 143:1–6

God's punishments are meant to draw us back to him. His discipline is designed to help us realize our faults and return to the life he has planned for us. He deems our temporary discomfort worth our spiritual health. God is not afraid to punish when the time is right. That does not mean we must always be looking over our shoulders waiting for lightening to strike, but it does mean we should be sober about our decisions to disobey him.

Talk with God

Forgive.

"Listen to my cry for mercy . . ."
God, forgive me for my failures, have mercy in my mistakes . . .

Tweet using #IASrelief to share your prayers.

Day 1: Nineveh

Watch the David McKenna Film

www.iamsecond.com/
davidmckenna

What did you like about, identify with, or learn from David's story?

> *Jonah obeyed the word of the LORD and went to Nineveh.*
> *Now Nineveh was a very large city; it took three days to go*
> *through it.*
>
> —**Jonah 3:3**

Read the whole passage in Jonah 2:10–3:10.

What It Says
1. What did you like about this passage?
2. What did you not like or find confusing about this passage?

What It Means
3. What does this passage teach about people?
4. What does this passage teach about God?

Live It. How will you live more Second today?
Tell It. How will you share what you have learned?

Practice It. Get with a friend or someone in your group. Practice or role-play your "Live and Tell" commitments.

Day 2: **Worse**

You not only followed their ways and copied their detestable practices, but in all your ways you soon became more depraved than they.

—Ezekiel 16:47

Read the whole passage in Ezekiel 16:1–48.

Because of Jesus, we have *holy* penned across our souls. We are named unique and different, separate and special. God sees us as exceptional, untainted, unmixed, and pure. By our inclusion in God's family, we have the label of holiness. But though we hold the title, our lives are still in process. God insists we participate in that process, that we strive to separate ourselves from what the world loves and to refrain from the ways of our old lives. He calls us to live up to our title and to respond to his love. When we turn back to our old habits and our old gods, we grieve his soul and spurn his love. He considers it a personal offense and a grievous insult. How are we treating God with the decisions of our lives or responding to his love on a daily basis?

Talk with God

God, forgive my failures and give me the power to live up to your standard.

Live It. How can you live more Second today?
Tell It. How will you share what you have learned?

Tweet using #IASworse to share your thoughts.

Day 3: Pure

Blessed are the pure in heart,
for they will see God.

—Matthew 5:8

Read the whole passage in Matthew 5:3–12.

God has begun a work in us, a process of refinement that will result in our perfection. He requires that we strive for this impossible goal and that we grow and become stronger. He insists on our involvement that we may use our faith and practice our beliefs. One day, we will be pure. One day, the struggle with evil will end, and the war with temptation will cease. And though we will never attain this freedom in this life, the practice prepares us for the next life. He asks for perfection, purity, and absolute spotlessness; though we will always fall short, it is the struggle that he honors and the intent that he rewards, the purity of heart that he encourages. When we find ourselves saddled with addiction or wrestled down by sin, he asks that we fight back, and he demands that we work to win our struggles. In the end, our struggle is a tag team match. We fight and we wrestle, but our teammate will rescue us. God will finish the fight, but he asks we stay in the ring.

Talk with God

Keep me fighting the good fight, but when the match becomes too heated, save me.

Live It. How can you live more Second today?
Tell It. How will you share what you have learned?

Tweet using #IASpure to share your thoughts.

Day 4: **Commandments**

Therefore anyone who sets aside one of the least of these commands and teaches others accordingly will be called least in the kingdom of heaven, but whoever practices and teaches these commands will be called great in the kingdom of heaven.

—Matthew 5:19

Read the whole passage in Matthew 5:17–20.

The business world measures dollars spent versus dollars earned. The political world weighs popularity and power and votes. Our culture views greatness as the letters after our names, the beauty of our gifts, or the money in our pockets. But God measures only faith and obedience. Without faith we can never please him, and without obedience we can never claim true faith. He gave us our gifts and finds us completely without flaw. He created our talents and endowed us with all he ever hoped us to have. What he desires now is that we love and obey him. Greatness is nothing less and nothing more.

Talk with God

I do not seek the respect or honors of this world. I only hope to earn greatness in your kingdom, to win reward through faithful obedience and steady faith.

Live It. How will you live more Second today?
Tell It. How will you share what you have learned?

🐦 Tweet using #IAScommandments to share your thoughts.

Day 5: Living Sacrifice

Therefore, I urge you, brothers and sisters, in view of God's mercy, to offer your bodies as a living sacrifice, holy and pleasing to God—this is your true and proper worship.

—Romans 12:1

Read the whole passage in Romans 12:1–21.

God has given us everything. He gives us the air we breathe, the bodies we move, and the world we live in. And if all that was not enough, he provided a way for us to live eternally with him in perfect and unending peace. So what should our response be to such awesome grace? Our lives should be a living sacrifice for him, a constant act of worship and thankfulness. We should love others in the same way he has loved us. We should bless those who persecute us. Love those who do us harm. Forgive those who injure us. We should be humble, knowing our weaknesses and admitting our failures. While dying for God or his cause may sound like a glorious end, it is the everyday living for him that is perhaps the hardest.

Talk with God

God, teach me to live in constant worship of what you have done in my life.

Live It. How will you live more Second today?
Tell It. How will you share what you have learned?

🐦 Tweet using #IASlivingsacrifice to share your thoughts.

Day 6: **First Love**

Yet I hold this against you: You have forsaken the love you had at first. Consider how far you have fallen! Repent and do the things you did at first.

—Revelation 2:4–5

Read the whole passage in Revelation 2:1–7.

It is possible to know all the right answers and still fail God's test, to believe all the right things and still fall short of his expectations. God wants more than head knowledge and more than rote obedience. He wants love. That does not mean he wants warm, fuzzy feelings or infatuation, though that is a good start. He wants the kind of aged love that never forgets the honeymoon, the kind of deep-seated affection that continues far beyond the thrill of the first kiss. He wants a commitment that grows with time and sweetens with the years. He wants obedience that flows with pleasure and that beats with warmth. He wants our strength and our minds but also our love.

Talk with God

God, I love you. I am committed to you, and I am determined to never forget our first meeting.

Live It. How will you live more Second today?
Tell It. How will you share what you have learned?

🐦 Tweet using #IASfirstlove to share your thoughts.

Day 7: **Enthroned**

The LORD reigns,
let the nations tremble;
He sits enthroned between the cherubim,
let the earth shake.
Great is the LORD in Zion;
he is exalted over all the nations.
Let them praise your great and awesome name—
he is holy.
The King is mighty, he loves justice—
you have established equity;
In Jacob you have done
what is just and right.
Exalt the LORD our God
and worship at his footstool;
he is holy.

—Psalm 99:1–5

Our praise to God can be the recollection of divine intervention or a memory of a time when God came near. As old friends tell stories of past adventures, so can our praise be a retelling of what we have seen God do in our lives and in the lives around us. So take some time and tell God a great story of something you remember him doing.

Talk with God

Worship.

"The King is mighty . . ."
God, I worship you because of what I have seen you do . . .

Tweet using #IASenthroned to share your prayers.

Day 1: Rights

Watch the Pete Briscoe Film

www.iamsecond.com/petebriscoe

What did you like about, identify with, or learn from Pete's story?

> *You have been concerned about this plant, though you did not tend it or make it grow. It sprang up overnight and died overnight. And should I not have concern for the great city of Nineveh, in which there are more than a hundred and twenty thousand people who cannot tell their right hand from their left—and also many animals?*
>
> **—Jonah 4:10–11**

Read the whole passage in Jonah 4:1–11.

What It Says
    1. What did you like about this passage?
    2. What did you not like or find confusing about this passage?

What It Means
    3. What does this passage teach about people?
    4. What does this passage teach about God?

Live It. How will you live more Second today?
Tell It. How will you share what you have learned?

Practice It. Get with a friend or someone in your group. Practice or role-play your "Live and Tell" commitments.

Day 2: Hard Words

On hearing it, many of his disciples said, "This is a hard teaching. Who can accept it?" . . .

"You do not want to leave too, do you?" Jesus asked the Twelve.

Simon Peter answered him, "Lord, to whom shall we go? You have the words of eternal life. We have come to believe and to know that you are the Holy One of God."

—John 6:60, 67–69

Read the whole passage in John 6:60–71.

Jesus is not offering a life of fluffy clouds and soft kittens. He does not promise ease and comfort on this earth. On the contrary, he promises hardship and difficulty. He promises persecution and rejection. He tells us that if we really took him seriously, if we really obeyed his commands and followed his teaching, then friends will abandon us, family will hate us, and the world may prefer to kill us. But Jesus also wants us to know that despite the hardship, he, and he alone, holds the keys of life. While some may offer big screen televisions and mansions and cars and sweet, soft words of encouragement, only he can offer an eternity of satisfaction, only he can provide life beyond death, peace without interruption.

Talk with God

Give me the strength to follow your way and to obey your lessons no matter the hardships that come.

Live It. How can you live more Second today?
Tell It. How will you share what you have learned?

🐦 Tweet using #IAShardwords to share your thoughts.

Day 3: Loving Life

Anyone who loves their life will lose it, while anyone who hates their life in this world will keep it for eternal life.

—John 12:25

Read the whole passage in John 12:23–33.

We do not belong here. We are commissioned to stay here, to be salt in a bland world and light in a dark place. But we do not fit in this world. Our citizenship is not in America or Germany, Bolivia or Bhutan. Our passports read: *heaven*. We are agents of his government and servants of his kingdom. We have been called to sacrifice our lives on behalf of this new nation, in the duty of his call. We can choose the little pleasures of life, the bits of gold or tasty food this world offers. We can hold on to the applause and approval of our peers or the popularity we might find in our short lives, but in doing so we forfeit something so much greater. Our God and King will accept no defection. He expects us to sacrifice all on his behalf, to put ourselves second and to make him first, even above our very lives.

Talk with God

God, I choose you, above all that this life offers. I love you and your kingdom above all else.

Live It. How can you live more Second today?
Tell It. How will you share what you have learned?

🐦 Tweet using #IASlovinglife to share your thoughts.

Day 4: Keep Watch

Therefore keep watch, because you do not know the day or the hour.

—Matthew 25:13

Read the whole passage in Matthew 25:1–13.

While many do not plan for it as well as we should, most of us have set aside some money for retirement. We recognize that a day will come when work will cease to be an obligation or option. We squirrel our money into 401(k)s and Roth IRAs. We watch our savings accounts, stock investments, and mattresses, all in the hope that we will be ready for the day when our health fails, our senses deteriorate, or the golf course calls, the day of retirement. But a day of absolute and eternal retirement awaits us all, a day that inaugurates an eternal rest and a forever peace. Will we be ready? Have we kept watch with our lives? Have we invested for that retirement, made ready our judgment with God and our place in a world so different than this one? While many fail to adequately plan for an earthly retirement, even fewer plan for the heavenly one. What can you do to strengthen your heavenly investments?

Talk with God

Give me the wisdom to plan for the day when you return.

Live It. How will you live more Second today?
Tell It. How will you share what you have learned?

🐦 Tweet using #IASkeepwatch to share your thoughts.

Day 5: Talents

So take the bag of gold from him and give it to the one who has ten bags. For whoever has will be given more, and they will have an abundance. Whoever does not have, even what they have will be taken from them.

—**Matthew 25:28–29**

Read the whole passage in Matthew 25:14–30.

Few of us were born with a voice that can resound in Carnegie Hall or shoulders that can keep pace with Olympic swimmers, but we all are endowed with greatness. Each of us is given gifts and talent and opportunity. Whatever the level of our giftedness, we all are gifted. We are gifted by a benevolent and wise Creator who has a plan for each of his masterpieces, a strategy to bring beauty to his world. But we must hone that gift, invest it, and work it. We possess wealth, knowledge, relationships, time, and opportunity. We are given all these good things and given them for a purpose. He expects us to use them well and use them for him. What does our heavenly investment portfolio look like? Have we buried most of our talents, hidden most of our money or time? Have we wasted funds on our own plans or squandered opportunities out of our own fear? Or have we taken eternity seriously and invested accordingly?

Talk with God

God, give me the boldness to try great things for you and the humbleness to know it's all for you.

Live It. How will you live more Second today?
Tell It. How will you share what you have learned?

🐦 Tweet using #IAStalents to share your thoughts.

Day 6: **Least**

Truly I tell you, whatever you did for one of the least of these brothers and sisters of mine, you did for me.

—Matthew 25:40

Read the whole passage in Matthew 25:31–46.

Peter will not be serving lemonade at the pearly gates or polling us for our favorite ice cream flavor at the doors of heaven. God will be our greeter. It is God we will stand before and give an account for our lives. And he will take our failures personally. He will take the cruel words we threw at his creations as insults against him. He will take our neglect of the poor as neglecting him and our indifference toward the hurting as apathy aimed at his kingdom. If God is our final critic and our last auditor, then what defense should we prepare with our lives, what proof should we produce with our choices? What would we change about our lives and about our everyday task lists and priorities, if we really believed that God will take our decisions personally?

Talk with God

God, I want my goals, my tasks, my daily habits, and my accomplishments to make you smile. I want you to be First. Teach me how to live with you in mind.

Live It. How will you live more Second today?
Tell It. How will you share what you have learned?

Tweet using #IASleast to share your thoughts.

Day 7: Ashes

I know that you can do all things;
no purpose of yours can be thwarted.
You asked, "Who is this that obscures my plans without knowledge?"
Surely I spoke of things I did not understand,
things too wonderful for me to know.
You said, "Listen now, and I will speak;
I will question you,
and you shall answer me."
My ears had heard of you
but now my eyes have seen you.
Therefore I despise myself
and repent in dust and ashes.

—Job 42:2–6

God is God. What more can be said? When he makes a plan, who can stop him? When he questions, who can answer him? When he intends to do something, it is done. Our response must only be surrender and our answer always be yes. If God is God, what must you do to make that more of a reality in your own life?

Talk with God

Surrender.

"I know that you can do all things . . ."
God, you are God, and I am not. You are First above all else. I and all my concerns and desires are Second . . .

Tweet using #IASashes to share your prayers.

How Do I Become Second?

Becoming Second means recognizing God is First. It means believing and trusting in Jesus and accepting who he is and what he did. The stories of I am Second illustrate the peace, purpose, and freedom that many people experienced when they made the decision to be Second. But the thread that holds each of these stories together is not so much what they got out of their experiences but where they began.

They each began by understanding that they were broken people. They each believed that they were sinners. Nobody escapes the weaknesses of being human. No one is without failures and mistakes, pride or selfishness. Everyone fails to love as they should.

These sins or failures separate people from God. They also bring a punishment. According to Romans 6:23, the wages of sin is death. Because of sin, everyone will face judgment when they die. "People are destined to die once and after that to face judgment" (Hebrews 9:27). God does not judge whether someone did more right than wrong. Perfection is the standard. Sin at any level, any amount, makes one guilty. Even in the present-day world, a person who commits a crime is not judged by whether he has done more good than he has wrong. He is judged on whether or not he committed the crime. Those who depend on their own good works are destined to spend eternity separated from God in hell.

But God offers forgiveness for all these sins. He offers forgiveness through faith in Jesus. It starts with an admission of guilt, a change of mind, a willingness to start going God's way instead of going our own way. It is admitting we are full of sin and in desperate need of help. But it is not just any help we must look for, it is Jesus' help. It is Jesus we need. It is his message and sacrifice that we must accept and believe to experience forgiveness and a relationship with God. It is about faith in the God of the Bible and in his Son Jesus who came and died for the sins of the world.

So who is this Jesus?

Jesus Is First

It's not about us. It's not about our good deeds or religion. It's about who Jesus is and what he did. "For what we preach is not ourselves, but Jesus Christ as Lord, and ourselves as your servants for Jesus' sake" (2 Corinthians 4:5). It's about Jesus, always and fully God, who came to earth and was born a baby in full humanity, who later died on a cross for our sins, and who was raised to life on the third day.

Jesus Died to Forgive Our Sins

The message of Jesus is simple and is summarized in 1 Corinthians 15:1–4: "Now, brothers and sisters, I want to remind you of the gospel I preached to you, which you received and on which you have taken your stand. By this gospel you are saved, if you hold firmly to the word I preached to you . . . that Christ died for our sins according to the Scriptures, that he was buried, that he was raised on the third day according to the Scriptures." Without the death of Jesus, there would be no forgiveness of sins.

Jesus Rose from the Dead

The foundation of our faith is not our personal story. The foundation of our faith is a historic event: the resurrection of Jesus. Paul wrote, "And if Christ has not been raised, your faith is futile; you are still in your sins" (1 Corinthians 15:17).

We Are Saved by God's Grace, Not by Good Works

We do not earn forgiveness. It is a gift. "Now to the one who works, wages are not credited as a gift but as an obligation. However, to the one who does not work but trusts God who justifies the ungodly, their faith is credited as righteousness" (Romans 4:4–5). God expects our behavior and life to change, but this change does not save us.

We Are Saved by Grace through Faith

This gift is received through believing. "For it is by grace you have been saved, through faith—and this is not from yourselves, it is the gift of God—not by works, so that no one can boast" (Ephesians 2:8–9).

If you want to be Second, if you believe in Jesus, who he is and what he did, take a moment right now and tell him. Tell him what you believe and ask him for forgiveness. Ask God to make you a part of his family.

Bonus Content

For training tools, free downloads, group discussion guides and other bonus content register at iamsecond.com/livesecondbonus.